A USER'S GUIDE TO POSTCOLONIAL AND LATINO BORDERLAND FICTION

Joe R. and Teresa Lozano Long Series in Latin American
and Latino Art and Culture

A User's Guide to Postcolonial and Latino Borderland Fiction

Frederick Luis Aldama

UNIVERSITY OF TEXAS PRESS
Austin

Requests for permission to reproduce material from this work
should be sent to Permissions:
    University of Texas Press
    P.O. Box 7819
    Austin, TX 78713–7819
    www.utexas.edu/utpress/about/bpermission.html

⊗ The paper used in this book meets the minimum requirements
of ANSI/NISO Z39.48–1992 (R1997) (Permanence of Paper).

LIBRARY OF CONGRESS CATALOGING-IN-PUBLICATION DATA
Aldama, Frederick Luis, 1969-
    A user's guide to postcolonial and Latino borderland fiction /
Frederick Luis Aldama. — 1st ed.
        p.   cm. — (Joe R. and Teresa Lozano Long series in Latin
American and Latino art and culture)
    Includes bibliographical references and index.
    ISBN 978-0-292-71968-2 (cloth : alk. paper)
    1. American fiction—Mexican American authors—History
and criticism.   2. Commonwealth fiction (English)—History and
criticism.   3. English fiction—Minority authors—History and
criticism.   4. Postcolonialism in literature.   5. Fiction—History
and criticism—Theory, etc.   6. Narration (Rhetoric)   I. Title.
    PS153.M4A45   2009
    813'.540986872—dc22
                                                        2008053301

In memory of my friend and mentor Alfred Arteaga—one of our great borderland scholars and poets

CONTENTS

A USER'S GUIDE TO POSTCOLONIAL
AND LATINO BORDERLAND FICTION

PUTTING THE WORLD BACK
INTO POSTCOLONIAL AND
LATINO BORDERLAND
LITERATURE

As a Chicano teen far from homelands (Mexico and California) growing up in a 1980s London stretched large with all walks of
life I found myself irresistibly drawn to literature. With the guidance
of a gracious librarian and an Afro-Caribbean British-identifying English teacher, I indulged in the inexhaustible splendors, merriment, and
knowledge served up by the likes of Gabriel García Márquez, Jorge Luis
Borges, Max Frisch, Hanif Kureishi, Elena Garro, Juan Goytisolo, and
Salman Rushdie, among many others. I was living and going to school
in a part of London filling to the brim with peoples from the Caribbean,
Pakistan, India, and Africa. I was living in a time when many "postcolonial" authors were fast becoming visible in their creative reimagin-
ing of such a metropolitan space.

This was my introduction to the world of literature—and to "world
literature." At this stage, such readings were absolutely self-interested and
self-absorbed, drawn to the narratives because of a strong identification
with the characters and their settings. I was filled with questions about
my various experiences of dislocation (Mexico City to Sacramento to
London), and many of these authors seemed to imagine characters and
worlds that did not so much provide answers as provide some kind of
tellurian foothold.

At this point, too, after returning again and again to certain authors I
began to wonder what it was about them—and not others—that had me
going back for more. It surely was not that their novels and short stories
captivated me because they mirrored my personal experience and that
of my classmates and friends while schooling ourselves in the racially
mixed inner-city London. After all, how much more different could
García Márquez's Macondo be from Frisch's Zurich or Kureishi's South
London? And yet I loved them all.

It was only once I set foot on the University of California Berkeley campus as an undergraduate that I began to more formally seek answers to questions such as: Why my attraction—along with so many others'—to narrative fiction generally? How did my favorite authors reframe and make interesting experiences and people and environments anchored one way or another to the real world but at the same time patently not duplicating "real life"? In which way (ontologically, epistemologically, functionally) was this fiction I loved to read different from reality? What might fictional narrative and reality have in common—if anything? What can fictional narrative in the form of literature do (and not do) in the real world? Did these questions already have an answer? If so, where?

In this period and more so later, in graduate school, I identified the focus of study that would further allow me to teach and research so-identified Latino borderland and South Asian postcolonial literature and film as they engage with other literary and filmic traditions. In my first book, *Postethnic Narrative Criticism* (2003), I critique the "locational" theories that conflate narrative fiction—and cultural artifacts in general—with reality outside the text, choosing as my site of critical analysis the storytelling mode known as magical realism. In my second book, to a certain extent a theoretical sequel, titled *Brown on Brown: Chicano Representations of Gender, Sexuality, and Ethnicity* (2005), I build on and complicate this argument by investigating the ways in which race and outlawed sexuality have been theorized in postcolonial and ethnic queer theory. Herein I will share with you a third installment in this unofficial trilogy: *A User's Guide to Postcolonial and Latino Borderland Fiction*.

The premise of *A User's Guide to Postcolonial and Latino Borderland Fiction* shares much with those of my other works: that the study of ethnic-identified narrative fiction (novels, short stories, and comic books, in this volume) must acknowledge its active engagement with world narrative fictional genres, storytelling modes, and techniques. Such study must acknowledge as well the contextual and pragmatic dimensions of this fiction—the existence of real-life authors and artists doing the creating and real-life readers and viewers doing the engaging—and acknowledge that while author and reader, artist and viewer are as unique as the full and limitless range of experience our world allows, as a species we share a deep, universal capacity for emotion and cognition.

To explore (and test) this premise as fully as possible, I focus on the following: style, genre, and the multislant filter in Arundhati Roy's *The God of Small Things*, the function of history in Amitav Ghosh's novel *The Glass Palace*, narrative universals and cultural particulars in Zadie

Smith's *White Teeth* and Hari Kunzru's *The Impressionist,* the interplay of the visual and verbal double narrator in Latino comic books, and finally, the significance of peritext, point of view, temporal order, and place in shaping our emotional and ethical engagement with characters and their worlds in the short fiction of Luis Rodriguez and Dagoberto Gilb.

All of the narrative fiction I explore—and to which I refer in theme, setting, characters, and so forth as "postcolonial" (South Asian or Afro-Caribbean British) and Latino "borderland"—include within their contents details, to a greater or lesser degree of specificity, that speak to cultural particulars as well as formal details (genre, point of view, style, and mode, for instance) that announce an affiliation with and inscription within world literary crossings. Indeed, as with writers and artists generally, those studied here read other authors' work—proximate and distant in time and space—to create new narrative fictional utterances in ways that vitally engage readers and viewers close to home and the world over.

This is not to suggest that in this book I willfully neglect the site-specific grids of history, politics, and culture that uniquely inflect such narratives—those and other features are perhaps necessarily textured in all fiction and therefore appear in my discussions of theme, characterization, and plot. Nor do I willfully seek to sidestep consideration of the material conditions that affect the production, circulation, translation in some cases, and consumption of postcolonial and Latino borderland narrative fictions. The aim is rather to place the emphasis where I believe it rightly belongs: on the literature as such, from the point of view of the peculiarities of its production (material and formal) and its reception (emotive and cognitive).

The overall thrust of this book is to explore how "postcolonial" authors such as Roy, Kunzru, Smith, and Ghosh as well as "borderland" writers Gilb and Rodriguez and Chicano comic book author-artists Laura Molina, Rhode Montijo, Rafael Navarro, Javier Hernandez, Los Bros Hernandez, and Wilfred Santiago, among others, use the techniques available within their storytelling media to organize, frame, and richly texture characters, times, and places. I explore how they infuse a unique, engaging, and responsive aesthetic into their narrative fictions.

To mention aesthetics alongside postcolonial and Latino borderland novels, short stories, and comic books might appear as an appeal to some old-school evaluation of inherently good and bad literature. While I do consider there to be poorly conceived and written (and illustrated) postcolonial and borderland fiction, this is not why I wave the aesthetic flag.

Rather, I consider "aesthetic" a useful term to identify a function of art generally: how reframing an object (the literary transfiguration of real subjects, real experiences, and actual events that make up every-day reality) can be engaging, generate emotions, suggest thoughts, produce moral conflicts, and even reach out toward and shed light upon the world in which we live. The tasks at hand are to study the aesthetic function of postcolonial and Latino borderland narrative fictions and to avoid confusing their realism (their generic mode) for reality.

While I use the terms "postcolonial" and "borderland" as tags to identify themes (dislocation and racism, say), settings (such as London and East Los Angeles), and characters (South Asian British and Chicano, for instance) in the novels, short stories, and comic books of this study, I by no means want to slip down that slope of category confusion. Postcolonial and borderland are categories originated and driven by academia, media, and marketplace. They are tags that help get books published and sold as well as to advance careers. I therefore use the terms as a shorthand to describe fictional narratives that include themes, settings, and characters described above. I say "include themes" because a novel like Kunzru's *The Impressionist* could be read as thematizing colonial and postcolonial crises of identity in India, the evils of global capitalism, or unrequited love.

Today, however, the production and marketing of postcolonial and borderland literature follows two paths: the degree of exoticism ascribed to themes, settings, and characters; and the degree of political value ascribed to themes, settings, and characters in terms of opposition to colonialism, imperialism, and the like. One such tack that scholars and media critics follow is to identify a postcolonial or borderland protein sequence in the DNA, so to speak, of the fiction and of those creating it. If you are born Chicano, you and only you can write a borderland novel. While John Rechy resisted writing about Chicanos in most of his fiction, few other Chicano authors can say the same. When a "postcolonial" author like Hanif Kureishi chooses to write not about the South Asian British Londoner experience but rather that of middle-class white people, he has betrayed his genetic makeup. A case in point: when he published the middle-class, nonracially marked novel *Intimacy,* readers in London threw up their arms in anger. They wanted more *Buddha of Suburbia*. (For more on this controversy see my interview with Kureishi in "The Pound and the Fury.")

Another consequence is that scholars and critics alike either programmatically declare that we must only read a given novel within its own native tradition or accuse us of misreading a novel because we failed to do so. (See Elleke Boehmer's *Stories of Women: Gender and Narrative in the Postcolonial Nation*.) Of course, we know that authors are much more than their biographies and their fictions much more than postcolonial or borderland protein sequences; if it were not so, we would not have Raja Rao hailed as the great novelist of India, knowing of his taste for French wine and that he wrote most of his fictions in a thirteenth-century castle in the Alps.

Likewise, there is a slip from "postcolonial" and Latino "borderland" as classifications (and rather loose and baggy ones at that) to worldviews—knowledge systems, even. So, "postcolonial" and "borderland" express localized knowledge systems (Nahua, say) and stand against and resist dominant Western thinking. For instance, in *The Postcolonial Body in Queer Space and Time*, Rebecca Fine Romanow discusses how *The Buddha of Suburbia* and other works reveal "nonnormative spatialities and temporalities [of the diasporic Other and how they] dissolve and disrupt the constraints of colonial or national history in order to construct and situate the present" (15). Others like Walter Mignolo identify a borderland, mestizo gnosis resistant to empire-driven knowledge systems. The borderland as expression of a mestizo knowledge system and essence offers Rafael Pérez-Torres the "boundless possibility" of reading into many texts how they destabilize "racial and gender hierarchies [but] with a sense of constraint" (3). For Ana María Manzanas and Jesús Benito, borderland fictions—or in their words, "border dwellers"—perform "concrete acts of mediation" and promote "conversation across difference" (3). In *Crossing Borderlands* Andrea A. Lunsford and Lahoucine Ouzgane declare in the introduction to their edited volume how postcolonial and borderland narrative fiction, with its themes of dislocation and resistance and with its hybrid characters, will liberate students and teachers from regulatory systems such as rules of grammar, Western canonical reading assignments, and more generally, society's discursive structures that contain and control racialized subjects. (See also Roberto Ignacio Díaz's *Unhomely Rooms*, Azade Seyhan's *Writing Outside the Nation*, and Bishnupriay Ghosh's *When Borne Across*.)

The net effect: authors like Sandra Cisneros, Ana Castillo, Arundhati Roy, Anita Desai, Hanif Kureishi, Salman Rushdie are served up by academics and mainstream critics as representing *the* dislocated experience, *the* troubled private identity that disrupts the nation-state—the public realm of the political. Doing so risks abstracting into oblivion the real and urgent need of oppressed and exploited working people worldwide and in each country to build the political party that is necessary for them (for us) to further their (our) struggle against oppression and exploitation. Neil Larsen aptly comments that postcolonial criticism's approach promises "cultural revolution without social revolution" ("DetermiNation," 154). It also ignores historical fact. If more than 80 percent of the world's population is "formerly, recently, or still colonized by Europe," as Patrick Williams notes in "Post-Colonialism and Narrative" (452), then nearly the entire planet would fall under the category of "postcolonial."

And the near-total focus on issues of identity and Otherness (or alterity) in postcolonial and borderland narrative fiction misses a crucial fact: that identity and Otherness are "relevant to *all* narratives," as Monika Fludernik remarks in her essay "Identity/Alterity" (543, her emphasis). If readers do not have something to identify as different from something else—a character with traits that differ from another's—then in the best of cases the fiction leaves us nonplussed, and at worst we simply do not read. Indeed, identity and Otherness are less tied to a postcolonial and borderland worldview than they are an epistemological necessity. We cannot talk about color if there are not at least two colors. If all in the world is gray, then the category "color" would not exist; it can only exist if we can identify red as different from black, and so on. For there to be identity, there must be Otherness—always. When a postcolonial or Latino borderland author introduces very little identity in his or her characters and fictional worlds—and there is a seeming trend to increasingly abstract character, time, and place—we are left with less than zero, something akin to the Harlequin romance novel in which all is abstracted from time and place.

Either way we look at it, what happens is that the richness and complexity (if such is the case) of postcolonial and borderland narrative fiction are reduced to a simplistic evaluation: Does it meet the criteria of representing, say, dislocation and a resistant bicultural identity, or not?

The criteria for analyzing postcolonial and Latino borderland literature tend, therefore, to reflect exorbitant claims about what narrative fiction—and cultural phenomena generally—can do. Common sense, however, quickly tells us otherwise. We know "postcolonial" and "borderland" to be terms used to very generally describe the themes, settings (time and place), and characters of a certain number of fictional narratives. And their deployment has not and will not alter fundamentally our selves and our world. If I self-identify as a borderland subject, I do not change fundamentally who I am as a subject. I am still the individual, Frederick Luis Aldama. I am still a social and biological being informed by a shared genetic and evolutionary history with all of humanity—a single unit or species and a singular part of nature; 99.9 percent of my DNA is identical code to all others of my species. So while I differ from another in three million separate places inside each cell of his body, this one-tenth of 1 percent difference between myself and another is not because I identify as a postcolonial or borderland subject nor because I write and analyze fiction labeled as such. So while we are all unique members of our species, we are unique only in the way we use our commonly evolved universal biological endowment in our long history of transforming nature and its transforming us in return.

Categories like postcolonial and borderland can be useful (to a degree) as a way to delimit the themes, settings, and characters in our study of certain fictional narratives. However, as categories used to create "special" standards whereby we judge the quality of such fictions by equally "special" standards, they fail. In *Native American Fiction: A User's Manual* David Treuer nicely teases out the problem with his discussion of the triumphant reception and then harsh rejection by American Indian scholars of the novel *The Education of Little Tree.* Rather than focus on the controversy—that the author, allegedly Native American and writing under the pseudonym of Forrest Carter, was a Ku Klux Klan leader implicated in the castration of an African American in Alabama— Treuer is interested more in "how we (readers) are trained to interpret Native American literature. We are trained to interpret the genre the same way we were encouraged to 'read' the exhibit of Native art at the Weisman Museum: with our hearts, not with our heads" (163). This is a consequence of using identity politics and "perceived 'authenticity'" (ibid.) as the standard for judging the fiction.

It is not on the identity of the author we should focus nor the postcolonial or borderland genetic sequencing in the fiction, but rather how effective the author is at using language and technique to invent his or her storyworlds. Even if their ambitions might be grander, those authors who rest heavily on clichés of identity—the mystically inclined, "authentic," ancestral-rooted, borderland lesbian mestiza described in Anzaldúa's *Borderlands,* for instance—create Kleenex narratives: once we finish (if we finish), we find the nearest garbage can.

Meera Syal's *Anita and Me* opens:

> I do not have many memories of my very early childhood,
> apart from the obvious ones, of course. You know, my
> windswept, bewildered parents in their dusty Indian village
> garb standing in the open doorway of a 747, blinking back
> tears of gratitude and heartbreak as the fog cleared to reveal
> a sign they had been waiting for, dreaming of, the sign
> planted in the tarmac and emblazoned in triumphant hues of
> red, blue and white, the sign that simply said, WELCOME
> TO BRITAIN. (9)

Syal's narrator is smarter than this hokum, however. Two paragraphs later, she tells us,

> Of course, this is the alternative history I trot out in job
> interview situations or, once or twice, to impress middle-
> class white boys sniffing round, excited by the thought of
> wearing a colonial maiden as a trinket on their arm. My
> earliest memory, in fact, is of the first time I understood the
> punchline to a joke. (9–10)

Syal invents a narrator who from the get-go pokes fun at and deflates this marketing and myth-making material of Otherness.

The themes, settings, and characters in and of themselves, then, are not the problem. It is the publishers, scholars, mainstream critics, and authors who ascribe material existence to only themes, settings, and characters *out of* time and place. The theme of dislocation, for instance, can be modified depending on historical and geographic circumstance and as it suits the imagination and needs of the author; the theme has a history and evolves, changes guises and forms, and so on. However, when one ascribes a material existence to a theme—when one hyposta- tizes, say, dislocation—the scholar, publisher, critic give it an existence in itself, above and beyond history. The theme of dislocation is no longer modified according to time and place but becomes an eternal state—an archetype. This is why a serious author like Dagoberto Gilb calls most fiction he reads "tract"—because it is "rigormortised by some transpar- ent issue, about as inconspicuous as a banner" (*Gritos,* 146).

We see this tendency with the hypostatizing of the myth of Aztlán during the late 1960s and early 1970s Chicano movement. Chicano scholars and authors alike took a pre-Hispanic theme not only as a writerly constraint but as a way of existing; incorporating the myth had its consequences. The designation of a utopian theme—that we will one day be free of exploitation and oppression in a recuperated, spiritualized Aztlán—as a real, obtainable material goal serves the interests of the bourgeoisie: instead of organizing and striking for better labor conditions, one simply had to believe that out of the thin air of the page this utopia would arrive. Once again Gilb offers pointed insight: "If you want to be The Leader of the People, if you want to be a Saint, if you want to be The Guru, please don't pretend to be first of all a writer" (*Gritos*, 146).

How do we avoid taking such missteps? I suggest the following seven steps.

First: We need to develop a set of tools that will allow us to consider "postcolonial" and "borderland" narrative fiction as part and parcel of "world literature." Moreover, we develop an approach that demonstrates how world literature is the sum of its postcolonial and borderland fictions.

Second: We need to keep history centrally in mind. Just as historical circumstance and the imaginative needs of an author shape, reshape, and shape again the theme of dislocation, for example, so too must we consider how history has shaped those so-identified postcolonial and borderland authors and their affiliative "ethnic" or other groups. In the United States, Chicanos are today less identifiable as an ethnic group separate from the "mainstream" than during the time of the Chicano movement. In the late 1960s, Chicanos forged a unity as an ethnic group with a shared cultural heritage to assert the right for representation in the United States. Today, Chicanos and Latinos are increasingly part of the mainstream—even holding high positions such as Alberto Gonzalez as former U.S. attorney general and Jose Rodriguez as former director of the National Clandestine Service (D/NCS) of the CIA. The historical circumstances and particularities of Chicanos in the 1960s were such that a Chicano like Gonzalez, who ultimately "legitimized" torture in Abu Ghraib and Guantánamo, would never have sat in such a high office. Today, there is much more integration of Chicanos into the mainstream. That is, there is a flow from the particular (Chicano as different) to the general; like the Irish, Russian, Italian, and Jewish ethnic groups before us, tomorrow we will simply be a part of the general. Under capitalism, we see this mainstreaming of Chicanos as a corruption of Chicanos to do the odious, despicable work of U.S. capitalist imperialism. Along with this mainstreaming is the eventual loss over a couple of generations of Spanish as a natal tongue.

Third: We need to understand that the vast majority of the fiction written by postcolonial and borderland authors is written in English. Postcolonial and borderland literature is part and parcel of English-language literature. For example, the more borderland literature is written by third- and fourth-generation Chicanos, the less this literature will use the technique of code switching as a marker of ethnic identity. While much that we do in our everyday lives goes beyond language, "there is nothing beyond language in literature. Literature is language," David Treuer astutely remarks (76). We should therefore read, evaluate, and appreciate postcolonial and borderland literature as we would all other English-language writers. We do this because English is the language of everyday life for writers like Luis Rodriguez, Hanif Kureishi, Salman Rushdie, and Amitav Ghosh, among many others. We appraise their work alongside that of other writers in English also as a question of motivation. It is the case for many authors, from Joseph Conrad to Arundhati Roy, that writing in English was a conscious decision, that their stories could only be expressed using the instrument of English. And so our main consideration of postcolonial and borderland narrative fiction should be their use of language and its aesthetic devices—and here they are no different from any English-language authors. T. S. Eliot was born American and died British; Conrad was born Polish and died British. Just as with a Roy or a Ghosh, it is not the nationality that counts, it is the writer's use of language and aesthetics.

Fourth: We must decouple identity from the fictional world. While a Chicano author might feel comfortable drawing upon the particularities of the neighborhood or characters he or she knows well from proximate environs, this is not an obligation. If a Chicano author feels comfortable writing about a Chicano living in the United Kingdom, as does Daniel Olivas, or simply telling the story of an Anglo stockbroker working on Wall Street, he or she can do so. And today we have a whole series of so-identified postcolonial authors writing in English and writing in different parts of the world whose imagination has been captured by life in Asian countries. Tomorrow, these authors might be interested in something else altogether. However, what does matter is how well these authors put language to aesthetic use in giving shape to particulars of character, time, and space.

Fifth: We should attend to how postcolonial and Latino borderland themes reflect the particulars of character, time, and place (racism on the construction site in Dagoberto Gilb's stories set in El Paso in *Woodcuts of Women,* for instance) and trigger emotions that have contributed in many instances to our survival, evolution, and development. It is important for us also to keep in mind how emotions play a vital role in reinforcing our capabilities to feel empathy and to learn from another person's experiences. We can confidently say that emotions and the attendant rules of behavior toward others are very present in politics. The will to organize in opposition to the war in Iraq may be fueled by the sheer horror of the grief, the massacre of Iraqi children and adults, the destruction of homes, museums, schools, factories, and so on. This reaction may be followed by a deeper understanding of the oppressive and exploitive nature of capitalism and imperialism and the will to contribute to building trade unions and political parties capable of stopping all wars and of fighting capitalism. Thus, emotion can grow into an ethical stand that can in turn grow into a political one: organizing and mobilizing against capitalists as a class and against their instruments of oppression and exploitation. For the purposes of this book, however, I shall remain focused more on how our universal nature of emotions along with our universal fiction-making capacity has given rise to the development of narrative fiction in all historical periods and all over the world. In *The Mind and Its Stories,* Patrick Colm Hogan explains how storytelling works cross-culturally, how it affects and is affected by the emotions, and how it exhibits universal structures both from the point of view of the author/storyteller and the reader/audience.

Sixth: We need to distinguish the formal techniques used to convey the story's content, that is, to distinguish the two most general categories that constitute an inseparable unity in narrative fiction: form and content. This distinction does not mean identifying an essential postcolonial or borderland content, as already discussed. Nor for that matter does this mean identifying an essential postcolonial or borderland form. In his essay "On a Postcolonial Narratology" Gerald Prince attempts the latter when he considers how "narratological modalities" such as point of view, flashback, and mood might inflect and inform postcolonial concepts of "hybridity" and "migrancy" and vice versa in positing a "postcolonial narratology" (372). Rather, we distinguish form and content to bring them into our conversation about tools that will give a deeper and more informed knowledge of how they work in any postcolonial and borderland narrative fiction.

Seventh: We want to keep in mind that we have the capacity to transform the whole of nature, including its human component (human biological nature), and therefore we as a species are the sum total of all its makers—its poets and their creations (Greek *poesis,* the "maker"). One of our shared capacities is that of fiction making and fiction engaging. However, just as we share the universal capacity for language, the particular use and manifestation of this capacity is uniquely expressed. So while postcolonial and Latino borderland authors use the same cognitive and emotive architecture as we all do in our everyday activities—select, store, and access actual or virtual experiences; infer cause and effect; read from exterior gesture interior states of mind; feel and empathize— they know how to work within a given medium to cue and trigger like responses and activities in the readers of their fictional worlds, and each will do so uniquely. This is why we delight in recognizing that Roy and Ghosh variously and uniquely engage with narrative techniques and generic conventions also used before them—with completely different aims and effects—by Jorge Luis Borges, Carlos Fuentes, William Faulkner, George Eliot, and Stendhal, among many others. This is why we can step fully into the shoes of a character like Roy's Rahel, who grows up in Ayemenem (near Roy's hometown, Kerala, India) and feel the pains and pleasures of Ghosh's characters who inhabit Burma at the turn of the twentieth century or Luis Rodriguez's Chicanas who inhabit a contemporary East Los Angeles—and know all along that they are "only" fictional inventions, "lies." This is why we can imagine holographically spaces, events, and characters only minimally described or hinted at by a narrator. This is why we can experience certain ethical dilemmas. Finally, this is why each narrative fiction is itself and other in that it solicits individualized reactions and memories; one might imagine and connect with Roy's Ayemenem more forcefully than with Gilb's El Paso or Rodriguez's East L.A., if Roy's depiction of it has more cognitive and emotional resonances in one's mind.

Postcolonial and Latino borderland fiction continues to evolve and even have excellent products and results. But it can also have its most degenerate aesthetic manifestations. In postcolonial and borderland fictions we are seeing more and more abstraction of time and place typical of the romance and the formulaic magical realist novel. This is not entirely surprising. Today, with the destruction and degeneration of daily life under capitalism, we are seeing scholars and media pundits hypostatize the particular, be it the borderland or the postcolonial, and therefore eliminate any sense of the passage of time and its consequences—how we modify society through (class) struggle and how this struggle in turn modifies the creation and reception of these narrative fictions.

In the chapters that follow I hope to provide several tools that will highlight features of form and content to give us a better idea of what makes good postcolonial and borderland literature tick as well as how they inscribe themselves within all other postcolonial and Latino borderland literatures—that is, within world literature. To begin to systematize just such an approach, in Chapter One, "A User's Guide to Postcolonial and Latino Borderland Fiction," I provide a preliminary guide to devices authors can use to move their readers. In Chapter Two, "Putting the Fiction Back into Arundhati Roy," I turn to the importance of style as well as the use of a "we" character filter, among other devices in Roy's *The God of Small Things*. So while the marketing-blitz context (the Booker media buzz, reviews, and swift academic canonization) can straightjacket a reader's engagement with the novel, its commercial success should not sidetrack us from understanding better why and how we relish its rich aesthetic complexity. In Chapter Three, "History as Handmaiden to Fiction in Amitav Ghosh," I use the tools of narrative theory to distinguish between history and fiction in an analysis of Ghosh's *The Glass Palace* as well as to disentangle those faddish academic theories that confuse nation with narration. In Chapter Four, "Fictional World Making in Zadie Smith and Hari Kunzru," I attend to the formal techniques used in Smith's *White Teeth* and Kunzru's *The Impressionist* that make worldly the particulars of culture and history represented within their pages. To this end, I also explore how emotive responses such as laughter work to reach out into the world and engage readers cross-culturally. In Chapter Five, "This Is Your Brain on Latino Comics," I analyze how the visual-verbal double narrator works in Latino comic books to create certain pleasurable disjunctions and unities in the reader-viewer's mind. Finally, in Chapter Six, "Reading the Latino Borderland Short Story," I focus on a number of narrative theory concepts and tools (peritext and point of view, for example) to understand better how the "will to style" in Latino borderland authors Dagoberto Gilb and Luis Rodriguez allows them to craft fictions that richly texture the lives of twenty-first-century Chicano characters inhabiting El Paso and East L.A. (the particular) in English with minimal code switching (the general) in ways that appeal to readers the world over (the universal).

One	A USER'S GUIDE TO
	POSTCOLONIAL AND
	LATINO BORDERLAND
	FICTION

Using narrative theory—specifically the tools developed by narratology—to understand better how postcolonial and Latino borderland narrative fiction ticks is an important first move. Mieke Bal defines narratology as "the theory of narrative texts. A theory is a systematic set of generalized statements about a particular segment of reality. That segment of reality, the corpus, about which narratology attempts to make its pronouncements consists of narrative texts" (3). Already, distinctions of character slant and narrator filter, first- and multi-person narrator, implied author and ideal reader, narratee, time, duration, and mode allow us to break from the various hypostatized theme- and identity-based trappings outlined in the Introduction. The distinctions allow us to more fully appreciate the craft of certain postcolonial and Latino borderland authors' idiomatic and particularized texturing of character, time, and place in ways that actively participate in shaping world literature.

As we will see in the chapters that follow, authors including Roy, Ghosh, Kunzru, Smith, Rodriguez, and Gilb as well as various author-artists of comic books—Los Bros Hernandez, Rhode Montijo, and Frank Espinosa, among others—choose particular narrative approaches and techniques according to what they perceive as necessary to the act of narration and to the engagement of the reader's or reader-viewer's cognitive faculties. The decisions made and the paths taken are conditioned by innumerable factors. No detailed account of the author's biography (her life experiences; her social, political, economic, and historical circumstances; her gender and sexual orientation; her ethnic background and upbringing), accompanied by the most extensive account of the way the author has reacted toward every circumstance she has experienced, will ever explain why Smith, for example, chooses to begin *White Teeth* with the character Archie about to commit suicide or why Kunzru chooses to begin his novel *The Impressionist* with action aswirl in the middle of a great flood. Why these authors among others decide to present their narrations in the third person as opposed to the first—or even the plural character filter as with Roy. Why Rodriguez favors code switching in some stories and not in others. Why Gilb chooses words and rhythms that lack adornment and figuration. Why Roy is more inclined to tell multiple stories simultaneously and others prefer sequential chapters.

Given that I want to avoid slipping into an "identity politics" approach as well as to sidestep that move that judges literary merit based on discussions of felicitous or infelicitous representation of race, ethnicity, gender, and so on, in the so-identified postcolonial and borderland experience I turn to those tools developed in "classical" narratology and "cognitive" narratology. My aim is to heighten our pleasure of reading postcolonial and Latino borderland novels, short stories, and comic books by getting to know better how they work and which procedures allow them to connect with our living realities, here (locally and countrywide) as well as globally.

      In analyzing postcolonial and Latino borderland literature, I do not intend to exclude judgments of value and political and moral arguments. On the contrary. Again, there is good and bad postcolonial and Latino borderland narrative fiction, but I do not want to use a rule of measure whereby that deemed good and worthy of our attention is simply that authored by a postcolonial or borderland Other or because its sentimentalizing of a given identity politics moves us.

Before moving into a discussion of the different narratological tools I consider useful in this analysis, first I want to expand on some of the key concepts and categories such as the particular, general, and universal.

For all practical purposes, human beings are universally endowed with the same biological and psychological equipment. Therefore, at the basis of human activities, be they scientific, artistic, productive (prehistoric scavenging, hunting, gathering; Neolithic fishing and cultivating; Modern Age manufacturing, building, and so on), one and the same anatomical, physiological, and neurological configuration is at work. It is this configuration that accounts for all our psychological, cultural, and sociohistorical universals. Take the senses. Sight, hearing, smell, taste, and touch are by and large the same in all human beings. Their bioneurological function is identical, while their "education" varies among individuals and from one historic moment to another. For example, if one's hearing has been educated by listening to Bach in the Los Angeles of the late twentieth century, it will differ from that of a person who has never listened to Bach and has been educated only by *corridos, boleros,* and pop music from Mexico. However, as is obvious, from the biological point of view nothing would impede the latter individual from becoming educated by Bach. For thousands of years, the hearing of the Chinese has been educated by instruments and musical traditions very different from those that shaped Bach and that Bach in turn shaped; yet today Chinese musicians such as ehru soloist Ma Xiaohui and members of the Shanghai Quartet are among the best interpreters of baroque music in the world, particularly of Bach. The same influence of education applies to the other senses. In matters of taste, the particular (local) and even the idiosyncratic may become universal when biologically based.

We know that narrative has been present in human societies since the dawn of time. Narrative consists of two primary kinds: fiction and nonfiction. They are both universal and they both exhibit universal forms. These forms are the subject of intensive research and discussion, but so far very few results have gone beyond the stage of classification. However, the work accomplished is very important already, for it provides the necessary means to begin delimiting specific branches of knowledge concerning many aspects of narrative and to delimit as well an overall science of narrative. Among the groups of approaches is a universal "syntax" as a taxonomy and incipient explanation of the structural, functional, and logical order of narrative as such. The findings in this field are due in considerable part to research done under the name "narratology." Another group is one formed by the complicated and complex research concerning a universal "semantics" as an inquiry into theme (or topic), plot, and genre. Then there is the group of approaches in relation with a universal "pragmatics" as an analysis of the relation between reader or audience and narrative. Lastly, there is the group of approaches related to a universal "phonetics" as an inquiry into rhythm, metered speech, onomatopoeia, and prosody.

No barrier separates one group of approaches from another. As will become clear, they are connected in myriad ways, but it helps to see them as distinct conceptual classes to keep instruction and research manageable. A common experiential link among these four groups of approaches is emotion. Recent neuroscience has given a solid basis to the hypotheses that emotions are also universal, notwithstanding the notion held by some, for instance among the military, that people in the former colonies "do not feel the same way we do"—as infamously claimed by General William Westmoreland when he stated that the Vietnamese have a different attitude toward death and life and feel pain differently, to justify napalming them. Now, after the pioneering work of Joseph LeDoux (*The Self: From Soul to Brain*) and Antonio Damasio (*Looking for Spinoza*), many neuroscientists have extended our knowledge concerning the functioning and role of emotions in human beings.

Emotions are of central concern in the study of narrative. That is one reason we must look closely at recent research in neurobiology. The discovery of a mirror neuron system in humans (after its discovery in macaque monkeys in 1996) opened the way to a multitude of new explorations concerning the brain and our social behavior. The mirror neuron system in humans has been consistently reported as being related to imitation, action observation, intention understanding, and understanding of the emotional states of others, to mention a few of the human faculties that are essential for the right perception of fictional narratives and, of course, for the survival and evolution of the human race.

And there seems to be even more to it. In a 2004 journal article titled "A Unifying View of the Basis of Social Cognition," Vittorio Gallese, Christian Keysers, and Giacomo Rizzolatti explore the possibility that the mirror neuron system, by providing us with an experiential (precognitive) insight into other minds, could provide the "first unifying perspective" of the neural basis of social cognition (401). The mirror neuron system is apparently the basic mechanism that allows us to grasp the intentions of others and to experience similar emotions (empathy). They write, "A crucial element of social cognition is the brain's capacity to directly link the first- and third-person experiences of these phenomena," that is, its capacity to link "I do and I feel" with "he does and he feels" (396). Would then art not be but a specific and specialized activity aimed at firing the mirror neurons in a certain direction? Would the "will to style" displayed by postcolonial and Latino borderland authors be the deliberate use of "syntax," "semantics," "pragmatics," and "phonetics" to trigger the mirror neuron system in specific and predetermined ways to elicit specific and predetermined insights and emotions in the reader and the audience?

The study of postcolonial- and Latino borderland-identified narrative fiction is a comparative study. There is nothing on this planet that it cannot touch. In matters of form, subject, and creative and receptive mechanisms, such a work does not stand alone. From neurobiology to psychology, from socioeconomic to historical circumstances, *all* works of fiction are overdetermined, complex systems. Nothing human is alien to postcolonial and Latino borderland narrative fiction in terms of subject matter and presentation: it deals with everything and anything under the sun, by any and all means possible. Nor is anything off limits when talking about the kind of knowledge brought to bear in its study and analysis.

Also, as is the case with ideas and with the findings of science, narrative fiction (postcolonial and Latino borderland or otherwise) knows no geographical boundaries, no frontiers. Ideas pertaining to science or to fiction and fiction making are in constant and unfettered movement. They know no borders, no political blockages, no race, no ethnic origin or destination, and no identity politics. Ever since *Gilgamesh* and the *Iliad*, narrative subjects and procedures are common property and, potentially at least, universal property.

Therefore, I ask, can there be, in *strictu sensu*, a literary tradition of only what is identified as the postcolonial and Latino borderland? Do postcolonial and Latino borderland narrative fictions, in their tireless travels around the globe and their permanent interactions with other "ethnic" narratives from all corners of the world, not participate within world literature? Is not world literature the outcome of thousands of years of various incarnations of what today we identify as postcolonial and Latino borderland narrative fiction?

Of course, there are postcolonial and Latino borderlands, and there are *postcolonial* and *Latino borderlands*. The birth and expansion of the capitalist mode of production in Europe gave way to that veritable explosion of creativity known as the Renaissance in the Old World but stifled it in the New World and other colonized areas. The original inhabitants of the American continent were almost completely wiped out, and the survivors were pushed more and more to live in the most inhospitable lands in a state of barbarism they had surpassed thousands of years before. When anthropologists in the Americas or Southeast Asia declared that they were studying the present mirror of humanity's prehistoric past, they forgot to indicate that what they were seeing in this "mirror" was not a remote past but the present outcome of four centuries of exploitation and oppression by the developing capitalist system. Only one anthropologist, the Mexican Gonzalo Aguirre Beltrán, stood up to the challenge of doing a scientific study of this phenomenon of forced retrogression to a state of barbarism, which he explained in his almost unknown and rarely discussed book *Regiones de refugio*.

Our twenty-first-century existence is no guarantee of a continued flourishing of the arts and the sciences. The twentieth century showed

us how we can fall back into barbarism, and the present century is show-
ing us how we are risking global destruction of our civilized creations.
Yet in spite of this, today narrative fiction in all its guises is still a shared
worldwide achievement. Postcolonial and Latino borderland narrative
fiction belongs to narrative fiction in the global village, to use Marshall
McLuhan's expression. The world is one, the science describing and understanding it is one, and the arts representing and recreating it are one.
The divisions into branches of inquiry, professions, and academic dis-
ciplines are contingent and the result of our human limitations and of
our political, historical, economic, and other contingent circumstances
that we should not hypostatize, turn into facts of nature, or consider as
simply "given."

Postcolonial and Latino borderland studies, the development of the
notion of postcolonial and Latino, and the identification of postcolonial
and Latino borderland literatures are all politically and historically situated phenomena. They all took place first in the United States, one of
the world's most massively diversified countries in terms of ethnic and
cultural origins. All European countries are present in the United States
through emigration; so are the countries of Latin America, Asia, Africa,
and the Middle East. The writers and artists of such diverse origins who
live and work in the United States are grouped according to ethnicity
and studied in college as representative of their respective cultural back-
grounds. But this is an exceptional situation. Writers of African, Middle
Eastern, Asian, or Caribbean descent living in France or Sweden, for
instance, are not studied separately in different departments in French or
Swedish universities. And the authors themselves do not wish to be considered and evaluated in any way differently from their European coun-
terparts living in France or Sweden. Albert Camus and Jacques Derrida
were born in Algeria, they lived there during their decisively formative
years, their mother tongue was French, and they wrote in French. They
never asked to be considered "ethnic" writers in France, and they considered themselves as innovative thinkers and narrative creators in the
French language.

So in order to understand the place of postcolonial and Latino
borderland literary studies in academia and the political and economic
importance these studies have acquired in the United States, we must
study and know the particular circumstances that led to their conception
and establishment.

What does it mean to label a literature "postcolonial" or "borderland"? What does it mean to title a course "Survey of Postcolonial and

Latino Borderland Literature"? These labels are more a way to circumscribe a set number of texts to read and analyze in a manageable way than they are the assigning of an idiomatic quality that we can identify as "postcolonial" or "borderland" residing in the DNA of the fictional narratives at hand. Scholars and media pundits have made many attempts to locate various traces of a postcolonial- or borderland-inflected uniqueness. I have mentioned Rafael Pérez-Torres, Elleke Boehmer, and Walter Mignolo. But there are many others such as Homi Bhabha with his "mimicry," "interstice," "hybridity," and "sly civility" (*The Location of Culture*) and Gayatri Spivak with her question "Can the Subaltern Speak?" There is also Henry Louis Gates Jr. with his concept of an African American "signifying monkey," Arnold Krupat and his concept of a Native American trickster, and Luis Leal with his Chicano themes of social protest or a symbolic reclamation of Aztlán.

If we read, say, Luis Rodriguez's "Las Chicas Chuecas" (in his *Republic of East L.A.* collection) with only an "ethnic eye" or through a "borderland" lens, we risk reducing the story to only a set of ethnic themes and characterizations when the story and the author's imagination are much more than the directly experiential. This is not always the fault of the reader. Authors freely decide the subject matter and form of their fiction. John Edgar Wideman, certainly a careful stylist of the English language, has been subordinating his writerly imagination more and more to his own and his family's experience to a neighborhood Philadelphia. At what point do "self-fiction" (by the author) and a postcolonial and borderland approach (on the part of the reader) cease being creative and instead become egotist sentimentality or provincial narrow-mindedness?

To determine a postcolonial or Latino borderland narrative fiction through and through, one would need to find an "ethnic" or "race" component or substance as the identifiable and identifying feature. However, if we characterize or circumscribe postcolonial and Latino borderland narrative fiction *only* by sociological or political or economic notions and considerations, are we not making distinctions removed from the reality of how such fictions work? After all, from the point of view of the production and reception of fiction narratives, all such notions and considerations are secondary and contingent, for the analysis they furnish are subsidiary or ancillary to the study of narrative as such.

The tools of narrative theory can help us find our footing when exploring how the so-identified syntax, semantics, pragmatics, and phonetics of the postcolonial and Latino borderland author come together as a unified whole in his or her narrative fiction. Narrative theory furnishes us with the verifiable means to identify structures in a given narrative fiction that can be studied in comparison with literature conceived by all sorts of authors in all parts of the world and in many different epochs. It can provide us with the tools and key ideas to understand better the techniques all authors, including postcolonial and Latino borderland authors, use to create interesting stories that move readers; among their techniques are point of view, temporal structure, narrative speed, narrating instance, embedding, free indirect discourse, and reported, transposed, and narrativized speech. Narrative theory also reminds us of the artifice of the narratives, that stories are artifacts represented verbally in written form, graphically by means of images, or a mixture of both. While a Gilb, a Smith, or a Montijo chooses to represent a part of reality—a section dealing with dislocated and disenfranchised people—and to have that representation become the setting and the unfolding of his or her story, this choice is only justified in terms of its narrative merits (not its "narrative contents"), just as with authors' other choices concerning point of view, temporal structure, and so on.

So, in our analysis—and evaluation—we might begin by asking how Smith uses verbs and syntax to engage her readers—even move us to laughter. Or we might ask what Luis Rodriguez can do (and not do) when texturing the lives of a Chicana gang in the short story form as opposed to a novel. We could examine how the interplay of the visual with the verbal works to engage readers differently in the comic book series *Love and Rockets* than the black marks on the pages of Smith's novel *White Teeth*.

In exploring these general questions—keeping the author-artist and the reader-viewer centrally in mind—I offer here a guide to a variety of narrative tools useful for understanding structures and devices used ("first order") and how they move us cognitively and emotively ("second order") to help us really *read* postcolonial and Latino borderland fiction.

FIRST-ORDER NARRATIVE TOOLS

Peritext

Those outermost features that surround a given postcolonial and Latino borderland fiction—the cover, title page, and jacket blurbs as well as format, paper, and typeface—are identified by Gérard Genette as the "publisher's peritext": "the whole zone of the peritext that is the direct and principal (but not exclusive) responsibility of the publisher" (*Paratexts*, 16). The peritexts are not totally arbitrary: they establish initial reader contracts and cues that trigger in the reader's mind important scripts—comic or tragic, for instance—that we anticipate encountering once inside the story proper. While some authors (I think here of Mark Z Danielewski's *House of Leaves* and Dave Eggers's *A Heartbreaking Work of Staggering Genius*) exploit the peritext conventions, mostly this is in the hands of publishing house marketing departments.

Zadie Smith's *White Teeth* makes a good test case. Salman Rushdie's blurb (wedged between the title and author name in the first hardback edition, by Hamish Hamilton, 2000) reads: "An astonishingly assured début, funny and serious . . . it has bite." Not only does Rushdie's name give it an important assurance of top-shelf postcolonial quality, but it establishes a contract: that it will be at once comic and serious. In this instance, the novel actually is funny and serious—satirical; often, however, the blurbs can create false expectations and tensions with what actually unfolds in the storyworld. The peritext can create interesting sets of tensions between the biographical author, say, and the "implied author" (described below). For instance, in the black and white photograph of Zadie Smith on the jacket cover of the Random House hardcover U.S. edition she wears glasses that obscure or cut across her eyes, and her head is cocked slightly to the side; her face is round, her curly black hair is pulled back, high up off her slightly freckled forehead, and she is wearing a black turtleneck. On the back cover of the 2001 Penguin U.K. and Vintage U.S. paperback edition, a color photograph of Smith has her appear with very straight dark hair, chiseled high cheekbones, brown skin tone, no glasses, and looking unabashedly and seductively at the viewer. From one edition to the next, Smith morphs from serious author-intellectual (the black turtleneck is the cue of African origin) to International United Color of Benetton model.

What is interesting is not so much the way the peritext markets Smith—a topic discussed at length by Mark Stein in his *Black British Literature*—but that in either case the author photograph creates certain tensions with the image we construct of the "implied author" of *White Teeth*. In both author photographs, Smith is serious. This tells us something about her approach to fiction, that she takes it seriously—and we get this more so from the hardback edition—and that she confirms her smart and richly complex interviews. The seriousness of her author photograph is at opposite ends to the playful, "funny" with a "bite" narrator of the story. That is, the peritext here helps establish in the reader's mind that author Zadie Smith is not the same as the implied author persona projected in the novel—nor is author Zadie Smith the same as her narrator.

Story and Discourse

The distinction between story (the time of the events as occurring within the storyworld) and the discourse (the time and ordering of the narrative telling) allows us to keep clearly in mind that the postcolonial and Latino borderland author (biographical) has at his or her disposal many possibilities for focusing (panning in and panning out, third person and free indirect discourse or interior monologue, for instance) as well as slowing down or speeding up (omitting or including details and inserting flashbacks or flashforwards, for instance) the pace in which the reader builds the totality of the story. In this control at the level of discourse of the time (speed up/slow down) and space (stretch out/shrink down) of the story, we can identify important narrative devices and affiliative affects that cue us to read any given narrative as fiction and not nonfiction.

While we can in theory distinguish between a discourse and story level, in the act of reading they fuse. Indeed, for some scholars the fact that they are fused in the reader's mind suggests the possibility that it is less a "discourse" and more the medium itself that determines the story, that there is no story without discourse and vice versa. This lends support to the argument that "a narrative medium is any semiotic means that enables the articulation (as distinct from expression) of cognitive image schemata in narrative form," as Richard Walsh argues in "The Narrative Imagination Across Media" (855). Simply stated, no thought can be communicated without some kind of vehicle; communication implies the transmission from A going out to and being incorporated by B as materialized in whatever form. And this form (or vehicle) shapes the content necessarily.

In "Dreaming and Narrative Theory," Walsh once again reiterates the point that the story is not the essential feature, or deep structure, of narrative fiction as is generally held. Therefore the story cannot, according to Walsh, stay the same when translated across different media. And it might be a question of degree of change depending on how alike the media are. For example, in the Shakespeare plays that have been adapted to the silver screen—I think of several about which I have written extensively—Oliver Parker's *Othello* (1995), Tim Blake Nelson's "*O*" (2001), James Gavin Bedford's *Street King* (2002), and Uli Edel's *King of Texas* (2002)—the shift from stage play to film is close enough in media likeness that the film adaptation only alters the content (the story) minimally. However, in Julian Jarrold's 2002 made-for-television film adaptation of *White Teeth,* so much of the story is altered that it fails miserably. The novel medium, with its device of narrated monologue or free indirect style, determines the story in such a definitive way that it cannot be adapted to visually driven media like film without severe distortion; what an author can do with the narrated monologue a director has to show in film, and this usually does not work.

Duration

If we decide to use the story and discourse distinction, we can see more readily how a given postcolonial- and Latino borderland-identified author can stretch, speed up (elide), and summarize scenes and events within the storyworld. This stretching and shrinking is identified as "duration" and works at the level of the discourse to determine the rhythm, tempo, and overall feel of the fictional narrative. It can serve the function of a climactic buildup. For example, in the penultimate paragraph of Cristina Garcia's short story "Inés in the Kitchen" we see a descriptive shift to a detailing of Inés's childhood: a father, Gerardo, who wanted to keep his daughter "dolled up in her starched Sunday dress, all to himself" and a mother who dressed her up for pageants and held up Inés's winning the Little Miss Latin New York as her "greatest achievement" (156). This allows us to see more clearly Inés's actions: her marriage to a starched-shirt-wearing, controlling, gringo husband, Richard, not as a sellout but as predestined from childhood. And just as importantly, the flashback slows the narrative enough so that when we reach the final paragraph of the story, the narrative snaps us back to the dilemma at hand:

> Other times, mostly in the early afternoons, she feels like setting fire to the damask curtains that keep their living room in a perpetual dusk. She dreams about blowing up her herb garden with its basil leaves, then stealing a thoroughbred from the stable across the street and riding it as fast as she can. Inés finishes the last of her milk. She rinses the glass and leans against the kitchen sink. There is a jingling of keys at the front door. Richard is home. (157)

Mode

Again, if we use the story and discourse distinction we can understand how a given postcolonial and Latino borderland author chooses certain words and syntax to build a narrative discourse and how this narrative discourse guides the reader in creating the fictional world. Mode is the difference between narrative discourse and the world it evokes; it is the difference between the words used to build the world and the world those words evoke. The only element that allows authors to erase the distinction between narrative discourse and imaginary world is what Todorov calls the direct discourse: a page and a half into *salt and saffron*, Kamila Shamsie's narrator announces, "Confused? Would you rather I changed the topic to yak milk production?" (2).

Flashback and Flashforward

Again, if we consider the story and discourse distinction useful, then we can see the double temporal sequence in narrative fiction: the time of the thing told and the time of the narrative. The discourse level determines the order in which the reader receives the narrative events contained within the story. The typical manipulation of temporal order is in the flashback (looking back or anachrony) and flashforward (anticipation or prolepsis) or a combination of the two as in a flashforward within an extended flashback and vice versa. In *White Teeth* Zadie Smith frequently uses the flashback to order time:

> Once the car started to fill with carbon monoxide, he had experienced the obligatory flashback of his life to date. It turned out to be a short, unedifying viewing experience, low on entertainment value, the metaphysical equivalent of the Queen's speech. A dull childhood, a bad marriage, a dead-end job—that classic triumvirate—they all flicked by quickly, silently, with little dialogue, feeling pretty much the same as they did the first time round. . . . There was the war, of course. (12)

Smith uses this device not only to shrink and stretch narrative time but to provide a series of events that allow the reader to more fully realize even a seemingly dull character like Archie.

In the comic book *In My Darkest Hour* Wilfred Santiago uses two different color washes over its panels to identify its shift into an extended flashback. We see in both Smith's and Santiago's work that flashback and flashforward techniques not only provide a shift in temporal rhythm but also give a fuller sense of a protagonist in and through the actions of others he or she encountered in the past.

Implied Author

The "implied author" is not an entity inscribed in the text as such—as narrator or teller of any kind. The implied author, as Uri Margolin identifies this persona, "is nowhere to be found as a speech position, and remains an unanchored, elusive entity hovering above the text" (276). The implied author does not recount situations and events but is inferred from the text as a whole and is taken to be accountable for the selection, distribution, and combination of all its ingredients. In still another sense, the implied author is the image of the author constructed by the reader. My image of Zadie Smith is smart and devilishly playful, in contrast, as mentioned above, to her author photograph.

When we read *The Impressionist,* Hari Kunzru constructs a felt persona, a sense of someone standing behind the scenes, but this someone is constituted by the narrative itself. This is not Kunzru, the biographical author who has written many novels, each with its own distinctive implied author, but the constructed persona that the reader senses to be the master of ceremonies—the grand conductor. This implied author is centrally concerned with constructing a world whereby the ideal reader—that entity shaped in conjunction with the worldview of the implied author—gets fully the subjective experience of an uncertain reality conveyed by the narrative *in toto.* The world in *The Impressionist* is characterized by a contemporary racist xenophobia of India at the turn of the twentieth century and London in the early to mid–twentieth century. This tool is useful for us to keep in mind, separately, the actual author and his or her circumstances and actual readers, their own circumstances, and their cognitive and emotive responses to a particular narrative as a work of the imagination.

These distinctions are important because they remind us that when a postcolonial and Latino borderland author creates a narrative fiction, she or he engages in a problem-solving, goal-directed activity: to write a blueprint for the reader to follow whereby choices of vocabulary, what is described and omitted, subject matter, plot, subplots, and so on generate a gestalt image of an implied author. In this sense, the implied author is one of the most elusive and yet important categories in the narrative theory toolbox. Moreover, the absence of a specific marker for the implied author in the text leads Uri Margolin to formulate the concept of "cognitive style" (276). This is what I call the "will to style" and describe below. With the goal of creating "a certain epistemic and aesthetic (that is, artistic and cognitive) impact on his or her readers and providing them with a certain 'vision'" (ibid.), Margolin observes, the author must engineer a "mode of presentation" that is specific and personalized—a *"cognitive style"* by which the reader will receive and process the information (277).

It is the implied author and the cognitive style (or will to style) that function as a bridge between the internal and external perspectives, the individual (neurobiological) and the social (cultural), as the bridge between everything that pertains to the author as an individual in terms of sociohistorical reality—his or her public existence—and his or her neurobiological or personal experience. It is the will to style that functions as this bridge between the neurobiological and the cultural in the making of postcolonial and Latino borderland narrative fiction. The end result of our forming an image of the implied author is that we have a sense of this personality as a synthesis of the public and private, individual and social.

Ideal Reader

The "ideal reader" is also nowhere to be found in the text; it is the hypothetical reader who takes on the beliefs and knowledge that the implied author conveys, including the knowledge that he or she is reading a constructed text. The ideal reader is a hypothesis formed by the implied author in accordance with the implied author's values and cultural norms. As an image of the ideal recipient of the text, this reader is an assumed addressee who understands the text optimally, that is, in a way that fully matches its structure and its aesthetic and other values and norms. This is not the same as the narrative audience, the one implicitly addressed by the narrator; the ideal reader takes on the beliefs and values that the narrator ascribes to him or her, and in most cases this reader responds to the characters and events as if they were real.

One must not confuse the ideal reader with the narratee (described below). The ideal reader is the audience of the implied author and must be inferred from the text as a whole, while the narratee is the audience of the narrator and is inscribed as such in the text. In other words, the ideal reader is the reader inferred by the real reader to be an intended recipient of the narrative and the reader for whom the implied author writes. As such, the ideal reader has no commerce with the narrator and cannot create a distance between itself and the narratee. The ideal reader belongs to an ontological category totally different from the ontological categories of the narrator and the narratee.

Multiple Implied or Ideal Readers

In "Singular Text, Multiple Implied Readers" Brian Richardson importantly identifies the making of "a duality textured narrative that unfolds one meaning to the majority audience and another, deeper one to the minority community" (261). Not surprisingly, Richardson identifies postcolonial authors (with more surveillanced contexts of writing, producing, and circulating) as utilizing this tool to write to "an indigenous audience" and a "larger Anglo-, Franco-, or Lusophone audience" (262). The tool of the multiple implied reader or ideal reader is important and does appear in postcolonial and Latino borderland fictions. However, we need to also consider the use of this tool within historical contexts. For example, today more and more we see postcolonial and Latino borderland authors conceiving of their narrative fiction from the very beginning with an international, middle-class ideal reader in mind—one most likely to buy and read the fiction internationally. Even when local color is represented, it is usually served up in a clichéd form. So we get the avatars of the Terry McMillans and Isabel Allendes sporting their faddish wares in all variety of South Asian postcolonial and Latino borderland literature.

There are those with few pretensions to be anything but soap opera, such as Nisha Minhas's *Sari and Sins,* the front cover of which announces it as "The Sparkling New Romantic Comedy from the Author of *Chapatti or Chips?.*" Some purport greater aspirations; Anita Desai's narrator in *Fasting, Feasting,* for example, describes an occasion when "the blue oblong of electric light that hangs from a branch of the spruce tree over the barbecue is being bombarded by the insects that evening summons up from the surrounding green. They hurl themselves at it like heathens in the frenzy of their false religion, and die with small, piercing detonations. The evening is punctuated by their unredeemed deaths" (167–168).

After Rushdie flung wide open fiction's doors with *Midnight's Children* in 1981, many a postcolonial author hacked up inventive and original expression; strings of hyphenation—the Not-Quite-Daughter, You-Fill-In-The-Blanks—littered paragraphs of what amounted to romance novels with pretensions of high-brow postcolonial grandeur. That is, with this international ideal reader in mind, today we see less a multiple implied or ideal reader and more a homogenized (pasteurized, if you will), dull implied or ideal reader.

Narrator

Postcolonial and Latino borderland authors have choices regarding how they want to present their stories—through unreliable or reliable voices, in first, second, or third person, and as multiple narrators, to list a few possibilities. J. M. Coetzee's *Boyhood: Scenes from Provincial Life* uses a highly restrictive third-person narrator (in a present tense and often slipping into a future conditional tense) to give harsh immediacy to this coming-of-age fictional memoir: "He shares nothing with his mother. His life at school is kept a tight secret from her. She shall know nothing, he resolves, but what appears on his quarterly report, which shall be impeccable. He will always come first in class" (5). In the case of unreliability, an author can choose to craft a narration that connotes a contradiction between the image of the implied author constructed by the reader on the basis of stylistic, ideological, and aesthetic features exhibited by the text and the image of the narrator(s) of the story resulting from different and sometimes even opposing features concerning behavior and values. When an author uses this technique the way Oscar "Zeta" Acosta does in *The Autobiography of the Brown Buffalo,* he or she makes a radical break from typical Chicano borderland fiction constrained by a straightforward realism that is driven by identity politics.

Postcolonial and Latino borderland authors can choose a number of types of narrator vis-à-vis their positions within or outside the storyworld (each, in turn, addressing a different narratee or the same one): third-person omniscient or with limited omniscience, narrator within yet not a part of the story, narrator as protagonist of the story, among others. For instance, as we engage line by line Ana Castillo's short story "Loverboys" we meet a narrator as a character within the story who is a voyeur and whose voyeuristic acts call attention to the reader's act of voyeuristic intrusion. Castillo uses the character-as-narrator who stands slightly apart from the story and begins it as follows: "Two boys are making out in the booth across from me. I ain't got nothing else to do, I watch them" (*Loverboys. Stories,* 11). The narrative complicates the voyeurism of the character-as-narrator as we identify, then re-identify the narrator's voice and position as well as the title of the story—"Loverboys."

When I have taught this story, some students initially have identified the narrator as male. Soon, however, the reader discovers the narrator to be a woman—a woman who desires both men and women. Tuned in to narrator position and voice, we can better understand the thematic essence of the story: to blur the boundaries between gender and sexual preference. Moreover, by understanding Castillo's choice to create a character-as-narrator who desires and objectifies, we also come to understand how the story subverts and resists a politically correct reading: that to be queer and of color does not necessarily mean one is above reifying processes. The narrator unabashedly fixes her sights on a patron she describes as having "Indian smooth skin like glazed clay," "obsidian eyes," and the "offhanded manner of a chile alegre" (13).

Plural Narrator

A postcolonial and Latino borderland author can also choose a narrator who occupies a middle ground between first person and third person, the "we" narrator. In *Unnatural Voices* Brian Richardson uses this tool to analyze several postcolonial authors, including Raja Rao, Ayi Kwei Armah, and Edouard Glissant. Richardson asserts that "the vast majority of 'we' texts valorize collective identity in no uncertain terms; 'we' is almost always a favored term and a desirable subject position that is to be sought out and inhabited" (50).

There are many variations on the "we" narrator. Ben Okri opens *Songs of Enchantment* with:

> We didn't see the seven mountains ahead of us. We didn't see how they are always ahead, always calling us, always reminding us that there are more things to be done, dreams to be realized, joys to be re-discovered, promises made before birth to be fulfilled, beauty to be incarnated, and love embodied. (3)

Then this "we" voice transitions into a first-person narration:

> Yes, the spirit-child is an unwilling adventurer into chaos and sunlight, into the dreams of the living and the dead.

> But after dad's last fight, after his magnificent dream, my
> adventures got deeper and stranger. (4)

In Elena Garro's *Recollections of Things to Come* (originally published in 1963 as *Los recuerdos del porvenir*) the "we" narrator takes the form of an "I." The novel opens:

> Here I sit on what looks like a stone. Only my memory
> knows what it holds. I see it and I remember, and as water
> flows into water, so I, melancholically, come to find myself
> in its image, covered with dust, surrounded by grass, self-
> contained and condemned to memory and its variegated
> mirror. I see it, I see myself, and I am transfigured into a
> multitude of colors and times. I am and I was in many eyes.
> I am only memory and the memory that one has of me. (3)

The plural narrator further complicates our understanding of the relationship between implied author and ideal reader. It seems possible to have multiple implied authors without a corresponding number of ideal readers.

Moreover, Richardson is careful to point out that the "we" narrator is not inherently ideological. He remarks, "There is no inherent ideological valence in any narrative form" (*Unnatural Voices*, 59). This is important to keep in mind when reading, analyzing, and teaching postcolonial and Latino borderland fiction, in which there is so much marketing (academic or otherwise) pressure to read it ideologically. One can use any narrative tool, the "we" narrator included, to give shape to either the most reactionary or the most progressive of postcolonial and borderland novels. The plural narrator is not a marker of any kind of value. We can say the same with any device, including the much-touted progressive gender bending (lack of pronoun identification) in a novel like Jeanette Winterson's *Written on the Body*. No technique in and of itself will indicate a progressive or regressive politics.

Narrated Monologue

In her chapter, "Narrated Monologue," in *Transparent Minds,* Dorrit Cohn resuscitates an important tool identified early in the twentieth century by German analysts like Leo Spitzer: the narrated monologue (see *Leo Spitzer: Representative Essays,* edited by Herbert

Lindenberger). This is a device used by postcolonial and Latino borderland authors with many sensibilities and outlooks. Where interior monologue takes the form of the first person (Molly Bloom in the Penelope chapter of *Ulysses*), the narrated monologue is always in the third person. It is a very flexible and convenient device for allowing the reader to *feel* the presence of a character's voice without establishing a rupture (as with quoted discourse) in continuity of this voice and that of the narrator (omniscient third person). The narrator "speaks" in the third person while adopting his or her character's inner language; the narrator functions as a sort of ventriloquist of the thoughts, inner language, and idiom of the character, all while the narrator continues to do the job of narrating in the third person. J. M. Coetzee uses this device in an extended fashion in *Disgrace* to continually present an odd admixture of a third-person narrator with a progressive worldview intermingled with the reactionary worldview of the protagonist, David:

> Technically he is old enough to be her father; but then, technically, one can be a father at twelve. He has been on her books for over a year; he finds her entirely satisfactory. In the desert of the week Thursday has become an oasis of *luxe et volupté*. In bed Soraya is not effusive. Her temperament is in fact rather quiet, quiet and docile. In her general opinions she is surprisingly moralistic. (1)

More generally, the device of the narrated monologue can be used to clear some space for postcolonial and Latino borderland authors to craft narratives with two simultaneous worldviews (those of narrator and character) that can run together in a seamless way while speaking to two audiences.

Intermental Minds

In our everyday activities we are constantly filling in the blanks about other people's minds; in the process of inferring another's state of mind, we are closing gaps in our knowledge of their behavior. Some argue that this everyday activity also takes place when we read fictional characters. Alan Palmer contends that we use "frames, scripts, and preference rules" to "supply the defaults that fill the gaps" in narrative fiction and that allow us to "construct minds from the text" ("Mind Beyond the Skin," 325). This gap-filling process occurs to greater or lesser degrees depending on how much the information of characters' minds the author provides. In Kunzru's *The Impressionist* the third-person narrator provides ample detail about events and interactions external to the protagonist, Pran (Jonathan), but very little about his interior state of mind. More is required of the reader to use those scripts and frames to decode from Pran's actions and behavior his interior state. An extreme case of this would be Melville's *Bartleby, the Scrivener* or Camus's *The Stranger.*

Moreover, the reader's cognitive in-filling process relies on scripts and frames that spin out of our social, group thinking. Palmer's "intermental mind" or "mind beyond the skin" is a reminder that authors (and their narrators and characters) and readers are always decoding and engaging with narrative fiction at once on individual and social levels. The first line of Dagoberto Gilb's story "Maria de Covina" unfolds as follows: "I've got two sports coats, about six ties, three dressy pants, Florsheims I polish *a la madre,* and three weeks ago I bought a suit, with silk lining, at Lemonade for Men" (*Woodcuts of Women,* 3). There is enough narrative detail—first-person narrative with a syntax that pushes the rhythm of the words forward confidently, seamless code switching, and content—for a reader to infer a psychological type. This is a self-assured fellow who likes to look good. However, Gilb plays with this automatic script and framing of the reader, soon turning this image of the narrator upside down and inside out. While this is a first-person narrator as protagonist who talks much of his mind, the reader could not infer psychological nuance if not for a systematic overlap and intersection of the instrumental (internalist, individual) and the intermental (externalist, social) perspectives.

This overlap also demonstrates not only how thought and action are linked in postcolonial and Latino borderland narrative fiction but that they exist along a continuum: they can be very close together or very far apart but remain linked by a thread. While Gilb's "Maria de Covina" is more thought-driven and therefore has less action, several of his other stories are more action-driven and reveal less thought. Lastly, the "intermental" mind (the author, reader, character, and narrator) as individual and social constructs reminds us how a postcolonial and borderland narrative fiction conveys an implied moral norm as set against, or not, the common doxa. Such narrative fictions can present or not an "implied moral norm" established by the implied author against which the ideal reader is "invited to judge the norms of the various of the collective" (Palmer, "Mind Beyond the Skin," 344).

Visual and Verbal Narrator

The narrator of comic book narrative fiction—its most salient feature—uses simultaneously image and text to show and describe its storyworld. The verbal/visual narrator works as a gestalt, even when the reader-viewer sees first the image, then the text. Given that the comic book narrator is both verbal and visual, Latino borderland author-artists can play with various degrees of presence of one or the other to control the rhythm and flow of the story, the pace at which the reader-viewer constructs a narrative gestalt.

Filter and Slant

This is an important distinction that allows us to see how an event can be filtered by the character one way and presented by the narrator in another way. For instance, in *Brown on Brown,* I use filter and slant as a tool to analyze Rechy's *The Miraculous Day of Amalia Gómez.* What is described as a miracle by Amalia (her Catholic filter) is identified by the narrator as a "filmy cloud or streaks of smoke" caused by "a sky writing airplane" (3). In *Postethnic Narrative Criticism* I use such tools to determine the difference between a fantastical and magicorealist storytelling mode. For instance, the narrative strategy for the fantastic is characterized by its narrators or characters calling attention to the strangeness of the magical events, while the strategy for the magicorealist narrative is to not invent a narrator or character who calls attention to the difference between the "real" and "unreal" (38).

Narratee

The narratee is that construction within any given postcolonial and Latino borderland fiction to which the narrative is addressed. Like the narrator, the narratee may be represented as a character, but very often it is not. The narratee is also a purely textual construct, to be distinguished from the real reader. But as Gerald Prince remarks, the narratee nonetheless "exists and is never entirely forgotten" ("Introduction to the Study of the Narratee," 99). In the act of reading a postcolonial and Latino borderland narrative fiction the biographical reader, say, recreates in his or her mind the narratee along with the ideal reader, the narrator, and the ideal author. The narratee is an implied listener; the ideal reader is an implied reader. The narratee listens to the (reliable or unreliable) narrator or narrators; the ideal reader reads the text as a whole. Also, the narratee may be but usually is not a character in the story; either way, the narratee is a position or role overtly or covertly present in the narrative as the audience directly addressed by the narrator.

It is essential not to confuse narratee and real reader. The narratee perhaps listens to the narrator's story as a sympathetic listener or not. The narrator tells the story; the narratee listens to it. When the narratee is represented as a character, it can have all kinds of interactions with the narrator within the diegesis, including disagreement. The concept of the narratee is a very powerful tool as a means of classifying types of fiction: ironic, satiric, and so on. The narrator and narratee relationship can be close or far apart as indicated by various tensions and ironies. There are even postcolonial and Latin borderland narrative fictions in which the narrator wants to dominate the narratee.

Palimpsest

This can be useful for us to understand just how an author overlays, reaches out toward, and interweaves into his or her own another world literary text. When Kunzru opens the first chapter of *The Impressionist* with a great deluge, a cave, an Indian woman, Amrita (the protagonist, Pran's mother), and an Anglo colonial bigot named Ronald Forrester, it is hard not to see its British canonical literary underlay: George Eliot's *Mill on the Floss*, Forster's *Passage to India,* and Conrad's *Heart of Darkness.* Smith does the same with *White Teeth* and Melville's *Moby Dick,* among others.

When John Rechy sets his novel *The Miraculous Day of Amalia Gómez* during a twenty-four-hour period in which he follows the journey of a racially marginalized protagonist, a middle-aged Chicana single mother of three living in East L.A., he does so to have his readers interface his novel with James Joyce's *Ulysses.* That Rechy chooses the stream-of-consciousness narration and free indirect discourse solidifies in our minds this palimpsest. As I discuss in *Brown on Brown,* Rechy's overlaying of *The Miraculous Day* on *Ulysses* is not ironic, satiric, or in any way bent—it is straightforward. (See Gérard Genette's *Palimpsests.*)

Enstrangement

When a postcolonial and Latino borderland author or artist chooses to tell a story in narrative fiction form, he or she can use all variety of the above-mentioned devices (and many others) to push at the boundaries of convention, to deviate unpredictably from aesthetic norms. "Enstrangement" is what the Russian Formalists called this process—and this goal. Generally speaking, we are made in such a way that when we see something continuously, after a while we no longer see it all. Authors can choose devices to make us look again *at* and *into* those objects to which we have habituated ourselves. Russian Formalist Victor Shklovsky writes that art can be used as a tool "to make a stone feel stony" (*Theory of Prose,* 6).

An author's will to style, his or her knowledge of the world and of different narrative techniques, can be used to *enstrange* the reader, to deliver a narrative fiction in which we acquire a deeper knowledge of the object rather than passing over it automatically. Shklovsky explains the object as

> an artifact that has been intentionally removed from the domain of automatized perception. It is "artificially" created by an artist in such a way that the perceiver, pausing in his reading, dwells on the text. This is when the literary work attains its greatest and most long-lasting impact. The object is perceived not spatially but, as it were, in its temporal continuity. That is, because of this device, the object is brought into view. (12)

Shklovsky considers *Tristram Shandy* "the most typical novel in world literature" (170) precisely because the novel encompasses the prototypical devices used in world literature (the parody and direct address of Rabelais and Cervantes, for instance) that wake us from that state of habituation. This is the way art works generally: to distill (systematically eliminate that which is redundant or dispensable), then distort and exaggerate in ways that create pleasing effects in the brain.

Enstrangement is also why ballet can be so moving: it distills everyday body motion and movement, then reframes and distorts on the stage. We feel its beauty because it appears unnatural—even though the movements are possible and perfectly natural. As readers and viewers, this enstrangement triggers our perceptual problem-solving faculty. A postcolonial author's distilling and distorting in the search for a way to make a "stone stony" can stimulate a like process in the reader. When we figure out that Coetzee has used the narrated monologue device to present a complex and contradictory South Africa, our brains respond, "Aha." We experience that feeling of being puzzled by something anew with a cognitive

and emotive payoff for solving the puzzle. (For the neurobiology behind this see Vilanayur S. Ramachandran's lecture "The Artful Brain.")

Exposing the Device

Along with parody and direct address, exposing the device is a tool in James Alan McPherson's short story "Elbow Room." In
this story, which follows the lives of an interracial couple, white Paul
and African American Virginia, McPherson uses the "frame-breaking"
device over and over again (McHale). The story opens:

> Narrator is unmanageable. Demonstrates a disregard for
> form bordering on the paranoid . . . Flaunts an almost bar-
> baric disregard for the moral mysteries, or integrities, of tra-
> ditional narrative modes. This flaw in his discipline is well
> demonstrated here. In order to save this narration, editor felt
> compelled to clarify slightly, not to censor but to impose at
> least the illusion of order. (256)

When I have taught this story, my students typically find this opening more than odd; such a flaunting of the device is not a very frequent
practice in multiethnic literature generally. So I ask the students why
McPherson would use such a device: Is this simply a way to draw attention to its own fictionality, or does it do something more, like under-
score the already fragile—as if fictional and not real—sense of identity
the African American characters have in the story? Or does it do both?
McPherson's exposing of the device is an atypical technique in "ethnic"
American literature and also in postcolonial and Latino borderland narrative fiction. It pushes hard on readers to recall that the postcolonial and
Latino borderland literature they are reading is, well, fiction, that there
is no one-to-one correspondence with some kind of postcolonial and
Latino ethnic, vernacular experience. It announces that such authors can
choose to use the techniques of a Barthelme or Barth just as much as a
Steinbeck or a Dos Passos.

Puzzle Solving

Another form of enstrangement is for a postcolonial and
Latino borderland author to create a puzzle-solving fiction. This can
come in the form of an Alfredo Véa reshaping the mystery-detective

genre with his *Silver Cloud Cafe,* a Cecile Pineda defying the science fiction genre with her *Bardo99,* or a Michael Ondaatje who eliminates chapters and dates in his archeological murder mystery *Anil's Ghost.* Each presents various degrees of resolvability. In any case, these post-colonial and Latino borderland narrative fictions set in motion the reader's puzzle-solving capacity. They present fictional worlds that require and resist our parsing as we try to make them correspond with the referents that make up our real world.

In Elena Garro's *Recollections of Things to Come,* the narration is told from the point of view of a stone—a petrified Isabel Moncada. That is, we have a literally petrified narrator who immediately poses a puzzle for the reader: Isabel's speaking from the realm of the dead—or a rock, actually—but as one who sees things as if she exists in the realm of the living (storyworld). We ask ourselves, What was the process of getting her from a living state to a state of petrification? This triggers our puzzle-solving faculty. Importantly, we need to keep in mind that those narratives that resist totally our parsing—I think here of Isabella Rios's novel *Victuum*—are not only intolerable but *boring.* Their ultimate un-readability tends to limit their readership.

Style

Postcolonial and Latino borderland authors use syntax, diction, pace, reiterations, imagery, metaphor, and other linguistic features of the narrative to solidify in the reader's mind a particular, identifiable voice (and as the image of an implied author). For instance, when a Latino borderland author uses bilingual word play, not only does this give a sense of the character's cultural background—Chicano, say—but also it gives the narrative a general feel and pull. As mentioned above, in the story "Maria de Covina" Dagoberto Gilb's use of code switching— "Florsheims I polish *a la madre*" (3)—gives the first-person narrator an "ethnic" tag as well as a certain quick, confident flow to his prose.

Code switching can also be a way for an author like Abraham Rodriguez Jr. to personalize the story by investing the narrative with a unique rhythm. We see this dramatically in Rodriguez's story "Babies" in his collection *The Boy Without a Flag.* It begins, "It was good fucken-shit, not that second-rate stuff. It was really good shit, the kind you pay a lot for, so I stared at Smiley for a while cause I got real curious bout whea the money came from" (45). Through inference, the style of the narration gives the reader a sense of the urban, gritty, and marginal. Style here also functions to set the reader up for a surprise. We soon discover that this hard-edged voice is that of a *female* first-person narrator.

Style is in many ways the air we breathe when we enter into post-colonial and Latino borderland narrative fiction. Given that such authors use language—most of the time English—to create their fictional worlds, style is an important tool for us to keep in mind. It is style that determines, Robert Alter remarks, "the rhythm of relation of the represented objects and personages, the depth of field in which they are seen" ("Reading and Style in Dickens," 130–131). Elements of style can point us strongly in one direction or another in terms of conventions of genre. According to Alter, the "formal fluidity" of metaphor is unique to the novel, where the narration can "rapidly glide back and forth from grand overviews to the restricted and emotionally colored view of a single character. It can adopt . . . the spatial and temporal orientation of a fictional personage with a technical subtlety and conviction matched by no other narrative genre" (*Imagined Cities*, 66–67).

Likewise, David Treuer considers that the study of Native American fiction "should be the study of style" (4). It is not only that Native American literature should be judged *as literature* but that by doing so we can understand why some authors are effective and others not: "We don't, after all, believe in characters, images, or situations because they *are* authentic. We believe in them because they *seem* authentic. And it is the seemingness of literature that is interesting—where language meets and dances with belief" (193). Like Flaubert, who Treuer says "made a necessity of form" (35–36), Louise Erdrich creates in her novel *Love Medicine* a similar unity: "Intercutting freezes the novel in time, which makes it possible for both the characters inside the novel and the readers outside of it to analyze and inspect the situation. . . . It creates a delicious, heightened, and, indeed, foregrounded sense of the action" (Treuer, 36). It is the use of syntax, diction, pace, and imagery in *Love Medicine*—not identity politics—that Treuer considers relevant evaluative criteria. Finally, it is the author's will to style—her or his obsession and determination to precisely organize the words, syntax, paragraphs, and the work as a whole—that creates an image of the implied author in the reader's mind.

Genre

While we might consider an element like voice or point of view as determining genre, it can be considered as the interplay of

technique and context, or convention. Alfred Arteaga opens his borderland short story "Gun" as follows: "So when the police had my daughter
in an assassination position, kneeling, gun to her head, I took care to
choose and phrase my words precisely" (57). Does the voice identify this
as a short story? Could it just as easily be a personal vignette, essay, or
journalistic reportage? As the story unfolds, it becomes apparent that it
is not the techniques in and of themselves that identify genre but rather
the critical apparatus that surrounds the narrative. The critical convention of the Latin American *crónica* (a hybrid form of the literary essay and
urban reportage) allows us to see how much the context together with
technique can determine our understanding of the narrative fiction—
and therefore determine our pleasure in its reading.

SECOND-ORDER NARRATIVE TOOLS

Partial Suspension of Disbelief

Our cognitive faculty that distinguishes between fact and
fiction, reality and illusion is what allows us to partially suspend disbelief
when we enter into all kinds of postcolonial and Latino borderland narrative fictions—including even the most otherworldly, such as Amitav
Ghosh's science fiction thriller *The Calcutta Chromosome*. Our suspension
of disbelief is never total. We are always *in* the contextual space of our
environs. If it were a total suspension—a total immersion—we would
not know the difference between fiction and reality, which would lead
to all sorts of problems (some call this condition schizophrenia), and on
a more basic level, we would not be able to derive pleasure from our
readings. Context is ever-present in our reading experience. It is our
position within a particular context—our place outside or beside the
text—that provides the minimum distance necessary for us to be able
to experience in an "as-if way" thoughts and feelings in response to the
narrative fictional world. (See Katja Mellman's essay "E-Motion").

Emotion and Cognition

The above-discussed techniques and devices reveal just
how complex a postcolonial and Latino borderland narrative fiction can
be. One way or another, such devices (and there are many others) represent the large pallet of colors, so to speak, an author has when he or

she is crafting a narrative fiction to convey meaning and move readers in specific ways. On the part of the author creating and the reader engaging, emotions play a central role in all of this. Just as the author's selection of techniques to cue and trigger the reader's emotions requires thinking, so too does the reader look for coherence and logic in the narrative. If there is a smoking gun, the gun has to go off or we stop investing emotionally.

In Julio Cortázar's very short story "Continuity of Parks" we see this interplay of emotion and cognition at work in our reading of the story and as foregrounded by the narrative itself. The story opens: "He had begun to read the novel a few days before. He had put it down because of some urgent business conferences, opened it again on his way back to the estate by train; he permitted himself a slowly growing interest in the plot, in the characterization" (63). The story performs that constant and simultaneous movement between narrative technique and affect. The opening lines foreground the reader's own processing of the narrative's coherence (logic system) and whether we invest in the story (emotive system) as a result of this coherence.

The story raises the issue of what we actually do when reading narrative fiction: do we really suspend disbelief, or are we simultaneously aware of our environs and immersed in the fictional world? In Cortázar's story the protagonist

> tasted the almost perverse pleasure of disengaging himself
> line by line from the things around him, and at the same
> time feeling his head rest comfortably on the green velvet
> of the chair with its high back, sensing the cigarettes rested
> within reach of his hands, that beyond the great windows the
> air of afternoon danced under the oak trees in the park. (63)

At the story's end, the fictional world of the protagonist's world reading the novel and that of the novel fuse; his ontological spaces mix and he is killed by the character in the novel. The techniques of destabilizing conventions of the story-within-a-story and mixing planes of reality move us cognitively as a puzzle-solving narrative as well as emotively. All of this requires that our working memory (the details of the story) and our long-term memory (generic convention) interweave and feed into the story's end—an end that shocks and surprises.

Postcolonial and Latino borderland authors enstrange by distilling, then distorting features of reality with the aim of generating specific emotions in their readers. We might keep in mind that many narrative fictions marketed under the rubric of postcolonial or Latino borderland do very little distilling and distorting; they abstract from time and space characters and events—the Chicano character could be anyone anywhere—and therefore only generate tedium.

Paradoxically, then, the moment a postcolonial or Latino borderland author lets himself or herself be guided by emotions (sentimentality of identity politics, say), then he or she is no longer able to make art that moves. This is why Shklovsky states, "Art is without emotion" (159). That is, all the devices and tools should be at the service of crafting a narrative fiction for the reader to have certain emotions. The tools are artifacts that manipulate emotions or that provide instructions to follow in order for the reader to experience emotions.

Importantly, too, each narrative fiction medium will distill features of the real world differently from other media. And each medium will use its devices to cue and trigger differently a range of emotions. Those devices used in comic books rely both on static image of the panel and the eyes' movement from one panel to the next; its medium is more visual-perceptual and action-dependent than a novel and therefore will be better at triggering peak emotions concerning action. No matter how fast a pace the author writes into a novel, it will never match the pace of the comic book, where our perceptual faculties swallow whole panels and pages in one gulp.

Empathy

Tied tightly to emotion is our capacity to stand in the place of another—our empathetic capacity—through which postcolonial and Latino borderland authors develop their characters and imagine ethical circumstances and problems that the characters face. It may or may not be true that writers are more empathetic than others or that they get better at relating to others the more they write. While Suzanne Keen acknowledges that "fiction writing may cultivate novelists' role-taking skills and make them more habitually empathetic" (*Empathy and the Novel*, 127), she also mentions many novelists for whom this is not necessarily the case.

Now this ability of a skilled author to identify with another can lead to some rather severe reader reactions. Keen discusses Keri Hulme's *The Bone People* as being so effective in conjuring an image of an implied author's abuse of children that its critics and lay readers were shocked at the novel. They considered Hulme somehow as either an abuser or as sympathetic to an abuser. An author can feel with his or her villains, and a reader can feel with those villains as well. It is because of our capacity for empathy that there is no limit to the creativity of the postcolonial and Latino borderland author.

Whatever the authors' or readers' gender, politics, or sexual persuasion, they have the power to put themselves in the place of anyone and anything, including a stone, as with Garro's Isabel Moncada in *Recollections of Things to Come*. It is why Hanif Kureishi can write an appealing novel, *Intimacy*, with a misogynist as its protagonist. Again, it is only when the author slips into *sentimentality* as the main psychological resource that this sours. This limits the psychological range of the characters, who thus do not live very long in the reader's memory.

Theory of Mind

Likewise very much tied to emotion and empathy is our evolved capacity to read from exterior gestures and behaviors the interior state of mind of another—our theory-of-mind capacity. When we read narrative fiction, Lisa Zunshine argues, readers' brains are tricked, so to speak, and their theory-of-mind faculty is activated, all while knowing the characters to be fictional. For Zunshine, this theory-of-mind capacity is the reason we can make and engage with narrative fiction.

I would like to complicate this picture a little here. First, we often misread interior states of mind in our everyday activities. As social beings we constantly conjecture about others' states of mind—and have a high percentage of misjudging them (see Ellen Spolsky's "Narrative as Nourishment"). However, when we read *White Teeth* or *The God of Small Things,* for example, it is the author who deliberately guides us to read or misread interior states of mind.

This is to say, in narrative fiction there is no guesswork. As with dreams, so too in narrative fiction—we are not guessing what is going on in the mind of the character the way we often do in everyday life when we try to determine if people are being sarcastic, aggressive, or even affectionate. There is no guesswork in these fictional works because the authors, in this case Smith and Roy, respectively, have articulated the characters' state of mind. From the very beginning of *White Teeth,* Smith's narrator tells us how Archie woke up with the idea of committing suicide. Therefore the narrator whom Smith has willed into existence provides all sorts of information about how he feels, what he thinks, and so on. Smith or Roy or Kunzru or Ghosh creates narrators to *tell* the reader about the mental states of their characters. We as readers simply follow the author's scripts and cues. We understand that Archie is depressed. The character's mental state is what it is, and we know it to be so. This is why Colin McGinn reminds us that real people "may not have the mental states they purport to have," while fictional characters "have no narrative-independent being; they are as they are narrated to be, and we readers know their minds by knowing what the narrative says" (122–123). Some guesswork about a character's mind does take place, however, when an author chooses to use a device that lends itself to ambiguity, such as psychonarration and interior monologue, but this concerns only a fraction of the totality of any given narrative fiction. The extensive and all-encompassing use of psychonarration and interior monologue in Joyce's *Finnegan's Wake* and Isabella Rios's *Victuum* make them exceptions.

Emotive and Narrative Prototypes

Our evolved capacity for emotion is a key ingredient in our ability to make and engage with fiction as well as other art forms. Our ability to feel happiness, anger, disgust, fear, and sadness (directly and vicariously) is so powerful that such emotions can override reasoning. For instance, if we are about to be attacked, we do not contemplate running—we simply run. Because our minds are organized hierarchically, while we might respond emotionally, we share the universal capacity to *know* that we are reacting in such-and-such a way. We can become absolutely invested in a story because we feel (sometimes conflicting emotions) for a character and at the same time think beyond the character's direct experiences; we can simultaneously feel sad and angry as well as formulate positive outcomes for the character.

These evolved prototype emotions—especially the desire to realize happiness—have arguably had the most influence on shaping the prototype narratives we see around the world. Whether in Sri Lanka, Mexico, or the Netherlands, narrative fiction tends to express itself as romance, heroic, epic, sacrificial, or any number of combinations of these; here I am paraphrasing Patrick Colm Hogan's *The Mind and Its Stories*. His research of hundreds of elemental narratives from cultures around the globe shows the cross-cultural presence of narratives that end with the realization of a romantic union and the autonomy of the individual or community. For Hogan, realizing happiness (most prototypically embodied in a narrative that consummates the romance) is central to our biological and thus social survival and evolution as a species. These emotive patterns inform centrally the shaping of prototype narratives.

Ethics and Morals

Without emotions, there are no morals—those rules of behavior toward others that each individual internalizes to a greater or lesser degree of consciousness and that shift in time and place. When we read a Latino borderland story by Luis Rodriguez that follows a day in the life of a Chicano living in East L.A. and working as a chauffeur to the rich and famous, we are also reading about a social situation with moral dilemmas for this Chicano character that are different from yesterday's dilemmas. With moral dilemmas come emotions and individual reactions within a social context: a Chicana gangbanger in Luis Rodriguez's story "Chicas Chuecas" does not show her grief publicly. While the context might alter the way the emotion is expressed, the fundamental emotion is the same whatever one's social context. This is important to keep in mind when we think of how postcolonial and Latino borderland authors portray the shaping of rules of behavior and the expression of emotion. Kamila Shamsie opens her novel *salt and saffron* with her narrator declaring: "Of course, reduce all stories to their basic elements and you'll see all families are possessed of prejudice—that alternative name for 'fear'" (1). She is right. If morals are those rules concerning the relationships between individuals that they internalize or consciously reject (during adolescence, typically), the first circle of human interaction—socialization—is the family. It is within this nucleus of the family as social nexus that we internalize or reject a series of rules about how to interact with others. This is why family appears so centrally in narrative fiction.

Not surprisingly, literary scholars have put much emphasis on the study of morals or ethics in narrative fiction and on producing rules of behavior and attitudes in its readers. In "Why Ethical Criticism Can Never Be Simple" Wayne Booth remarks that "ethical criticism is relevant to all literature, no matter how broadly or narrowly we define that controversial term; and such criticism, when done responsibly, can be a genuine form of rational inquiry" (16). This interface between implied author and ethics is fully explored, among other issues, in James Phelan's

Experiencing Fiction. Here Phelan brings together the tools and concepts that he has been developing over the years to provide a unified theory of his "broader rhetorical approach to narrative" (3). He follows five principles that relate to and concern "narrative judgments" (7). By understanding how narrative displays itself and advances—he divides the beginnings of narrative fictions into "twelve aspects of narrative progression" (21) that include exposition, launch, and initiation—as a way to distinguish, for instance, lyric narrative from portrait narrative. He does so to understand better how any given fiction's moral implications, problems, dilemmas, and values engage and move readers.

In Phelan's work we see how closely connected narrative fiction is tied to morality and ethics and how this is inseparable from emotions. It follows, then, that the elucidation of the cognitive and neural mechanisms underlying neuro-emotional behavior generally has great potential to deepen our understanding of the *why* and *how* of fiction in general and of postcolonial and Latino borderland fiction in particular. It can offer a rational foundation for the discussion of matters such as moral rules and political outlooks and reactions.

Indeed, an important part of the identity of the implied author that we as readers form is achieved by the ethical deductions that we make about what we are reading; it is the ethical atmosphere that blankets the whole text. If reading a postcolonial novel about romance, our image of the implied author might be one with a limited range of emotions, ambitions, and moral dilemmas or one who is complex and sufficiently different from the ideal reader. In the former instance, the moral dilemmas are simplified and subordinate to commonplace thinking and feeling with respect to any kind of problems. In *Transmission,* while Hari Kunzru's command over language, syntax, and grammar is evident, the novel slips into common clichés and simplified dilemmas that gravitate around issues of migration, global capitalism, and technology that render a shallow, dull implied author. When Kunzru caps off the novel with some magical abracadabra—the protagonist Arjun Mehta steps across the border into Mexico and into a global hyperspace never-never land—formula and cliché wash away any shadow of an interesting moral conflict and dilemma.

Another aspect to this ethics category is the debate around fiction's social and political transformative power. Rather than deliberate on whether a postcolonial or Latino borderland narrative fiction transforms the world—as I argue in *Postethnic Narrative Criticism, Brown on Brown,* and *Why the Humanities Matter,* this is the work of hundreds of thousands of organized people moving against targets of oppression and not the reading of an *Uncle Tom's Cabin*—I would rather suggest that we consider the empathy and ethics in light of the problems of creativity and the distinctiveness of fiction, that is, what makes fiction *fiction* and not something else. Namely, instead of seeking literariness in the language or even in a formal procedure for narration (for narrating), we might pose the problem of fictionality and even literariness elsewhere: in the universal capacity for empathy on the one hand and the universal need to establish and follow ethical rules and behavior (by this, I do not mean a moral behavior that I approve or that I condemn) toward other individuals, a group of individuals, and even a society of individuals. This approach to empathy and ethics in postcolonial and Latino borderland narrative fiction allows us to integrate several levels of analysis: the most elementary and universal level, the neurobiological; the social level as manifest in ethics on the one hand and politics on the other hand; the personal level of the author, his or her creative capacity and the particular way this creative capacity manifests itself in the author's writing or comic book making.

The two orders of narrative theory tools I have described present but a mere sampling of the many tools and concepts that can enrich our study (and teaching) of postcolonial and Latino borderland narrative fiction. They provide a set of markers to keep us on the right track for understanding deeply how postcolonial and Latino borderland narrative fiction ticks and that they contain within themselves, as Tzvetan Todorov writes of fiction generally, "direction for its own consumption" ("Reading as Construction," 267).

The tools and approach remind us that postcolonial and Latino borderland narrative fictions do not imitate reality but rather create a reality that uses as its building blocks *anything* in reality. Such a narrative and cognitive theory toolbox approach drives home the crucial point that human beings are endowed with the biological and psychological equipment to produce and enjoy fiction, be it identified as postcolonial or Latino borderland or not. A Chicano reader may be moved by a Chicano author—as well as by a Japanese author. Along with biological and cultural universals, and attached to these or in close relationship with these, are those particular narrative devices used by authors to move their readers with shared universal emotions. It allows us to see more clearly, and less impressionistically, how postcolonial and Latino borderland narrative fiction is a "dialect" within world literature. This is to say, a postcolonial- and Latino borderland–identified author ultimately wants to be judged by the same aesthetic criteria by which his or her peers are judged the world over. Finally, the devices and arrangements I have described here are by no means prescriptive. In all postcolonial and Latino borderland art there should be total anarchy, to paraphrase Trotsky.

Two

PUTTING THE FICTION BACK INTO ARUNDHATI ROY

WORLD SYSTEMS OF LITERATURE

For Peter Hitchcock, the postcolonial condition finds expression in the genre of the novel; it is this genre of postcoloniality that uncovers "the lie of colonialism" ("The Genre of Postcoloniality," 326) and at the same time questions the very category of the novel as a genre. Thus the novel both threatens its own erasure as a genre—those "divisions that have produced it" (327)—and, given that it is bound up with a postcolonial identity, points to the threat of erasure of the "postcolonial" identity itself in its articulation.

Whew, what a mind-full—a seeming aim of Hitchcock's rhetoric that uses tautology to confuse categories of narrative fiction (genres) with subjectivity and reality (ontology). This is not a path I want to follow. In this chapter, I am interested in questions of narrativity (genre, style, voice, temporal, and spatial play) in Arundhati Roy's *The God of Small Things*. However, I begin with Hitchcock to point to a dominant trend in postcolonial literary studies that one way or another conflate concepts pertaining to narrative fiction (genre, point of view, fictional characters, and direct, indirect, and free indirect thought, for instance) with those pertaining to so-identified postcolonial subjectivity, geography, sociology, and history. While Hitchcock's exaggerated rhetoric that gives with one hand and takes with the other is a near-cliché of this approach, other critics are less inclined to follow this path. For example, Laura Moss's intentions are good and expressed with clarity in "'The Plague of Normality': Reconfiguring Realism in Postcolonial Theory." She seeks to recuperate the realist novel "as a viable form for resistance narratives" (n.p.). For Moss, realism should not be weighed down with the ideological baggage of a Western individualism à la Defoe's *Robinson Crusoe* that reinforces a "conservative ideology" and instead should be considered as another form for postcolonial authors to resist and radically oppose politics of containment.

Whether realistic or not, in the scholarship of Moss and others the postcolonial novel becomes a politics by other means. In Elleke Boehmer's *Stories of Women* it is the technique used by Arundhati Roy in *The God of Small Things*—her "extravagant realism and exuberant wordplay" (164)—that reproduces a "neo-orientalism" and simultaneously uproots such a restrictive impulse in its celebration of the private and public spaces where "women's politics can be located" (203). Boehmer finds that Roy's novel serves as an example of how women, too, can use "symbolic vocabularies of entitlement . . . to lay claim to the nation's public and imaginary spaces" (219). And Susan Stanford Friedman focuses on how Roy's "spatial poetics" reveals ways in which the novelist uses the local, Kerala, to address the "politics of regional, national and transnational landscapes through time" (198). By different means and focusing on different narrative features, Hitchcock, Moss, Boehmer, and Friedman, then, apply the same procedure: one way or another they conflate or confuse devices of narrative fiction with ontological identity categories.

Given that I have already said much on this topic in earlier books (*Postethnic Narrative Criticism* and *Brown on Brown*), I shall only add that the questions, problems, and deliberations mentioned briefly above are ultimately not interesting. Whether we decide that it is Roy's use of realism, symbolic vocabularies of entitlement, or spatial poetics, together or individually, that animate in compelling ways her storytelling, the fact remains that those narrative devices and her novel as a whole do not have the material power to open doors for postcolonial women to become full-fledged citizens (Boehmer) or change the world (Friedman and Moss).

Yet nothing in the world is alien to fiction. Everything we make and do and which transforms the world and in turn transforms us sooner or later finds its proper place in a work of fiction. Given that we are constituted through and through as social beings and that we transform ourselves and the world we inhabit in a social way and create thus our own sociality by doing so, it is no surprise that postcoloniality, oppression, and exploitation in their myriad most contemporary forms—wars, class struggles, financial unraveling of capitalism and imperialism, and the innumerable effects of these phenomena—are reflected and represented in all sorts of narratives and media (books, films, comic books, soap operas and other television shows, and computer games, for example). This is one of the reasons that today, in the full sense of the word, literature is always *world literature.*

Moreover, this world system of literature itself spins out of our cross-cultural capacity for language and fiction making. One can create fictions—narrate fictionally—about everything that exists in the world—and the world is full of everything. An author's choice to tell her story of a particular place in India in a particular time, in a particular style, and in a particular genre might or might not reflect the condition of the people of that place (workers or otherwise). Either way, building an evaluative scaffolding based on whether a novel is ideologically for or against the people straightjackets the limitless domain of fiction.

Evaluating according to a for/against ideological position not only neglects this complexity, such evaluation mistakenly simplifies the persuasive effect of a given novel; common sense tells us that reading literature—especially complex literature—allows for a vast range of interpretations and experiences; this experience does not necessarily lead to making a better Indian citizen subject, for instance. In fact, sometimes labels like "postcolonial" or "borderland" and the like that are placed on a given text because of its autobiographic or geographic ties can lead to gross misreading. Anita Desai's novel *Baumgartner's Garden* has been applauded as a progressive postcolonial revision of Conrad's *Heart of Darkness.* However, a careful reading will reveal, as Patrick Hogan does in *Empire and Poetic Voice,* that *Baumgartner's Garden* remapping leaves readers with a deeply reactionary worldview of Indian people as a threatening swarm of unindividuated subjects; there is not an ounce of progressive politics here, yet its de facto "postcolonial" label pronounces it as such.

I will follow up this broad-stroked statement with a deeper investigation into the question of fictionality. First, however, to begin to put the fiction back into postcolonial literary studies, I will discuss the context in which Roy's *The God of Small Things* was conceived, written, published, circulated, and received both within and outside the academy. Then I will turn to what I consider a more interesting and productive path to follow: analyzing *The God of Small Things* as a novel, that is, as a carefully designed interplay of worldly narrative techniques borrowed and reshaped—from Faulkner, García Márquez, the Kerala storytelling tradition of *kathakali*—that aim to engage readers in specifically directed ways.

Context is important. *The God of Small Things* did not appear out of nowhere; nor did its making happen by divine grace or some sort of tapping into a Platonic *topos Uranus*. Nor did its production and circulation take place magically outside of capitalist economic exchange systems and its mass media appendages.

In October 1997, *The God of Small Things* picked up Britain's prestigious Booker Prize, billowing up a storm of fame and infamy. The first South Asian woman and Indian citizen to take home that award coincided with India's celebration of fifty years of independence from British rule, two facts that led many a roiled author and critic to claim it an act of Booker paternalism and a great deed of imperial retribution. Also, when newspaper headlines worldwide announced that Roy had accumulated two-plus million dollars in publishing advances from the rights to publish her prize-winning novel in nineteen countries (it has since been translated into twenty-seven languages), many chose to guffaw instead of applaud.

With such puffed-up pandemonium permeating the publication of *The God of Small Things,* it is understandable that Roy has not put forth another novel. (Often, the only way for incipiently published writers—postcolonial or otherwise—to quiet the naysayers is to issue a "brilliantly successful" second novel.) This is not to say that Roy has abstained from writing. She has been typing up reams, but in the form of hard-biting political essays. Published in a variety of scholarly and mainstream journals—many of which have been published as collections such as *Power Politics* (2001), *War Talk* (2003), and *An Ordinary Person's Guide to Empire* (2004)—her essays variously attack global capitalism and its nefarious consequences (a case in point being the multimillion-dollar Sardar Sarovar Dam project in western India that is displacing millions of people), the role of the International Monetary Fund in spreading and deepening poverty, the significance of nuclear bomb tests in India, and cronyism and corruption in the BJP, India's Bharatiya Janata Party. In *The End of Imagination* Roy asks how it is possible for the Indian government to spend millions of dollars developing and building nuclear bombs when more than four hundred million citizens in India live in poverty and remain illiterate.

If the post-Booker Arundhati Roy put on hold the writing of fiction, she has been penning indispensable essays that call out social injustices and that cry out for the basic implementation of democratic demands: for all to have access to decent jobs and decent wages, food, shelter, transportation, education, medical services—and for all to have the right to freedom of expression, organization in trade unions and political parties, and real representation. As she points out in one of her essays, "Ahimsa," it is imperative that India have *"more modernity, not less . . . more democracy, not less"* (*War Talk,* 12).

Indeed, without more democracy, without the people's freedom and organized capacity to put a stop to the disastrous present course of building and testing nuclear bombs, waging war between nations, and spreading corruption at all levels of government and the rest of society, not only will the people continue to suffer, but all that civilization holds sacred—science, ethics, music, art, literature—will be destroyed. As a writer today, Roy advocates that the fight for social equality and justice come first to ensure that the sculpting of fiction can follow.

In 1997 Arundhati Roy appeared as if out of nowhere, but of course, we all come from somewhere. In 1960 Arundhati Roy was born in the multicultural masala pot of Kerala, India, aswarm with Hindu, Muslim, and Christian people. Herself the daughter of a Bengali Hindu father, Rajib, and a Syrian Christian mother, Mary, meant that a deep sense of cultural relativism and sensitivity were the order of Roy's childhood. Growing up surrounded by her schoolteacher mother's books and having the middle-class means also provided by her father, a tea plantation overseer, led Roy to attend university in New Delhi. Here, however, rather than study literature or writing, she chose the path of architecture. With her degree in hand, she worked a stint for the National Institute of Urban Affairs but soon tired of its humdrum politics and affairs.

As chance would have it, another door opened for Roy—that of the arts. She landed a small role in the film *Massey Saab* directed by her husband-to-be, Pradeep Krishen. With Roy's appetite for the arts whetted, she began writing screenplays and documentary film scripts. Several made it into production, including *Electric Moon* and *In Which Annie Gives It Those Ones.* During this period she began publishing essays on art and culture; in one such essay, "The Great Indian Rape Trick," written in 1994, she leveled vitriolic critique against director Sekar Kapur's misrepresentation of Phoolan Devi in *Bandit Queen.*

Roy's involvement in the early 1990s with the arts in India, as she tells Taisha Abraham, was "warming up exercises" (90) for writing *The God of Small Things.* And once she sat down and began to write the novel, she could not plug its torrent of words for four and a half years. More than acting, screenplay writing, and essayistic critiquing, it was writing the novel, as she stated in several interviews (with Praveen Swami, for one example), that allowed her to give creative and memorable shape to the complex world she wanted to bring to life in the minds of her readers. By May 1996 Roy handed a finished manuscript to fellow novelist Pankaj Mishra, an editor for HarperCollins India. He considered it the first masterpiece to appear since Rushdie's *Midnight's Children.* The result: by April 4, 1997, *The God of Small Things* had already begun to fill bookstore shelves in India and soon after those of Europe and the United States.

Months before winning the Booker, *The God of Small Things* received a blaze of media attention—good and bad. Many celebrated the novel's storytelling inventiveness and postcolonial historical revisionism, the narrative seen as implicating British imperialism and Christianity in deepening the oppressive caste system. *New York Times Book Review* critic Alice Truax celebrated Roy's "shape-shifting" narrative and her use of "rogue capital letters, nonsense rhymes and unexpected elaborations" (5). And Ramlal Agarwal was especially appreciative of Roy's lack of "sentimentality" (209).

However, there was also many a disgruntled critic. In the *Electronic Telegraph,* Paul Rutman considered the novel derivative, wishing that "some kind soul had confiscated all copies of James Joyce when Ms. Roy was a little girl." In the *New Statesman,* Amanda Craig expressed irritation at Roy's "wonky" style and fondness for "capitalized clichés." Rankled by Roy's "overwrought" style, John Updike concluded in *The New Yorker* that this was "one more example of William Faulkner's powerful influence upon Third World writers, his method of torturing a story, mangling it, coming at it roundabout after pretentious detours and delays" (159). Others were more than critical of Roy's depiction of a caste-transgressive act: the forbidden sexual encounter between Ammu and the Untouchable Velutha. One lay reader even filed a lawsuit against Roy, and others turned to violent protest in attempting to ban its sale in bookstores across India. Many an Indian media pundit expressed dismay at Roy's "filthy" and backward representation of Kerala. And some, like Aijaz Ahmad, held the novel accountable for misrepresenting historical fact, critiquing the novel specifically for its representation of the Communist Party.

The God of Small Things certainly did more than simply survive its critics—by 2002 it had sold more than six million copies. A 2003 BBC reader poll voted it one of Britain's one hundred best-loved novels. Perhaps, then, there is more to the novel than first meets the mainstream media eye. Perhaps there is more to Roy as an author than the many critics could see who commented on her photogenic appeal and marketability as one reason for her success. Elleke Boehmer in *Stories of Women* is critical of such short-sightedness and the marketing machinery that transformed Roy into the multiracial exotic. The book could hold more meaning than was picked up by the knee-jerk reactions to "yet another novel" of the postcolonial exotic. Roy's experience could fit Amanda Craig's description:

> The Indian novelist is confronted with a paradox. Our feelings about India are so complex that a novel is rarely judged on its own merits rather than on a mixture of guilt, anger, defiance and sneaking envy. Those such as Rushdie, who stress the exotic, profit by it; Rohinton Mistry, on the other hand, is accused of writing flat prose—presumably because critics, when confronted with a thick book about poor people, simply cannot cope with too much reality.

Not only was *The God of Small Things* swarmed by mainstream media criticism, but in a remarkably short period after its publication there appeared a glut of academic scholarship on the novel—especially in India. With Prestige Books in New Delhi, R. K. Dhawan published an edited collection of essays titled *Arundhati Roy: The Novelist Extraordinary* (1998); Indira Bhatt and Indira Nityanandam published the collection *Explorations: Arundhati Roy's* The God of Small Things (1998); and editors Jaydipsinh Dodiya and Joya Chakravarty followed closely by publishing their collection titled *The Critical Studies of Arundhati Roy's* The God of Small Things (1999). This interest did not cease. In 2001, R. S. Pathak published another collection, *The Fictional World of Arundhati Roy.*

The novel seemed to provide the reflective surface on which many an Indian scholar sought to sound out a particular theoretical reading: feminist, postcolonial (Bhabhaean *inter dicta* or Saidean orientalism), deconstructivist, Marxist, New Historicist, Bakhtinean, post-Freudianist, nativist, and, well, you name it. Whether the proliferation of readings had to do with the novel's appearance coinciding with postcolonial studies' hitting a strong midstride in the academy worldwide or with other factors, in a matter of only a couple of years dozens upon dozens of essays were written on *The God of Small Things.* So many had so much to analyze about the novel that, on one occasion, Praveen Swami remarked how all the criticism was telling us more about the critics than about "the book itself" (102).

Many such scholars were particularly interested in focusing on the narrative fiction as a "Third World" artifact swept up into a global book marketplace, variously leveling critiques at its so-identified exotic packaging and a suspect "orientalist" representational politics. Alluding to Kurtz's going native, one scholar considered that the novel had gone "international," for example. Other scholars turned their critical gaze from the novel (empire-writes-back or not) to the critics themselves. Elleke Boehmer turned her critique toward those critics from the West who judged the book's value in terms of a European novel (civilized) versus a South Asian novel (primitive and hypersexualized) that reproduces an age-old orientalism. In "East Is East and South Is South" Boehmer states how such critiques—even if laudatory—abstract, stereotype, and exoticize "the once-colonized" and thus "commodified and made [them] safe for a western readership" (67). To reclaim the novel and its author from the "neo-Orientalist underpinning of postcolonial literary criticism" (*Stories of Women,* 165), Boehmer situates them within a nineteenth-century tradition of Indian writing, specifically linking the novel to the poetry of Sarojini Naidu, a South Asian author who wrote within a Western-identified poetic tradition but against the West's tropicalization of South Asia.

Many scholars chose to explore the novel's anticolonial (and antipatriarchal) representational features. Given the author's gender and the novel's focus on (mostly) female characters, much of the South Asian postcolonial scholarship used Western feminist approaches (poststructuralist and otherwise) to tease out the novel's resistant texture and its against-the-grain narrative sensibility. For example, M. K. Ray turns to a Luce Irigarayean "gynocriticism" in an exploration of how narrative technique such as stream of consciousness and voice such as syntax and rhythm express a resistant feminine psyche that is, Ray states, "so different from that of men" (105). The time leaps, syntactic reconfigurations, and narrative tempo reflect "the fractured sensibility and the broken and fragmented world of women" (106).

Anita Singh, among others, more deliberately couples the novel to a postcolonial feminist frame, reading how the novel powerfully moves those who are otherwise kept at silent margins, such as women, children, and Untouchables—"all those dispossessed of an identity or a speaking voice" (133)—to authoritative narrative centers. For Singh, Roy's retrieval of subaltern voices becomes a postcolonial "act of liberation" (ibid.). Many other postcolonial feminist critics who appeared during the period of this novel's canonization have discussed its use of Western-identified novelistic conventions to write against neo-Orientalist representations, and they have examined the way it gives texture to localized epistemologies—small histories and everyday struggles—that are seen as resisting the homogenizing flow of a patriarchy-identified global capitalism.

Added to the views of the feminist and postcolonial readings of *The God of Small Things* are the analyses focused on the novel's use of the storytelling strategies associated with postmodernism. Rather than addressing the novel's play with temporality or its focus on dispossessed peoples posited as being anticolonial rather than more generally anticapitalist, such analyses have concluded that the novel participated in and extended the line of the traditionally Western-identified postmodern approach: anachronistic narrative collage, fragmentation of self, multiplication of centers of truths of history, to name a few of its conspicuous characteristics. Thus, for Akshaya Kumar the "video-graphed montage of the splintered self," the narrative's "pastiche of the petty," its "perversity and irresponsibility," and its refusal of the "grandeur of sublimity" (69) locate *The God of Small Things* within the cosmopolitanism of postmodernism—not, as some Western criticism would have it, within a quaint Indian parochialism. For Yogesh Sinha and Sandhya Tripathi, the novel's blurring of fact and fiction, its play with language, and its sense of truth as a "hall of mirrors" (154) both convey a postmodernist sensibility and express the "experimental type of knowledge" (152) that typify the postcolonial narrative that "outwits" an "imposed Western colonial impression" (156).

THAT SMALL THING CALLED FICTION

In the academic canonization of *The God of Small Things* few interpretive angles were left untapped. Quite expectedly in view of the origins and gender of its author, the themes it develops, and the particular actions and reactions of its characters, it was the postcolonial critical frame that most strongly adhered to the novel: not only how the narrative writes back against neo-Orientalist representations, for example, but also how it constitutes an allegory of nation, how it should be seen as an act of symbolic resistance to metropolitan nation-state and neo-imperial discourses, and so on. Thus while seemingly nothing was left out in the canonization process, little attention was paid to the novel's *literary* ground.

The identification of *The God of Small Things* as postcolonial and feminist hinges on the psychoanalytical, sociohistorical, and political concepts and themes chosen as the lens through which to read the novel as a whole: to interpret its characters and their behaviors, attitudes, and actions as well as to attach a certain meaning to its descriptions and narrative comments. Such a choice to analyze *The God of Small Things*—and all narrative fiction—as produced by an author (an individual) addressing herself to readers (other individuals) as determined by nationality or postcolonial status, class, location within a caste system, ethnicity, and gender, assumes that it is the sociopolitical forces at large that shape and determine the novel's making and engaging. Now, Roy's novel not only bears other readings—it requires them if one wishes to be able to account for its accomplishments as a literary work of art and to perceive accurately the elements that complicate its relationship to certain approaches to criticism (postcolonial, feminist, or otherwise).

The novel is generously roomy, capable of fitting in anything and everything from the external world and from the subjective world of feelings and thoughts, while using all the narrative techniques humankind has invented, including free indirect speech, stream of consciousness, dramatic narrative, lyrical narrative, and prose poem, to name a few. Roy states,

> Rule One for a writer, as far as I'm concerned, is There Are No Rules. And Rule Two (since Rule One was made to be broken) is There Are No Excuses for Bad Art. Painters, writers, singers, actors, dancers, filmmakers, musicians are meant to fly, to push at the frontiers, to worry the edges of the human imagination, to conjure beauty from the most unexpected things, to find magic in places where others never thought to look. If you limit the trajectory of their flight, if you weigh their wings with society's existing notions of morality and responsibility, if you truss them up with preconceived values, you subvert their endeavor.
> (*Power Politics,* 5)

So Roy chose to tell her story in the form of the novel, not the autobiography or the short story or the epic poem or the essay or the journalistic article. And the storytelling mode she used is the one we identify broadly as realism. Informing the realism of her novel are not just verifiable facts of history—the Naxalite revolt and Indira Gandhi's imposition of a state of emergency—as well as those culled from Roy's own life: the character Rahel, who grows up in Ayemenem (near Roy's hometown, Kerala) shares many of Roy's experiences (she studies architecture, for example) and attributes (she refuses to conform and marches to a different beat). As such, Meena Sodhi identifies the novel as a "personal book" (41) that chronicles Roy's "life reconstructed out of the memories of the past" (42). Now, to continue with the obvious, neither historical facts nor autobiographical traits appearing in the narrative transform the novel into a historical document or a "disguised" autobiography. Both the critic and the general reader are to engage with *The God of Small Things* first as a fictional narrative.

Roy's sources are varied, both individual and universal. She draws from the treasure trove of personal experience, history, and stories read and heard to invent her plots, settings, and characterizations. As the novel unfolds, we see the influence of Dickens (playfully precise imagery and metaphor), Faulkner (layered voices and multiple filtered events), Fitzgerald (tragic romance and a theme of capitalist production and waste), Thomas Hardy (rural realism and character fate), Jamaica Kincaid (colonial history and coming of age), and Gabriel García Márquez (syntax and temporal play), to name a few. We also witness the narrator's explicit references to classic Indian epics such as *The Mahabaratha* and *Ramayana*. And, as Julie Mullaney identifies in her reader's guide to the novel, the narrative unfolds like the stylized dance-dramas known as "kathakali"—a storytelling tradition that originated in Kerala in the seventeenth century.

The God of Small Things situates itself quite overtly within world literary traditions—often, the narrative directs its reader to signposts that indicate a wealth of affiliations. One of the paratextual blurbs that appears along with others just before the story proper begins picks up on this, identifying the novel's allegiance as "Faulknerian in its ambitious tackling of family and race and class, Dickensian in its sharp-eyed observation of society and character." To restate the obvious: Roy and all contemporary novelists of value resist the ghettoizing of their work, no matter where it is accomplished or where the author lives or was born. While texturing a South Asian subjectivity and using postcolonial aesthetic sensibilities, Roy is the opposite of a parochial writer, and her sophisticated novel both engages and disengages with world literary canons.

One of the dominant plots in the novel is that of romance. This age-old, universal, and somewhat conventional plot line, however, becomes interesting and vital once again thanks to Roy's narrative skills and to the focus on two lovers not just from across those proverbial tracks that divide families and class, but from across caste lines. Also, as the novel spirals into its center and goes on to reveal the mystery of Velutha's murder, the romance plot is made to intersect with a mystery suspense plot; this puts an interesting and engaging new spin on the classic love story as it gravitates around the tragic consequences of loving within a caste-structured society. (Indeed, the final, sensual scene of caste-transgressive lovemaking suggests that the lovers will be metaphorically reunited after death and aligns the story with that of a similar suggestion at the end of the *Ramayana*.)

Romance and intrigue are the dominant containers and motivators of *The God of Small Things*, a story that unfolds along two temporal planes. The most chronologically present narrative takes place over twenty-four hours: adult Rahel's return from the United States to Kerala (identified fuzzily as 1992–1993) and her reunion with her twin brother, Estha. The most chronologically distant past narrative takes place during the two weeks in 1969, when Rahel and Estha are seven, that lead up to the drowning of their cousin Sophie Mol and the murder of Velutha, their mother's lover. The two chronological lines intercalate as the novel unfolds. As the narrator moves back and forth between these two temporal zones, the narrative gives more and more detail to scenes, events, and character interactions that make up the 1969 moment. In contrast, since the narrative present does not contain any plot-shifting events, the reader senses that whatever happened in 1969 must have put a choke hold of sorts on Rahel's and Estha's lives. Most of the novel concerns the past and hinges on it, and as the details accumulate, the reader slowly and strategically is made privy to the *who* and the *why,* not just of Velutha and his murder, but also of Sophie's death, of Estha's sexual abuse, and so on.

MULTIPERSON CHARACTER SLANT

As the narrative interweaves past into present, it also uses the device of the narrated monologue (free indirect discourse) in new and interesting ways. The multiple-person or "we" narrator, as Brian Richardson identifies it, occupies a middle ground between first person and third person. Moreover, even if the technique itself does not identify a postcolonial essence, it is used by a great many postcolonial authors who seek to, as Richardson writes, "valorize collective identity in no uncertain terms" (*Unnatural Voices*, 50). In Roy we see this "we" presence as a character filter. In Roy's first chapter, "Paradise Pickles and Preserves," in which the reader experiences eleven instances of temporal shift and rupture, Roy introduces a number of narrative voices. It opens: "May in Ayemenem is a hot, brooding month. The days are long and humid. The river shrinks and black crows gorge on bright mangoes in still, dustgreen trees. Red bananas ripen. Jackfruits burst" (3). The third-person narrative voice in the present tense continues in this straightforward manner for two more paragraphs, one of which is quite short—a sentence. The narrator's voice and tone then shift:

> It was raining when Rahel came back to Ayemenem. Slant-ing silver ropes slammed into loose earth, plowing it up like gunfire. The old house on the hill wore its steep, gabled roof pulled over its ears like a low hat. The walls, streaked with moss, had grown soft, and bulged a little with damp-ness that seeped up from the ground. (4)

While still in the third person, the tense shifts here—and so does the language. We are no longer seeing the world through the eyes of the first (third-person) narrator but rather through a third-person narrator focalized through the perspective of Rahel. She is the one who has just arrived. While the narrator tells us this is Rahel returning to Ayemenem "years later" (5) as an adult, the way the house and its environs are described capture the way Rahel and her twin brother, Estha, would see the house on the hill *as* children; we know this retroactively only once we have read far enough along in the novel to hear the words and images they use as children to know them and the way they see the world *as* children. That is, in the first several paragraphs of the novel, we readers already feel the presence of Rahel through the third person narrator's voice, but it is the presence of Rahel as a child.

Moreover, it is the presence of Rahel *and* Estha, even though it is Rahel with whom we identify more strongly given that she is the one of the two who still uses words. Estha, through her, feels and thinks in his silence on a train returning to Calcutta: "Rain. Rushing, inky water. And a smell. Sicksweet. Like old roses on a breeze" (32).

The narrative runs home this point on the following page:

> Now, these years later, Rahel has a memory of waking up one night giggling at Estha's funny dream.

> She has other memories too that she has no right to have.
>
> She remembers, for instance (though she hadn't been there), what the Orangedrink Lemondrink Man did to Estha in Abhilash Talkies. She remembers the taste of the tomato sandwiches—*Estha's* sandwiches, that *Estha* ate—on the Madras Mail to Madras.
>
> And these are only the small things. (5)

Rahel and Estha feel and think as one. So if it is Rahel's perspective that we feel within the third-person narration, then it is both his and hers.

As this chapter unwinds, along with giving a faint outline to the major events that shape the novel's plot, we encounter yet another narrative voice. The narrator tells us,

> She had forgotten just how damp the monsoon air in Ayemenem could be. Swollen cupboards creaked. Locked windows burst open. Books got soft and wavy between their covers. Strange insects appeared like ideas in the evenings and burned themselves on Baby Kochamma's dim forty-watt bulbs. (11)

Here we have Rahel's thoughts and perspective *as* an adult but not in her voice. After several more like passages seeing Ayemenem as filtered through an adult Rahel's perspective, the reader once again feels the presence of the Rahel/Estha voice projected through that third-person narrator:

> Once the quietness arrived, it stayed and spread in Estha. It reached out of his head and enfolded him in its swampy arms. It rocked him to the rhythm of an ancient, fetal heartbeat. It sent its stealthy, suckered tentacles inching along the insides of his skull, hoovering the knolls and dells of his memory, dislodging old sentences, whisking them off the tip of his tongue. (13)

Roy invents a third-person narrator wherein the reader feels a "we" character filter (Rahel and Estha). The narrated monologue is the device that allows a third-person narrator to ventriloquize the character's thoughts and perspective. Dorrit Cohn defines this as the device that suppresses all marks of quotation that set it off from the narration, and this self-effacement can be achieved most perfectly in the milieu where the narrative presentation adheres most consistently to a figural perspective, shaping the entire fictional world as an uninterrupted *vision avec.* The narrated monologue itself, however, is not *vision avec,* but what we might call *Pensée avec:* here . . . tightly woven into the texture of third-person narration. (500–501)

Indeed, in Roy's hands this *pensée avec,* or "thinking with," is made plural with Rahel and Estha's childhood thought and perspective interwoven into the third-person narration. Refashioned as such, the "we"-narrated monologue in *The God of Small Things* works as a device that allows Roy to create a narrative whereby the reader *feels* the presence of Rahel/Estha as children in an extensive and extended way. This along with the dreamlike ordering of time—the seamless movement between past and present—remind us once again that Roy has put the fiction back into the postcolonial.

Once the narrative gets under way, this narrator with its third-person objective as well as its narrated monologue "we" (Rahel/Estha as children) and "I" (the adult Rahel) perspective breathes life into the major characters that populate the novel: the independent-thinking Ammu (mother of Rahel and Estha), who defies law and has an affair with Velutha, the Harijan Untouchable, a skilled carpenter trained by a European builder to sculpt Bauhaus furniture and the son of a glass-eyed father; Ammu's brother, Chacko, a conflicted pickle-factory owner, his ex-wife, Margaret, and his British-raised, Anglo-Indian daughter, Sophie Mol; Mammachi, Estha and Rahel's grandmother whose skull exhibits permanent scars from her husband's beatings; Bennan John Ipe, their grandfather whose dashed dreams of becoming an important entomologist for the British government (pre-Independence) lead to his death; Baby Kochamma, who lusts for Father Mulligan and embraces Christianity; Kochu Maris, the superstitious houseservant; Comrade Pillai, a local politician who in the name of Marxism actually brings more suffering than good to those disenfranchised like Velutha. As the narrator reveals the nuances of each character, the reader begins to see how ideology and social status (Anglophilia, heterosexism, caste, class, for example) form different expressions of alienation, shame, self-loathing, violence, sexual abuse, and death.

For the most part, by the end of the first chapter the reader already has a good sketch of the plot (romance and mystery/suspense) as well as an overview of the themes and characters. What continues fueling the reader's interest is the way the narrative fills in details as shaped variously by the third-person narrator and its various ventriloquisms of the "we" (Rahel/Estha) and the "I" (Rahel as adult) perspectives. This colors the questions we have as readers about the cause and effects in the various plot turns, how those "little events, ordinary things, smashed and reconstituted, become imbued with new meaning" (32). And it asks us to relinquish control to its own logic—a logic of dream whereby the narrative sometimes gives us a discernible cause/effect configuration and sometimes does not. Lastly, the narrative sets up various tensions between what the third-person narrator knows and what the "we" (Rahel/Estha) and "I" (Rahel as adult) narrated monologues reveal.

WRAP-UP

Since the publication of *The God of Small Things* and its worldwide success, doors have opened to many other young South Asian women writers, among them Kiran Desai, Manju Kapur, Ameena Meer, and Shauna Sing Baldwin. Often these new authors allude to Roy's novel, extend and complicate her narrative line, and enrich the South Asian literary genealogy in new and exciting ways. When in an interview Roy explains that her novel is not "specifically about 'our culture'—it's a book about human nature" (Abraham, 91), she is inviting the reader and the critic to take a more careful look into the contents, the underlying themes running through the multiple labyrinths in *The God of Small Things*.

Because the novel as a literary genre has an unlimited capacity for world making, it can show us and make us feel everything and anything existing in the universe, including our personal imaginings and fantasies. And with no concern for veracity, for scientific probability or plausibility, or even for everyday commonsense realism, the novel opens unlimited opportunities to realize thought experiments of every sort, to test emotions and thoughts and instincts of all kinds against wholly imagined worlds or quite real life circumstances. This is what makes the novel such a formidable laboratory of human sciences and psychology and such a delightful depository of suppositions, hypotheses, and knowledge concerning all aspects of what we are, what and how we feel, and what we do or are capable of doing. Such are the properties, the function, and the origin of the "realism" and the "antirealism" peculiar to fiction and above all to the fiction shaped by an author like Arundhati Roy with her strong will to style.

If *The God of Small Things* has been a powerful catalyst for many writers, it is certainly because it has been efficient in the sense previously mentioned. Through the careful architecture of Roy's novel, the expansion of contact zones between postcolonial/ethnic and the Western Anglo-American and European canon, the inventive use of narrative procedures (focalization, temporality, free indirect discourse, multiple plot lines, characterization, and so on) and style (rhythm, atmosphere, tone, chiastic repetitions, lexical register and innovation, and so forth), Roy has furnished tools for others to use and improve, and she has incorporated in the literary laboratory areas of the human psyche for others to continue to explore. This is certainly one of the reasons her novel has rapidly become a "classic" and will probably remain so for a long time to come, not because it is deemed an allegory of nation, a writing back against empire, or a selling out to global capitalism.

Stephen Alter remarks that works of fiction in general have had no "measurable social or political impact. Their readership, in most cases, is limited to the middle class and seldom reaches the poor and oppressed population, most of whom are illiterate" (24). Indeed, it is rather naively utopian to believe that novels and their interpretation are as such agents of social change. Moreover, this illusion can work very much against the literary writer in the first place. That is why Salman Rushdie warns of the author who "sets himself or herself up as the voice of nation," as this leads to stifling creative possibilities (*Step Across This Line*, 60). And that is why Roy, too, considers that being identified as a "writer-activist" diminishes "the scope, the range, the sweep of what a writer is and can be" (*Power Politics*, 23).

I leave the last word to Roy herself, who states in *War Talk* that "when writers, painters, musicians, film makers suspend their judgment and blindly yoke their art to the service of the nation, it's time for all of us to sit up and worry" (47).

Three

HISTORY AS HANDMAIDEN TO FICTION IN AMITAV GHOSH

It may be said that writers in my position, exiles or emigrants or expatriates, are haunted by some sense of loss, some urge to reclaim, to look back, even at the risk of being mutated into pillars of salt. But if we do look back, we must also do so in the knowledge—which gives rise to profound uncertainties— that our physical alienation from India almost inevitably means that we will not be capable of reclaiming precisely the thing that was lost; that we will, in short, create fictions, not actual cities or villages, but invisible ones, imaginary home-lands, Indias of the mind.

—SALMAN RUSHDIE, *IMAGINARY HOMELANDS*

WHAT NARRATION IS *NOT*

Salman Rushdie identifies a narrative impulse to invent "imaginary homelands" that springs from loss. In response to "talk about Third World novels as essentially about nation and nation build-ing," Amitav Ghosh highlights the family as the "central imaginative unit" in his fictions (Aldama, "An Interview with Amitav Ghosh," 89). For Rushdie and Ghosh and other South Asian diasporic writers gener-ally, the family and home are central to their crafting of fictional lands. To engage powerfully their readers, such writers employ a variety of narrative points of views, genres, storytelling styles, and techniques. They organize their complex fictions not as documents aimed to alter or replace reality—the reality, say, of existing nations—but to enliven the imagination with unreal worlds that cohere.

This is not to say that such writers offer escapes into never-never lands. It simply means that a writer like Ghosh carefully organizes his narrative elements so as to simultaneously engage the reader's creativity and disengage him or her from confusing invented worlds with the world that exists outside the narrative fiction universe. As Ghosh reminds us, his novels are centrally about family, but the fictional family members and their vicissitudes, the settings where the stories take place, and so on have nothing to do with "real" families and everything to do with a very skilled and intellectually captivating narrative style. Ghosh and his fellow writers do not pretend that their novels have the same ontological status and power to alter the world out there as the texts (constitutions, legislations, decrees, treatises, political documents, and regulations, for example), the sociopolitical institutions (political parties, trade unions, and executive, legislative, and judicial powers), and the class struggles and their embodied results (Social Security and medical care, public education, labor codes and guarantees) that have made and in most cases preserved their existence and unity. This most obvious clarification seems necessary in view of the opposite notion very widely held by a cadre of literary theorists who read the complexly crafted and imagined postcolonial narrative fictions as "real" or equally reductively as only an "allegory" of nation. In Ghosh's words, this view is "lopsided"—and not an "alert reading" (ibid.).

Indeed, much poststructuralist-informed postcolonial theory looks to cultural phenomena (the preferred subjects being nowadays music, fashion, sports, and especially literature) as signifying systems that either work with or against hegemonic power structures such as capitalism, colonialism, and the modern nation-state. All those phenomena are "theorized" as discursive constructs that, after such-and-such idiosyncratic decodings, are "revealed" to be equal in ontological status and agency as the identified hegemonic power structures. Thus, for poststructural postcolonialist critics such as Homi K. Bhabha the text (be it a novel or a political document) is the world (real and imagined), and the world is the text.

Amitav Ghosh throws down the gauntlet with *The Glass Palace,* challenging such postcolonial critics to confuse narrative fiction with reality of nation by writing a historical novel, a narrative whose fictional edges bleed more readily into the empirically verifiable facts of the "real" historical record. *The Glass Palace* unfolds over a hundred years of precolonial, colonial, and postcolonial Burmese history as families are formed and individual characters experience loss and joy. Social organizations such as feudalism are destroyed and new ones formed in the guise of the colonial and postcolonial nation-state. *The Glass Palace* is not, as Frederic Jameson claims generally of all "third-world texts," to be read as a "national allegory" (69) projecting de facto a subaltern epistemology that is an "allegory of the embattled situation of the public third world culture and society" (ibid.).[1] Also, it does not serve as a vehicle to articulate, as Azade Seyhan writes generally of such postcolonial narrations, a "countermemory" that resists and radically reforms "ethnocentric epistemologies" (154). Neither is it an expression of an "exilic ontology," as Emily Apter identifies of the postcolonial novel (92). Nor is it the resistant and revolutionary voice of a subaltern "third space," as Homi Bhabha would have.

The Glass Palace is a narrative that gravitates around the experiences of a variety of multigenerational, diasporic Indian-Burmese characters during a historical period (the late nineteenth century to the end of the twentieth) filled with battles won and lost over Burma's territories such as the British, then Japanese invasions. It is a novel that reflects obliquely the great tectonic shifts in rulers and national policy that affect the everyday of its characters' lives. As such, *The Glass Palace*'s characters, plot, and events can open its readers' eyes to acts of forced displacement and even genocides of peoples that took place historically; it can revisit grand historical events from different perspectives, such as that of Gandhi's attempt at a social revolution seen from the angle of vision of the female character Uma. The novel acts as a creative response to and reflection of experience in this world by a process of empathy with the characters and their circumstances and changing fortunes. But *The Glass Palace* is not a symbolic representation of nation, nor is it an expression of the "real" experiences of real people, rich and poor, during such tempestuous times in Burma. It is a work of fiction, a novel whose complex organization deftly balances the referential—characters described alongside real people; places that have houses, mountains, rivers, and so on, like real locations; and historical events that can be recognized as such—with the imaginary to open its doors for readers to enter and engage with its fictional storyworlds.

NARRATION AS NATION?

The boundary between literary study and political praxis has dissolved for the poststructuralist postcolonial theorist. For this to happen, the subject and its products and the material and social world

A User's Guide to Postcolonial and Latino Borderland Fiction

must be theorized as texts or discourses. Narrative fiction and political and historical discourse must be held to be equal. Accordingly, Azade Seyhan identifies literature "as one signifying system among others" (152). For this to be so, all texts and cultural phenomena must be seen as signifying constructs, a point of view based on a very peculiar interpretation of a linguistic theory formulated almost a century ago by the Swiss linguist Ferdinand de Saussure. For many poststructuralist postcolonial theorists, to act against colonialism or to unseat Western ontology, say, it would suffice simply to decode their signifying systems: to decode the discourses that naturalize hierarchies of difference (Western as civil versus non-Western as primitive, for example).[2] Consequently, if text and world are nothing but a signifying system, then the narrative titled *The Glass Palace* is as (ontologically) real as the reality outside the text; so the mere act of interpreting the novel not only destabilizes exoticist narratives of difference but generates a counternarrative with the power to disrupt those master signifying systems that make colonialism *mean* in the real world.

In *The Location of Culture* Homi Bhabha proposes a number of these decodings—variously identified as "mimicry," "radical hybridity," "colonial nonsense," and "sly civility," to name a few—of novels such as V. S. Naipaul's *The House for Mr. Biswas* and Salman Rushdie's *The Satanic Verses.* For example, he identifies "mimicry" in the postcolonial novel as a sign of "double articulation" (86) in which the text (the written text of the novel and the spoken text of the character) exists within, uncritically replicates, and threatens to disrupt the regulative rules of a disciplining colonial signifying system that imposes the English language as the standard and that exercises a close surveillance of subaltern bodies and knowledge systems. To confer to a novel like *House for Mr. Biswas* such power to resist and/or conform to a colonial hegemony, Bhabha, taking his lead from Derrida's *différance,* must muddle up de Saussure's linguistic theory.

Ferdinand de Saussure considered that a sign was an indivisible (psychological) unit formed by a signifier (acoustic image/phoneme) and a signified (mental image/concept), representing an aspect of reality (referent). To repeat: according to de Saussure, the two components of the sign (signifier and signified) are inseparable psychological entities, and the sign is the most basic element for communication to take place within a given linguistic community (Spanish or English, say). When Bhabha mistakenly identifies a "slippage" between the signifier and the signified, he is speaking nonsense in any accurate interpretation of de

Saussure's theory of the sign. Within this slippage, Bhabha considers meaning deferrable and the subject and world experienced by the subject unstable and fragmented. However, according to him, in order to make the subject and the world seem coherent and whole, those with power construct master narratives of wholeness that ideologically manipulate the sign to naturalize difference.

Homi Bhabha theorizes an "interstitial gap" between signifiers (mistaking acoustic image/phoneme for the sign) where resistance to meaning can take place ("meaning" as Derrida formulates, not in the presence of the sign and the referent but in the gaps between signifiers). He also theorizes the subaltern subject's formation by and through a colonial discourse, but one that can resist *inter dicta* (89). Therefore, to identify the "interstitial passage between fixed identifications" (4) is to reform dominant signifying systems. To inhabit such interstitial passages with a "radical hybridity" is to radically alter the master narratives of oppression and subjugation. At the end of *Location of Culture,* Bhabha positions postcolonial discourse generally—textual texts and textual subjects—not just in said gap that is "neither signifier nor signified" but also "outside the sentence" (181) and therefore outside of discourses of power. To posit such a mysterious resistance strategy, Bhabha must mistake the signifier for the sign (the part for the whole) and quite simply distort the nature of the relationship between signifier and signified in language as conceived by de Saussure.

As I discuss at length in *Why the Humanities Matter,* to say that there are gaps between words is true, and to say that it is often difficult to find the right words to express a concept is also true. However, to say that meaning is made in a gap between one acoustic image (or phoneme) and another acoustic image (or phoneme) is plain nonsense from any linguistic point of view; to say that the signifier and signified can be separated and then manipulated to change reality is equally sheer gibberish. If somehow one were able to rip apart de Saussure's signifier and signified, words within a given language community would become mere meaningless sounds. Absolute nonsense (better still, muteness) would preside. No communication could take place, and there would be no possibility for exchanging information concerning, say, oppressive conditions, and that would impede the necessary organization of people in need of a real social transformation.[3]

In order for subaltern subject and text to resist or destabilize hegemonic signifying systems *inter dicta,* Bhabha must muddle a very simple and primitive linguistic theory, but he also must add to this a misconception of how power functions within colonial rule and, more generally, within capitalism and the capitalist nation-state. According to Bhabha, who takes his lead from Michel Foucault's conception of power, there is room for contestation and resistance because colonialism is an unstable system of signification. The subaltern subject as a construct of colonial discourse is, for Bhabha, a "repertoire of conflictual positions" (204) that can intervene or not in the struggle against colonialism because this form of domination is constructed through discourse and therefore is uneven and incomplete. Thus, the moment colonialism exerts its force is precisely the moment that resistance forms in its interstices. But why even posit such an intervention if, by a logical extension of Bhabha's formulation, colonialism by its very existence as an unstable entity of power will ultimately fail? It is the same question we might ask of Foucault, who identifies in his *History of Sexuality* a "plurality of resistances" (Bhabha's "radical hybridity") that is formed de facto within a dominant power structure (a capitalist surveillance system that normalizes heterosexuality, for example).

By this token, we no longer need to locate power in the ruling class or the state it controls or the institutional structures it creates and handles, nor do we need to look for the "source of all rebellions, or pure law of the revolutionary" (Foucault, *History of Sexuality*, 96). Bhabha, following Foucault, considers that power is everywhere, but if that assertion were true, then power would be nowhere.[4] Like Foucault before him, Bhabha must theorize the simultaneity of power with resistance in order to make his "radical hybridity" work; to this end he must theorize out of existence the "real" exploitive and oppressive systems of colonial rule. (Foucault's intellectual missteps and the subsequent influence of his ideas on postcolonial theory generally is a topic I address in more detail in *Why the Humanities Matter*.)

This self-deconstruction of an oppressive and exploitive social structure, however, does little but promote a lack of real social mobilization and resistance; it ultimately celebrates symbolic forms of resistance in cultural phenomena and literature and dangerously dislocates and permanently erases the real site (the state apparatus) of the real ruling class (the private owners of the means of production and distribution) asserting its power through its all-too-real institutions (mainly the executive, legislative, and judicial branches of the state) that are used to dominate, oppress, and exploit the very real subaltern subjects.

If colonial power is a discursive construction and its simultaneous resistance textual, then it is not surprising that Bhabha considers that a nation is itself a narration—and concomitantly, that narration is nation. In the introduction to his edited collection of essays *Nation and Narration,* Bhabha defines the nation as formed by "textual strategies, metaphoric displacements, sub-texts and figurative stratagems" (2). To confront the nation, then, is to encounter it "as it is written" (ibid.). Again, like his formulation of colonialism as signifying system, the nation is fragmented. Bhabha must formulate the nation as made up of "scraps, patches, and rags of daily signs" ("DissemiNation," 297) to identify a resistance in the "language of metaphor" (291) in postcolonial novels that reimagine postcolonial histories and "nation-people" (ibid.). Finally, for Bhabha, then, the "double-writing" form of the postcolonial novel acts as a site of contestation and "dissemi-*nation.*"[5]

Bhabha is not alone in this textualist idealism. We see this impulse also in Edward Said's *Orientalism.* Among concepts, Said proposes how scholars from all walks of life devoted their time and energy to the study of what they called the "Orient," thereby creating not only the concept of the Orient but a *conceptual* Orient. According to Said, such assigning of a series of characteristics to the Orient coincided with the work done by bureaucrats from Western imperialist states along with the exploitive activities of private companies like the East India Company. Now for Said to consider the study of Sanskrit or archeological digs as having the same importance (materially and cognitively) as, say, topographic studies used to build forts to violently oppress native peoples (or even the study of caste to better divide and rule), he erases those differences that make a difference; he places everything (novel and judicial document, say) at the same level. Since such fields of inquiry are extremely diverse and create radically different outcomes, Said's brand of idealism requires that they all be reduced to one common denominator: the world as a text. By doing so, he himself creates a category or classification of the Orient as a textual product with no distinction made between the different so-called "texts." So, to level the differences between the nineteenth-century scholarly studies of social or natural phenomena in areas that had been or were being colonized by European capitalists and imperialist acts of exploitation and oppression of those areas and their peoples, Said transforms all reality into a text. And by textualizing all reality, he posits that the "Orient" and the "Occident" are constructs.

One way or another such scholars reject any concrete study of historical phenomena of the development of capitalism, how it develops and spreads all over the world.[6] Thus they can only resort to an idealist

A User's Guide to Postcolonial and Latino Borderland Fiction

position that declares: It is not on material reality that we need to focus but rather on the development of ideas and the effects of ideas on reality. In this approach to postcolonial studies, then, what we begin to see is the formulation of a material reality transformed not by people situated in and actively shaping history, but simply by ideas. Ideas and narratives become nations; ideas and narratives become the motor of social and political transformation.

AGAINST THE GRAIN OF HOME AND NATION

If *The Glass Palace*—or any novel, for that matter—is a narrative fiction that is bound only to the conventions of narrative aesthetics and not to a radical transformation of the reality beyond its pages, then what else follows from the assertion that nation is narration? What is entailed from the compulsive need to fantasize about counternarratives that resist the nation?

The nation is not an imagined community. Many attempts at defining a nation have been defective because they have failed to embrace the great variety of fundamental traits observed in the hugely diverse existing nations and have not identified what could be called the necessary and sufficient elements that would characterize a particular socioeconomic and historic phenomenon as a nation. According to a most general but useful definition, a nation is a geographical space inhabited by a population that shares a common history, a common language, and a common set of customs or habits, that is, a common culture. The problem with this definition is that it carries many exceptions. In some nations, for example Switzerland and India, the population speaks not one language but several. In many countries it would be difficult to say there is a common culture—the cultural diversity of countries like the United States or Mexico are examples here. A more general but perhaps better definition could be this: a nation is on the one hand a material reality and on the other a psychological affiliation; it is a space forged by history and class struggles, leading to the establishment of stable institutions: a constitution, laws and regulations and general legal codes (labor, sanitary, and so on), courts, independent judiciary, legislative, and executive bodies. A nation is a space forged by history and class struggles that have led to the establishing of infrastructures and means of communication for its people and that offers its people peace and security as well as a sense of affiliation, belonging—patriotism.

The nation is not a signifying system or linguistic construct. In fact, in modern times the nation has represented the most positive drive toward democracy. (See also David Miller's *On Nationality*.) Without the nation as a political framework in which wage workers struggle to obtain and to protect their basic rights, exploitation and oppression would be complete. So, when Bhabha proposes that a radical hybrid narrative actually destabilizes and transforms the nation, even if it is no more than hot air or perhaps utopian fantasy, the proposal itself is politically regressive. It would entail the full application of the policy that the American administration and the American ruling class are seeking to apply today worldwide: the destruction of all institutional structures and laws that protect the working classes and the exploited and oppressed populations in every country. The only way these populations can hope to fend off exploitation and oppression is to continue the fight that they have been fighting for more than two centuries: the organized struggle for the right to build their own politically independent parties, to build their own independent unions, to obtain and preserve the equal right to a secular education, to free medical care, to public transportation services everywhere, and to the total freedom of organization, expression, and representation for all—in short, to fight for and to maintain those institutions and laws that make for a democratic nation and that are being eroded by the bourgeoisie in India and the United States, in Asia and the Middle East, in Africa and Australia and Latin America.

The destruction of nation-states without the destruction of capitalism would not translate into a utopian world filled with radical hybrid subjects but rather into the worldwide spread of barbarism, of the warlordism and slavery that we have already seen in places like Somalia and the former Yugoslavia, in Iraq and Afghanistan. Moreover, to theorize a utopian hybrid space of resistance that supposedly exists between the lines of signification is to disrespect the memory of the millions of people who struggle and have been struggling for generations with massive costs to lives in order to establish and maintain the democratic rights that they have forced the capitalist nation to adopt and to uphold.

Because capitalism cannot do without its own foundational principle— the right to privatize property—the bourgeoisie has had to accept reluctantly the existence of laws generally, including those that protect the laboring class. Hence, the importance of the nation not as enemy to subaltern struggles worldwide, but as the very political framework in which all the wage-earners and the oppressed peoples can fight to obtain and preserve—even against the most violent opposition of the ruling classes—their democratic rights. So, in the name of radical hybridity and revolutionary "third space" narrations, Bhabha and others could be actually positing the destruction of a most fundamental barrier that remains between the working class and peasants and their complete and total enslavement.

Bhabha's formulation of postcolonial narrative as counternation relies on the highly speculative idea that the nation is made up of narratives that gel together and create imaginary or discursive communities. One might simply ask what literature actually has done to create the nation of India, or even closer to home, the nation of Mexico or the nation of the United States of America. Narrative fictions did not alter or contribute to altering the northern boundaries of the territory of Mexico in 1836 and after the U.S. invasion of 1846–1848. Narrative fictions did not alter Spanish rule in Mexico during the eleven-year war of independence that led to Mexican sovereignty. Narrative fictions did not create the upper-, middle-, and working-class uprisings that led to the American War of Independence from the ruling British class. Narrative fictions did not create nations in Africa when the continent was mostly divided up by lines traced with rulers on maps in political drawing rooms in France, Belgium, and England. Narrative fictions did not create nations in Central Europe such as Yugoslavia. Literature was not the agent behind Great Britain and the United States deciding after World War II that the territory inhabited by both Jewish and Palestinian peoples should become a theocratic state, Israel, a decision that resulted in the expulsion of hundreds of thousands of Palestinians and has created an atrocious conflict that lasts until today. The main problem with the highly speculative statements made by Bhabha and others is that they not only cover over the harsh facts of material reality— among them the massive rivers of blood that poured in the creation of nations and the millions of people involved in that process— but they also resist the most elementary confrontation with historical reality: that literature has never been a material force in the formation of a nation.

Narrative fiction, then, for scholars like Bhabha does not just reflect or recreate reality and bring to the table events that happen; they invest it also with a godlike power to create and transform reality. At best, this can be read as a response to our contemporary world that promises little in the form of real social change; to that extent, the utopian impulse can be justified. At worst, this is an extremely dangerous promotion of an arm-chair political "praxis" that denies the real need for class struggle against concrete, actual, present-day problems that have plagued the working classes worldwide since the rise of capitalism and that have only grown more severe. Antony Easthope writes of Bhabha's radical hybridity and its destabilizing of discourse, knowledge, and power that this "theorizing" coincides "with one of the more pervasive fantasies of our time: that reading texts otherwise changes the world" (60).[7]

READING *THE GLASS PALACE* AS LITERATURE

The Glass Palace is chock full of hyphenated (Burmese-Indian, Anglo-Indian, for example) characters who seek a sense of place and belonging—a home—within homelands torn apart by colonialist and imperialist invasions and civil wars. It is a novel whose story stretches out from and around the experiences of South Asian hybrid characters as grand historical events of nation unfold. In a review of *The Glass Palace* Chris Higashi calls the novel "a multigenerational saga" that "is a wonderful, satisfying blend of history and storytelling" (132). When all is said and done, however, *The Glass Palace* is more storytelling than history. Ghosh's primary concern is for the story to engage and move its readers.

The Glass Palace is filled with unrequited love and passionate consummation of desire; it is a narrative of dramatic adventure, great migrations, and unbelievable chance encounters. It is packed with historically verifiable details, such as colonial India's invasion of Burma, and dates in chapter headings remind readers of the plot's imbrication with historical chronology. However, its thematic material is carefully organized according to the principles that govern the crafting of fiction: language, narrative technique, and genre. Contrary to what many poststructural postcolonialists venture to say, even at the most basic understanding, the biographically verifiable author Amitav Ghosh does not correspond one-to-one with the fictional characters he invents nor with the narrator he employs to shape the narrative. Nor, for that matter, do his characters represent real people.

Characters are not, as Dorrit Cohn comments, "free subjects who can potentially escape their graphic prison and make fictional subjects of—or even talk back to—their author or narrator" (*The Distinction of Fiction,* 171). They are, Cohn remarks, "equally inhabitants of the same conflicted fictional world" (ibid.). And those disciplinary spaces—colonialism, capitalism, and otherwise—in *The Glass Palace* are only representations and not the real disciplinary spaces where the powerful rule over the powerless in the real world. Finally, language—the very substance of *The Glass Palace*—has, Lubomír Dolezel aptly reminds us, "weak performative power" (253). While it can help solidify a group and communicate its needs to bring about changes in everyday social relations and affairs, Dolezel continues, "it cannot create the actual world that exists and goes on independently of language and any other representation. The only kind of worlds that human language is capable of creating or producing is *possible worlds*" (253). That is, *The Glass Palace* is the stuff of fiction that can open eyes to the brutalities of colonialism—and more—and not a text that can resist, intervene, or fundamentally transform anything, much less the everyday reality of millions of people living within a national space shaped by history and governed by laws.[8]

The Glass Palace includes a recorded history, and the immediate impulse, then, would be to read it as a postcolonial text that revises and dramatically transforms Anglo-colonial-biased histories that traditionally have silenced or erased the subaltern presence and agency. The novel's revisiting of historical events might be read as a symbolic and real restoration of subaltern history and cultural memory that, as Azade Seyhan comments generally, "accord meaning, purpose, and integrity to the past" (15). To read accordingly, one must blur the boundary between the categories of fiction and nonfiction, novel and history.[9] However, the organization of the narrative components and of characterization in *The Glass Palace* does the opposite. It educates its reader to reinforce the border between the empirically verifiable historical reality and the narrative fiction. For example, Ghosh invents a third-person narrator who relates a story in a helical fashion that simultaneously fictionalizes and makes real historical subjects and events. By making them real, the narrator represents the characters (whether factually based, like the Burmese King Thebaw, or fictionally based like the protagonist, Rajkumar) as "real" according to the terms of the fictional narration. As such, the narrative often slips into free indirect discourse to open up a free flow of information between the reader and the character's interiority.

The narrator of the historical novel can see and enter into all characters' minds; the author of a factual historical narrative cannot. So although Ghosh employs a third-person omniscient narrator who exists at a remove from the storyworld, the narrator is not bound by the conventions of the work of history. Such a work of history also uses a "third-person narrator," but it does so announcing explicitly that the narrator is the point of view of the trained historian with a scholarly interest in historical document and ethnographic material. This historically bound narrator is tied to referential obligations that aim at establishing a one-to-one correspondence between the facts represented and the verifiable reality of the world. Ghosh's narrator is not bound by chronological convention; he even makes huge leaps in history—1919 to 1929—with the turn of a page. When a historically bound narrator does not know something, the scientific aims are not abandoned; on the contrary, the narrator announces to the reader the lack of knowledge. (See also Kale Pihlainen's "The Moral of the Historical Story.")

And so where the narrator of historical narrative is constrained by the demands of truth and the facts found in archival, autobiographical, and anecdotal sources, the narrator of the historical novel is free to imagine and invent the "facts." Lubomír Dolezel further clarifies the distinction, identifying "historical noeisis" as writing that constructs "models of the past that exits (existed) prior to the act of writing" and "fictional poiesis" as the invention of a "possible world that did not exist prior to the act of writing" (262). *The Glass Palace,* then, uses "models of the past" to enrich the creative invention of a "possible world." Here, factually verifiable characters acquire fictional dimensions and can interact with those of purely invented flesh and blood. The fictional Rajkumar can fall in love with the invented handmaiden of the real historical figure Queen Supayalat. And, as the narrative unfolds, the reader witnesses such a "real" figure as the queen increasingly migrates over into the "semantic and pragmatic conditions of the fictional environment" (Dolezel, 264). The force of fictional narrative is such that it pulls the factual characters into its world without asking its readers to question such a move, without asking its readers to look beyond its pages for a one-to-one verification between textual representation and an ontologically independent and temporally prior set of events—archived data—that existed prior to the act of writing.

HISTORY PERCOLATES . . .

At the outset, *The Glass Palace* educates its reader to interpret its narrative as a historical fictional narrative. But before entering the storyworld proper, history is foregrounded. The following titles appear as paratextual preface material: W. S. Desai's *Deposed King Thebaw of Burma in India, 1885–1916;* Patricia Herbert's *The Hsaya San Rebellion Reappraised;* and Majjhima Nikaya and Amyutta Nikaya collection, *The Buddhist Tradition in India, China, and Japan.* Verifiable historical figures and events as well as dates and cultural documents begin to condition the reader's approach to the text—a text situated within the historically and culturally verifiable. The list of texts identifiable as historical and cultural documents is far from exhaustive, however. And given the discrepancy between the length of *The Glass Palace* (five-hundred-plus pages) and this short list of archival material, the reader quickly grasps that narrative fiction is central and that the narrative which has a one-to-one correspondence with the historical record is subordinate to the purposes of the fictional storytelling. This paratextual frame (and as described earlier, there are subclasses of "peritexts" that enhance the total paratextual effect, such as the jacket cover blurbs and the publisher's identification of the book as a novel) helps pave the way for a reader's first encounter with the text itself. The narrative begins:

> There was only one person in the food-stall who knew
> exactly what that sound was that was rolling across the
> plain, along the silver curve of the Irrawaddy, to the western
> wall of Mandalay's fort. His name was Rajkumar and he was
> an Indian, a boy of eleven—not an authority to be relied
> upon. (3)

Unlike the narrative conventions found in historical narratives, here the third-person announces its omniscience—commenting on a character's knowing what the sound was that rolled across the plain and also having a knowledge of this character's unreliability—and quickly shows its deft control over an in medias res flow of information. The narrator does not plainly relate the information but uses language, syntax, imagery, and sequence to engage the reader with dramatic effect. Cannon fire does not just happen—its sounds are described as "rolling across the plain"; the Irrawaddy river does not simply exist—it is given a poetic attribute ("silver curve") that helps the reader imagine the cannon sound as it weaves in and out of the river's glistening serpentine shape. The narrative has established the contours of its contract: that the reader will give priority to reading the text as a narrative fiction first and secondarily to reading it as historical document.[10] From the beginning to the last sentence of the book, the reader is to acknowledge the presence of historical fact but not to privilege it over fictional invention.[11]

To solidify the privileging of fiction over fact in the reader's mind, Ghosh's narrator spends the first three pages of the novel breathing life into the invented character Rajkumar. The narrator does not introduce the historical figures King Thebaw and Queen Supayalat until after he has introduced Rajkumar. The story of the historical figures (who after the British invasion of Burma experienced life as dispossessed exiles in India) becomes increasingly fictionalized as it interweaves with the lives of the fictional characters and their stories. Fiction overwhelms fact as the reader submerges into the story of Rajkumar's Horatio Alger–like rise to monetary glory, his romancing the queen's handmaiden, Dolly, and the subsequent adventures and romances of their sons: the naive photographer, Dinu, and the pragmatic materialist, Neele. Within this world the reader also meets the character Arjun, an Indian soldier fighting for the British army who realizes that his use of Britishisms like "yaar" and "spiffing" simply mask his own complicity in the oppression of South Asian people. And the reader encounters the politically active character Uma, whose adventures in India open the reader's eyes to India's early-twentieth-century campaigns for independence.

The verifiable historical event that percolates through the fictional narrative functions not solely to open reader's eyes to, say, Gandhi's 1942 Quit India movement, but as part of Ghosh's toolbox for creating a dramatic narrative that engages the reader. For example, the Japanese invasion of Burma cuts short the deeply moving romance between sympathetic characters Dinu and Alice, causing the reader's emotions to surge. Historical events also act as a springboard for a creative reinterpretation of history. While the real British invasion of Burma was a violent act of imposing a brutally oppressive colonial regime through much shedding of innocent blood, in the world of the novel it can be this as well as the seed event that leads to the love stories of Burmese princesses with those of a lower caste. The First Princess falls in love with the royal family's former coachman Sawant, and the Second Princess elopes with "a Burmese commoner" (204). Ghosh intersperses historically verifiable events such as the British imperial fleet crossing the Indian/Burma border "on 14 November, 1885" (25) and the 1942 Japanese bombing of Rangoon, which become kernel events, and these in turn seed new plots or turn stories in different directions.

Historical events can give cause for deep psychological probing of a character's interiority. For example, it is not until the Japanese Inspired Fifth Columnists (JIF) defeat the British army in Burma (historically verifiable) that the character Arjun has his epiphany, realizing his own complicity with colonialism. And on other occasions, historical event clears the space for a character to speak critically about the world. When the character Uma talks to Dinu about Hitler and Mussolini, the reader learns that such fascist dictatorships have already been a lived reality for Indians since the British conquest: "How many tens of millions of people have perished in the process of the Empire's conquest of the world—in its appropriation of entire continents?" (294). Finally, the presence of history as discipline gives shape to a third-generation character, Jaya, who studies history and "the huge collection of the documents and papers that Uma had left her, in her will" (449) to make her life and the world better.

. . . BUT ROMANCE PREDOMINATES

Grand historical events of colonial and postcolonial nation pull at and stretch out the fictional canvas of *The Glass Palace*. However, it is the romance narrative that predominates. When Rajkumar sees Dolly for the first time, the narrator remarks that she was "by far the most beautiful creature he had ever beheld, of a loveliness beyond imagining" (34). It is his vision of Dolly that sets his quest in motion. That is, romance leads to the rise and fall of three generations of family in grand epic proportion. It begins at the end of the nineteenth century with Rajkumar setting out to build his fortune—always with the idea that his acquired wealth will win the hand of Dolly, that his upward mobility—from street urchin to teak mogul—will enable him to provide for a family and ensure his legacy. It finishes three generations later at the end of the twentieth century with the character Jaya re-collecting a record of family through shards of archival documents.

For such characters as Rajkumar and Jaya, there is the impulse toward family—biologically and culturally—to find a sense of belonging. It is their lack of family that both generates this desire to create one anew and frees them of the traditional constraints of this institution. On one occasion, Rajkumar tells his loved one, Dolly: "I have no family, no parents, no brothers, no sisters, no fabric of small memories from which to cut a large cloth. People think this sad and so it is. But it means also that I have no option but to choose my own attachments" (147). He reads this lack of attachment as "a freedom of a kind" (ibid.) that allows him to remake family not according to racial, caste, or national dictates: the first son is named Sein Win (Burmese) Neeladhri (Indian) and looks "more Indian than Burmese in build and colouring" (202), and the second son is named Tun Pe (Burmese) Dinanth (Indian) and described as inheriting Dolly's "delicate features as well as her ivory complexion and fine-boned slimness of build" (202). Both sons affirm the forming of a new family populated by racially and culturally mixed subjects.

The novel charts the positive side effect of crumbling family structures that allows for the making of new communities based on common social understanding. After the character Uma's husband dies and she moves from India to New York, she begins to build an ad hoc family. In a new land and free of oppressive gendered roles and duties, she becomes the new matriarch for a "small but dense net" of "explorers" and "castaways" whose lineage is that of political and social change.[12] Finally, then, in *The Glass Palace*, family is more than biological; it is that which allows one to build social matrices through nonreproductive means.

Family is central to *The Glass Palace* in terms of content but also form. Its narrator uses the realist storytelling mode to give texture to its characters' experiences in the storyworld and uses historical event to fill out this telling; but it is the romance genre that functions as its narrative container.[13] In a review of the novel, Pankaj Mishra is critical of the novel's overreliance on the "idea of sexual love as redemption from history" (7) and is critical of the characters because, as he writes, "king and peasant alike in *The Glass Palace* lack a complex inner life" (ibid.). And finally, Mishra is critical of the novel's "childish" representation of people who lack "self-knowledge" and that are characterized as having only "simple longings and frustrations" (ibid.).

Mishra, however, misses the mark. While it is true that many of the characters lack full psychological and emotional depth and complexity— Queen Supayalat is easily identified as one—this type of nonrounded characterization is part and parcel of the romance genre convention. This has nothing to do with representing the characters as child-like or undeveloped and everything to do with generic convention. As we know from its long history, the romance novel is one that is characterized not just by a storyworld filled with quests and courtings, but a form that is deliberately episodic and that can cover massive social, historical, and geographic landscapes. The deep psychological character development that characterizes the bildungsroman is the means to an entirely different goal.

The romance is less concerned with individual psychology than with archetypes. In his taxonomy of different storytelling modes, Northrop Frye nicely sums this up, writing, "the romancer does not attempt to create 'real people' so much as stylized figures which expand into psychological archetypes" (304). And, unlike the bildungsroman that often provides a smooth veneer to cover over its generic borrowings, the romance often make visible its cracks and seams to disengage ever so slightly the reader's engagement with its storyworld. Robert Kiely identifies the romance genre as a "patchwork" of storytelling devices, themes, genres, and aesthetic aims that sometimes "produces the literary counterpart of Frankenstein's monster" but that can nonetheless reveal a new glimpse into life and fashion a "new idea of art" (3). Pankaj Mishra's dismissal of the novel is based on a misreading of the novel's participation within the conventions of this genre. *The Glass Palace* can both engage the reader at the level of the storyworld and disengage and remind the reader that they are reading narrative fiction at the level of form. *The Glass Palace* wants to tell us more than the psychological transformation of a protagonist. It wants to give the reader a sense of a massive historical and social landscape.

WRAP-UP

While critics such as Pankaj Mishra are dismissive (indirectly) of the romance gene, theorists such as Doris Sommer and Nancy Armstrong have identified it as a genre that has the power to critique and uncritically resist patriarchal, capitalist nation-state formation. For Sommer it naturalizes a patriarchal nationalism that valorizes heterosexism and biological reproduction (see her *Foundational Fictions*). For Armstrong, it allows a writer like Jane Austen to wrest power (at least symbolically) from a patriarchal state (see her *Desire and Domestic Fiction*).[14]

More radically, in *Atlas of the European Novel 1800–1900*, theorist Franco Moretti identifies how a careful decoding of the romance genre can reveal it to be a participant within a "geonarrative system" (17) that seductively masks capitalist nation formation. Moretti contends that it is the romance—and novel generally—that has the unique capacity to represent the nation. He interprets Jane Austen's romance plots that begin with family and home about to be disrupted as rewriting in the form of a "seductive journey" the "painful reality of territorial uprooting" (18). And he reads her happy endings as the joining together of "a *local* gentry, like the Bennets of *Pride and Prejudice,*" with the "*national* elite of Darcy and his ilk" (18, his emphasis), concluding that her novels "take the strange, harsh novelty of the modern state—and turn it into a large, exquisite home" (18).

The preoccupation with the romance genre as somehow tied to nation formation is not surprising. There is no doubt about the historical coincidence between the appearance of the romance novel and the formation of the modern capitalist nation-state. Cervantes's *Don Quixote* appeared at the moment when the bourgeoisie was beginning its long struggle to take power in Spain, for example. And in this historical conjunction, this seminal novel can be read as a matrix for the modern novel—growing out of the parodic opposition and engagement with earlier medieval romance conventions—that follows the life of neither peasant nor aristocrat, but rather an average individual with enough money to own books and have the leisure to read them and to go out to see the world. So while *Don Quixote* appeared at the very early stages of capitalist growth and the novel started to crystallize as the storytelling vehicle capable of describing this new reality (more democratic in content and form than, say, the courtly romance or the epic poem), it ultimately does not prove a useful model for reading a postcolonial avatar of a romance novel like *The Glass Palace.* Reading *The Glass Palace* as participating within "geonarratives" that critique or uncritically reproduce the nation—colonial, imperialist, postcolonial—leads one back to a Jamesonian reduction of narrative fiction to allegory or historical document. Moretti's approach misses the fact that Ghosh uses the romance genre to chart the stories of a panoply of characters who may or may not *reflect* on a history of colonialism in Burma and the formation of the present Myanmar nation. Also, the novel may affirm the reconstitution of family as hybrid (culturally and biologically) and postcolonial, but the romance genre also powerfully reminds the reader—with its use of "flat" characters and visible juxtaposition of genres—that *The Glass Palace* is to be read as narrative fiction told from a different angle and that sheds new light on the world we inhabit.

In his essay "Notes on Writing and the Nation" Salman Rushdie writes of the dangers of authors aligning their fiction-writing endeavors with political agendas like nation building, as this ultimately leads "to the murder of thought" (*Step Across This Line,* 60). To this I add: Beware the critic who sets up the nation as narration, for doing so flattens out those grand cartographies of the imagination. It cuts short the life of narrative fiction's great capacity to map an infinity of worlds. Reading *The Glass Palace,* then, not as a document of nation but as a narrative fiction that employs a complex helical narrative structure to richly texture its many characters' identities and experiences in a world marked by colonial oppression and exploitation allows us to see how this novel is able to revitalize the power of the romance genre and of the historical novel as told from a new point of view.

To read *The Glass Palace* thus is to enlarge the narrative contact zones between those genres and to shatter the interpretive lens that systematically confuses aesthetics with ontological facts—to shatter the wish-fulfillment fantasies of certain critics who choose to conflate narration with nation and nation with narration.

Four

FICTIONAL WORLD MAKING IN ZADIE SMITH AND HARI KUNZRU

NARRATIVE DOUBLE HELIX

In U.S. borderland and postcolonial theories of literature, much critical debate and discussion swarm around the issue of representation. Some consider the novel, as opposed to the prose poem, a more appropriate form for narrativizing postcoloniality or ethnicity, that one is more able to "strike back" against a Western canon than another.[1] Others consider the postcolonial identity and experience best represented in the storytelling mode of realism as opposed to magical realism, fabulism, naturalism, or metafictionalism, and vice versa. Some consider this experience best plotted as tragic and not comic, or vice versa. And yet others contend that postcolonial and ethnic characterization be only positive and affirming or that certain characters are more suitable as typical of a postcolonial narrative. Others debate the identity politics of language: writing in a precolonial tongue is more "authentic" than writing in a colonizing tongue like English. Ultimately one might ask whether there is a postcolonial "narrative essence." Can we unravel a unique postcolonial-borderland narrative code? To this end I ask, Where—if anywhere—might a borderland-postcolonial narrative essence reside? Is it a category imposed from scholarly Olympic heights? Is it to be found in the form? The content? Both?

To explore these initial questions, in this chapter I will focus on Hari Kunzru's *The Impressionist* and Zadie Smith's *White Teeth*. In a first step toward unraveling their narratives' double helix, I will examine how like and unlike narrative ingredients (universal and particularized) work to create the two novels' respective postcolonial storyworlds in ways that engage those who are reading cognitively and emotively.

On the one hand, Smith's *White Teeth* and Kunzru's *The Impressionist* are as unlike as any two novels could be. *The Impressionist* follows more directly the bildungsroman format: stretched over a wide canvas of time (half of the twentieth century) and geographic space (India, Britain, Africa), this narrative chronicles in a linear chronological fashion the seminal events that inform the development of the outcast and "half-baked" (35) protagonist, Pran Nath. From his early struggles as an androgynous sex slave (*hijra*), his by-day teenhood as adopted son of missionaries and by-night ladykiller pimp/grifter persona (Bobby), to the Oxford-educated scholar who assumes the identity of a deceased orphan named Jonathan and comes into a final reckoning of self while on an ethnographic field trip to Africa. It is told with acuity and wit and in the style of stolid realism. The novel opens:

> One afternoon, three years after the beginning of the new century, red dust that was once rich mountain soil quivers in the air. It falls on a rider who is making slow progress through the ravines that score the plains south of the mountains, drying his throat, filming his clothes, clogging the pores of his pink perspiring English face. (3)

Its narrative slant is one of smart omniscience; its mood is serious; its humor is reined in.

White Teeth follows in near-simultaneity the lives of a handful of characters from three families. The Joneses include Archibald, Clara, and their daughter, Irie; the Iqbals include Samad, Alsana, and twin sons Magid and Millat; the Chalfans include Marcus, Joyce, and their son, Josh. The narrative is set almost exclusively in Northwest London; with the exception of a few extended flashbacks—Archie about to commit suicide in 1975, Archie and Samad in Romania at the close of World War II, Clara's biracial roots in Jamaica at the turn of the twentieth century— it unfolds largely within an early 1990s epoch.[2] It is told in many different styles, from carnivalesque wit to dead-pan, dirty grit. It opens:

> Early in the morning, late in the century, Cricklewood Broadway. At 0627 hours on January 1, 1975, Alfred Archibald Jones was dressed in corduroy and sat in a fume-filled

> Cavalier Musketeer Estate facedown on the steering wheel,
> hoping the judgment would not be too heavy upon him. . . .
> He was resigned to it. He was prepared for it. He had flipped
> a coin and stood staunchly by the results. This was a decided-
> upon suicide. In fact, it was a New Year's resolution. (3)

Its third-person narrative slant is limited as well as pop-culturally in-the-know, hip, and personable; its mood is at once tragic and comic.[3]

While certainly different, the two novels share an important common ground. In their different narrative approaches, they both focus on the body: how, in academic-speak, the gendered, sexualized, and racialized act and are acted upon in the world.

In *White Teeth* it is the body that throws those most estranged from their bodies for a loop: Samad's faith in Islam and purity of mind and body are disrupted by his masturbation (115); Irie's internalizing of whiteness as ideal of beauty frustrates her when she cannot hide the kink of her hair,[4] returning her again and again to her embodiment as Jamaican:

> Now, Irie Jones, aged fifteen, was big. The European propor-
> tions of Clara's figure had skipped a generation, and she was
> landed instead with Hortense's substantial Jamaican frame,
> loaded with pineapples, mangoes, and guavas; the girls had
> weight; big tits, big butt, big hips, big thighs, big teeth. (221)

And we are told that Irie's grandfather, Darcus Bowden, was one of the original Windrush generation (those who came over during and after World War II because of a high demand for blue-collar workers) now settled into an odd bodily paralysis as an "odoriferous, moribund, salivating old man entombed in a bug-infested armchair from which he had never been seen to remove himself, not even, thanks to a catheter, to visit the outdoor toilet" (26). The description of his affliction as an "illness that no doctor could find any physical symptoms of, but which manifested itself in the most incredible lethargy" (26) more than hints that Darcus's émigré experiences with a 1950s xenophobic Britain has led to psychic paralysis.

In *The Impressionist* it is the body that passes or does not pass racially—a body that is white, or brown, or black depending on social context, a body that returns to itself constantly in the odyssey of its protagonist's kinesis of consciousness. It is such a body that allows Pran/Bobby/

Jonathan to pass into certain social spaces with their various attendant psychological schisms and chaotic unravelings and that ultimately propels the plot forward. Indeed, as the novel unfolds, what we discover is that Pran/Bobby/Jonathan's journey is one whereby he moves from a blinding belief in civilized order to a sharply focused awareness of the power of chaos and his own racial hybridity. At the end his release, so to speak, comes at the moment when he vision-quests into chaos and confusion and comes out the other side embracing fully a hybrid state of being. It is this "half-baked" body that rushes the reader, not so unlike that of *White Teeth,* into the chaos of a postcolonial identity and experience.

Clearly the moods differ from one novel to the other, yet both stories gravitate around characters who one way or another have a heightened sense of living in outcast bodies. And while the narrators' voices differ in tone, there is the overwhelming sense that they sit on the same side of the table as their outsider characters. They are not narrators who judge negatively the Prans and Iries of the world (as, say, a Kipling) but rather who sit sympathetically alongside them. And they do so from a certain tempered remove.

For example, Pran's outsiderness allows the narrator to take a certain side against colonial violence. During a rebellion, the narrator's abhorrence of the excessive force is evident—"one thousand six hundred and fifty rounds" (148) fired into the people. The narrator further describes the perpetrator's mindset:

> Like the deputy superintendent of police the general thought of his bullets in pedagogical terms. Ethnically, the dark-skinned races are like children, and the general was fulfilling the primary duty of the white man in Asia, which is to say that he was laying down a clear line. His bullets were reminders of the meaning of Law. Repeat after me. (148)

And yet, the narrator depicts violence as a two-way stream. On another occasion, Pran/Bobby is spit on and called a "Mongrel, English lackey" (206) by those subjects colonized by the British. And his outsiderness allows him to uncover the deep hypocrisies that underlie English society in Britain. While attending Chopham Hall boarding school, he writes in his diary: "Englishness is sameness" and "The comfort of repetition" (252). The narrator remarks, "Week by week his understanding of this world improves, the white spaces on his map filling up with trails and landmarks" (253).

Smith's narrator at once affirms the outsiderness—the racial mixings of Irie's generation represented by those like Danny Rahman and Quang O'Rourke[5]—but does not get swept away by happy-go-lucky multicultural jingles. In spite of "all the mixing up" (271), there are still those Others like Magid who aspire to a certain middle-class Englishness;[6] and there's his brother, Millat, who models himself after the "pacino-deniros, men in black who looked good, who talked fast, who never wiped a (mutherfuckin') table, who had two, fully functioning, gun-toting hands" (181) and who belongs to a crew called the Raggastanis who "spoke a strange mix of Jamaican patois, Bengali, Gujarati, and English" (192). And there's the mother, Alsana, who fears that her son will marry white. There are those angry white men "who will roll out at closing time into the poorly lit streets with a kitchen knife wrapped in a tight fist" (272). Also, there are xenophobes who fear "infection, penetration, miscegenation" (272); there are still those émigrés who fear "dissolution, *disappearance*" (272). And so, the narrative is careful to sully a too-romanticized view of racial mixing as the panacea to all social ills.[7]

The outsiderness and attendant critically sympathetic narrators of both novels push the narratives beyond individual self-enclosures and into the world. One might argue that it is this outsiderness that infuses both stories with a postcolonial worldview: one marked by a conflictive and contradictory racialized experience rooted in long stretches of history (Irie's mixed-race Jamaican heritage, for example) but that also offers from this vantage point the possibility of ultimately breaking with (colonial) fated determinism and coming into a space of creativity and freedom, a sense of optimism in the ability to shape this outsider status.[8] Smith's narrator closes with a celebration of Irie's newly claimed self-confidence, her requited love, and the promise (impregnated either by Magid or Millat) of new adventures to come.

Some might identify this outsider status as less postcolonial and more the angled vision of the satirical novel. According to Charles Knight, for example, those novels generally told from the point of view of the colonial, tyrannical, or war-dislocated, are "satiric exile" narratives (96) that reflect an uncertainty of place and carry a pessimism that reveals universal dehumanizations at the same time that they affirm "dissent" and proclaim the "urgency of change" (114–115). In *Black British Literature* Mark Stein identifies the themes of intergenerational conflicts, diasporic dislocations, and ethnic divisions and erosions in a novel like *White Teeth* as the special ingredients that make for what he calls "the novel of transformation"—not just of character but of the world by working in particular ways that "reach beyond the text" (171).

The Impressionist and White Teeth certainly brim with outsiderness, but neither has the pessimism that marks satire; and while both affirm possibilities and change, one might ask if this is a trait particular to these novels as postcolonial or more specifically "black British literature." Could we say the same of a Kundera, Dickens, or McEwan novel?

Paradoxically, to sharpen our focus, we must first enlarge the picture. This sense of postcolonial outsiderness is expressed in very specific ways from novel to novel, narrator to narrator, setting to setting, and character to character. At the same time that White Teeth and The Impressionist express uniquely different settings, experiences, and characterizations, there is a reader who can recognize and inhabit (to lesser or greater degrees) such outsiderness. Why? Because the particular is never too far from the universal.[9]

What does this mean exactly? It means that whether or not your particular experience of a 1990s Northwest London is one that matches that of, say, Irie's specific experience, this ultimately matters less than your capacity to infer, emote, empathize, holographically imagine disparate times and spaces. It is the universal capacity to feel and think, read minds, empathize, and communicate beyond the individual self so sharply attuned in Kunzru and Smith that allows readers to imagine so fully and empathize so deeply with the particular experiences of fictional characters like Irie and Jonathan.[10]

There is an added particular/universal dimension here, too—that we as individuals can read somebody else's words that turn into phrases that shape specific characters and settings that convey emotions (character feelings and narrative moods) are all subjective and objective facts that in each of us necessarily require a shared social memory. The same holds for the word "India" as referring to a mass of land located in a determinate place on the globe. And given that the readers might not share the cultural memory of the characters concerned, the narratives provide certain signposts and information to enrich their imagining experience.[11]

The particular and universal function on another level, too. To a certain degree Smith and Kunzru generate narratives out of stock storytelling conventions and recognizable character attributes. A certain degree of prototype recognition is necessary for the reader to be able to make the step into any fictional world (*Finnegan's Wake* is a good example of a closed-door novel—so much so that we cannot even say that it alienates the reader). The ideal reader of *White Teeth* and *The Impressionist* is one who relishes novelty. This is not the same ideal reader of, say, Mary Higgins Clark. So, prototypes are mixed up, exemplum disrupted, and schemas rescripted. *The Impressionist* and *White Teeth*, respectively, re-engineer the disobedient schema of the picaresque exemplified by *Don Quixote* and the hybrid Menippean mixtures exemplified by *Gargantua and Pantagruel*.[12]

Both novels include ingredients typical of the picaresque and Menippean schemas. However, each novel has a dominant mood, and this is determined by the greater degree of presence of the ingredients of one schema over the other. Kunzru's choice of particular narrative structures, devices, characters, and events primes, cues, and triggers the reader's identification of the presence of the picaresque—episodic plot, outsiderness, movement across multiple social spaces to reveal social hypocrisies and contradictions.[13] Smith's particular choice to employ a carnivalesque artillery of linguistic registers and zany mixed styles and to focus on bodily function in encyclopedic and majestic detail trigger in the ideal reader an identification of the presence of Menippean satire.

And yet, neither simply follows the picaresque or Menippean prototype narratives obediently. Both offer new cues and triggers that reschematize even these exemplary schemas. Smith divides *White Teeth* into four main sections that shape the individual journeys of the characters and their transformations. Thus, rather than simply giving readers tickets to a carnivalesque free-for-all, she blends Menippean and bildungsroman schemas to engage readers anew. And at novel's end, Kunzru's protagonist does not follow the typical *pícaro* path of continued delusion and lack of self-awareness. Rather, his Jonathan experiences the type of psychological transformation we expect of the bildungsroman schema.[14] He vision-quests—"the land skims beneath him as he rushes over it, white as bone in the moonlight" (378)—then experiences a massive disintegration of self:

> As he is pulled apart the world is pulled apart with him
> and he screams again, because without anything to screen
> it reality is unbearable and he is an abyss, and the thing he
> thought was himself is plucked out and flung away, leaving
> only a nightmare, a monstrous disorder. (379)

Suddenly, in the eleventh hour, Kunzru's picaresque narrative turns into the narrative of self-transformation, leaving that massive mark of the bildungsroman as Jonathan, the erstwhile (postcolonial) *pícaro,* returns to the primal matter of the earth "molten, formless, and in flux" (376). He is reborn into a "monstrous disorder" that allows for the opening of a new sense of himself in the world: "For now the journey is everything. He has no thoughts of arriving anywhere. Tonight he will sleep under the enormous bowl of the sky. Tomorrow he will travel on" (383).

BACK TO THE READER

The novels lay out signposts to prime, cue, trigger the ideal reader's responses in specific ways.[15] Robert Alter, so finely tuned in to city novels including those about Dickens's London, is one such ideal reader. In a review of Smith's more recent novel, *On Beauty,* Alter offers an illuminating passing comment on *White Teeth:*

> [I]t bustled with energy, evinced a rare generosity of imagination, and rendered the wildly various multicultural scene of contemporary London with unflagging satirical zest as well as sympathetic understanding. One readily forgave the moments, and there were more than a few of them, when the book's profusion of florid detail began to seem a little excessive because the book as a whole was such fun to read. (29)

Alter adds that *White Teeth*

> appealed to many readers precisely because it seemed such a full-throttle expression of a postmodern sensibility, given to energetic improvisation, to an extravagant mélange of human figures and situations, and to a certain deliberate and delightful looseness of form. (Ibid.)

Alter concludes, "As a novelist, she can marshal shrewd understanding, stylistic flair, vivid description, and a lively sense of comedy" (ibid.).

James Wood speaks of big contemporary novels like that of Smith's *White Teeth* as a "perpetual-motion machine that appears to have been embarrassed into velocity. It seems to want to abolish stillness, as if ashamed of silence. Stories and substories sprout on every page, and these novels continually flourish their glamorous congestion" (178). He identifies such fictions as "hysterical realism" (179) whereby the storytelling becomes the propelling force and not that of characterization or verisimilitude: "they clothe people who could never actually endure the stories that happen to them" (180). In comparing Smith's characters to Rushdie's, Wood remarks that hers are at times "externally comic" and at other times sympathetic in their "move in and out of human depth" (182). Claire Squires likewise reads the novel as "comic, sympathetic, and—essentially—optimistic" (13); its "intertextual largess" (20), Squires remarks, is inclusive of allusions to Kingsley Amis, Charles Dickens, Lawrence Sterne, Jeanette Winterson, Julian Barnes, and Vladimir Nabokov, among others. And as she astutely points out, this is a novel in which "common geographical location overrides [the characters'] disparate heritage" (7). Finally, because of its "urgent postcolonial themes of immigrancy and multiculturalism" (67), *White Teeth* is decidedly a historical novel for Squires.[16]

Kunzru's ideal reader would be one who can pick up not only on the picaresque conventions but also on how the use of an omniscient narrator with full control of the events adds to the sense that Jonathan is completely *not* in control of the world; he acts passively within a world that constantly acts on him—at least, that is, until the novel's end. In an interview Kunzru states:

> I was writing a picaresque very consciously with books on my mind like *Tom Jones, Candide,* and Nash's *The Unfortunate Traveler.* The central character is very much this type of hero—an outsider with a skewed pair of eyes looking on a crazy world. And, like the heroes of picaresque novels, he is something of a blank slate; he lacks an identity. So, the color of the book doesn't come out of any psychological depth of his character, but rather as he moves from set-piece scene to set-piece scene as the pageantry of empire plays out all around him. (In Aldama, "Hari Kunzru in Conversation," 12)

Kunzru discusses how he fooled around with canonical colonial literary representations of India and how in the final stages of the novel the travel upriver in Africa is not so much *Heart of Darkness*—"that's all about verticality and closing in"—but an opening outward toward a "terrible blankness" (ibid.). Finally, *The Impressionist* is, Kunzru concludes, "a book about books" (13). It is safe to say that the reader who picks up on its picaresque and other reschematizings (Kipling's *Kim* and Forster's *Passage to India,* among others) is the book's ideal reader.[17]

Readers of *White Teeth* and *The Impressionist* are constantly moving back and forth between the novel world and everyday life experiences and memories, activating and decoding constantly representational and behavioral schemas; we move between the actions of the characters and our memories of actions of people generally. Emotion plays a central role in our everyday experience and navigation of social worlds. It is our capacity of empathy that allows us to read minds, to step vicariously into another's shoes, to infer meaning from action. We are constantly inferring from such actions interior states of mind of a character—an activity we do in our everyday lives; we are constructing storytelling schemas—picaresque, say, or bildungsroman or Menippean—and deriving pleasure from following how the narratives reshape these schemas and from the ultimate reframing of the general categories within which these narratives operate.

For this cognitive and emotive activity to begin, the reader picks up on and deciphers the different signposts—those that blend and refashion the Rabelaisian, the bildungsroman, and the picaresque—to engage with the particular reschematizings at work in these novels. The ideal reader of both novels is one who enjoys the way the narrative's ironic reversals, direct addresses, unreliable narrations, and the like remind him or her of the artifice of the narrative—narratives that are built on truths within the fictional world. This ideal reader is the figure who will relish the way the novels refashion and particularize (postcolonialize, say) universal narrative prototypes in new cognitively and emotively engaging ways.

Clearly, both authors demonstrate a massive range of knowledge of literature and history, music, art, and more. This is displayed not only overtly—in a direct allusion to Conrad or an indirect allusion to Melville—but also in the distinct styles of their narratives. I ask here, Are their styles distinctively postcolonial? Is it the making of authors who seek to give shape from a postcolonial vantage point to their storyworlds? Do their individual styles create an effect that asks the reader to participate in specifically postcolonial-inflected ways?

Smith's narrator deploys a style that feels like a talking narration—its colloquial direct addresses, playful tangents, and mixings of linguistic registers. The narrator asks, "What else? Well, Archie hadn't always folded paper. Once upon a time he had been a track cyclist" (13), and on another occasion mentions how Archie

> drove straight past his flat, straight past the street signs (Hendon 3¾ miles), laughing like a loon. . . . In this manner, a new Archie is about to emerge. We have caught him on the hop. For he is in a past-tense, future-perfect kind of mood. He is in a *maybe this, maybe that* kind of mood. (15)

Colloquialisms abound: "Archie was at work when he heard the news. Clara was two and a half months up the spout" (57). And the narrator describes Clara at seventeen with her first love, Ryan Topps: "A typical teenage female panopticon, she knew everything there was to know about Ryan Topps long before they ever spoke" (24).[18] This not only establishes a relationship with the reader but also guides the reader's meaning-making process: a particular synaesthesia—the life sense, or awareness of being alive in the world.[19] Smith's talk style certainly creates a dense vision of the world that moves that reader who is interested in seeing the world through the eyes of the outsider—and this outsider is identified as postcolonial.

Perhaps, however, it is not so much that we have found the key that unlocks a postcolonial style. Perhaps what Kunzru and Smith do is craft language in his and her respective "will to style" that gives texture to specifics of time and place that nicely balance the particular (ethnicity, race, gender, and postcoloniality) with the general (English-language fiction) and the universal (our evolved and cross-culturally shared cognitive and emotive capacities as authors, readers, and all others).

NO MOTION WITHOUT EMOTION

I have mentioned the verb "move"—how the narrative moves the reader emotively and cognitively. For this to happen, the narratives must hold together in their internal logic; if suddenly Irie turned a corner and a woolly mammoth appeared, as a narrative constructed in the logic of straightforward realism—and not that of the fantastical or magical realism, say—its coherence would collapse, and we would not continue to invest our mental and emotional energy into it. There would be no moving of any kind and no final payoff. This is not the case, of course, with either *White Teeth* or *The Impressionist*. The internal

A User's Guide to Postcolonial and Latino Borderland Fiction

logic holds. The reader invests. The postcolonial worldview and sensibility are conveyed.

This coherence happens within the storyworld—when Jonathan travels to the U.K. in the early twentieth century, it is not in a Boeing 747 but by ship—and more generally (and cross-culturally) at the level of prototype narrative based on three prototypical emotional scenarios that operate "to prime or activate the personal memories and their affiliative feelings" of the reader (Hogan, 65). Romantic tragicomedy is characterized by conflict usually between lovers, the parents of the lovers, or the society in which the lovers live, the subsequent separation and exile of the lovers, and their final unification. Heroic tragicomedy is characterized by an individual like King Lear who is usurped politically or economically and whose territories are invaded; in these the usurper and the invader are defeated. Sacrificial tragicomedy is characterized by a character or entity whose hubris leads to the punishing of the community typically through drought, famine, or plague, and harmony and plenitude are restored only once the offending character or entity is punished. All such prototype narratives, Patrick Hogan convincingly argues in *The Mind and Its Stories,* are driven and structured by emotion prototypes; the aspiration for happiness is the strongest—it governs how we plan, plot, and organize our everyday lives—and the one that guides most heavily the "overall shape and outcome, its tone and so on" (88).

In *White Teeth* or *The Impressionist,* when the universal aspiration of happiness is foiled, the reader's response will be strong; the type of response will guide how we are to identify the narrative mode and genres. In the case of *White Teeth,* it is largely comic; in the case of *The Impressionist,* it is largely heroic.[20] Both combine to varying degrees any number of the three prototype narratives—this is what gives them their individual novelty and rhythm—but each leaves the reader with a set of prototype emotions and their affiliative prototype narrative. If storytelling functions to convey a message as well as to affect readers, its prototype narratives must necessarily be tied in some way to emotional prototypes. Hogan sums up nicely how emotion prototypes "help guide our decisions as to what sort of story is tellable, what is of interest, what is valid, and what is effective and engaging" (88). He further argues,

> This is true whether the narrative in question is fictional, biographical, or historical; set in the form of an epic, a drama, or a novel. In each of these cases, due to the emotive purpose of the tale, emotion prototypes will provide central

structural principles for the story, partially guiding its overall shape and outcome, its tone and so on. (Ibid.)

So while *White Teeth* sets in motion a whole range of emotions and
narrative types that vacillate among romantic, heroic, and sacrificial
tragicomedy, they ultimately subordinate to each other. If Smith or
Kunzru were to only deploy one prototype narrative without introducing, even if subordinately, one or both of the others, the reader would
quickly become bored. For their novels to remain interesting, they must
vary their intensifications—happiness and sorrow, say—and this is done
(among other ways) in the particular combinations and subordinations
of the three narrative prototypes.[21]

PLOTS AND AGENTS

Comic and heroic prototypes are nothing without agents.
Achieving goals of individual and/or collective fulfillment (or not) rests
on the shoulders of Smith's and Kunzru's characters.[22] And certain tensions should be created by a character's achieving fulfillment in different
areas of his or her life. Kunzru's Jonathan achieves the goal of social (and
racial) integration and can be said objectively to have made it professionally: from the gutters of India he ends up an Oxford graduate. This
is achieved, however, at a certain price. He learns to racially pass for
white by altering his mannerisms and voice. He is successful at holding
the voice of his former sex-slave master, Major Privett-Clampe, "inside
his mouth" (150) when passing from a brown Indian social enclave into
a colonial white one, and "no one questions him as he passes by" (151).
The narrator describes him as a late teen in the U.K. at Chopham Hall:

> He no longer lives in constant fear of discovery. He is
> becoming what he pretends to be, realizing that the truth is
> so unlikely that, despite his occasional oddities and lapses,
> no one would ever divine it. He is starting to coincide with
> his shadow. (254)

This passing allows him to assume different white identities, but at the
same time his deeper goal of personal fulfillment is slipping through his
fingers. So, while he becomes more professionally successful, he in turn
becomes less personally fulfilled; one of the great moments in this tense

play of professional and personal fulfillment is when his love interest, Star, dumps him because he is too safe, unlike the African American musician she falls for.

Jonathan's realized and unrealizable aspirations propel the narrative forward and also our reading: we want to feel Jonathan's twists and turns; we want to immerse ourselves in that paradoxical pain his professional success brings. As the narrative unfolds and Jonathan's passing deepens in order for him to realize his professional goals, we want to feel that conflict between his sense of himself as Indian or brown and his sense of himself as feigning whiteness. We want to judge him as well, that in his achievement of professional goals and aspirations he has lost touch with his brown, Indian self, and how this too stands in the way of his realizing a personal happiness with Star. The greater the degree of Jonathan's frustrated personal aspiration, the greater the degree of reader empathy. That is, the less cookie cutter and absolute the character, the more the character will trigger the reader's empathetic involvement.

Situation is everything in *White Teeth*. In the same way that the narrator asks the reader to be friendly and sympathetic toward Jonathan as well as angered by his choice to pass at the expense of losing a sense of himself, so too do Smith's main characters ask readers to vacillate between sympathy and anger. The novel is divided into three main sections that follow sets of characters: Archie and Clara; Samad and Alsana; Irie, Magid/Millat/Marcus, and Joyce. Each section contains its own miniplots that eventually weave into a main plot at the novel's end; we still feel the same range of feelings—sorrow and happiness, anger and sympathy—depending on whether the character is able to realize an aspiration. Archie is a failure in his personal and professional life; this is best expressed in his hoarding of things he intends to fix, as the narrator says, "if only to show that he was good for something" (8) but never does. Yet, as the narrative unfolds, the narrator reveals enough parts so that we can figure out the puzzle to this sense of personality; the long-term debilitating effect of his failure to shoot a mad Nazi doctor in Romania at the close of World War II, for example. And the narrator gives us enough information about his goals that his lack of ability to realize these goals evokes our sympathy.

While the triggering of emotive responses is largely the same in both novels, *White Teeth* requires more cognitive labor than *The Impressionist* does. With a multiple cast of central characters in *White Teeth*, we must keep track of multiple ups and downs, of goals and their realizations or not. This, too, presents a certain pleasure. The more the reader retains of each character, the greater the emotional rhythms he or she will feel throughout the reading, and the greater the emotive payoff will be when all the threads weave together at the novel's end.

PLACE, TIME, AND SOCIAL ORDER

Smith's and Kunzru's characters exist in different epochs and move through different geographic spaces, big and small. Each character has a particular relationship to his or her position in time and place; the twins Magid and Millat are connected through time and space like Corsican brothers, but their individual personalities determine different relationships to time and space. And Smith and Kunzru vary the rhythm of the time and space delineated with those that characterize personal attributes of their protagonists.

The dominance of spatial description in the narrative can have the effect of flattening out temporal textures of plot, and vice versa.[23] Very often the authors use descriptions of inhabited space as ways to provide such character attributes. The Chalfens' house is big and excessively ordered, the Joneses' and Iqbals' disorderly. Irie desires the order of the Chalfens; the Iqbals fear that they will lose their children to the Chalfen household—that is, to middle-class whiteness; this is ironized when the reader discovers the Chalfens' own covering over of chaotic desires and disorders: Joyce desires Millat, and Marcus fetishizes the exotic difference Irie represents. Without the narrator having to use more direct character descriptions, spaces (restrictive or open) affect character and how characters relate to one another in ways that complicate character typology.

The reader also is situated in a specific time and place, and this will inflect how he or she experiences the time and spaces of the characters. The reader is, in a sense, asked to deal with the characters and their given interactions because of the confined spatial conditions that reading presents.

Smith to a greater degree than Kunzru suspends the course of time; this is why both narratives feel episodic—even though Kunzru's takes place over a larger chronological stretch, it shares a propensity to amplify the place of the character and his or her interactions within this place as the engine of plot. Smith prepares the reader for this with the novel's opening. After setting the scene of Alfred Archibald's intended suicide, Smith continues:

> Squeezed between an almighty concrete cinema complex at
> one end and a giant intersection at the other, Cricklewood
> was no kind of place. It was not a place a man came to die.
> It was a place a man came to in order to go to other places
> via the A41. (3)

When action (time) happens, it is during moments when the narrative tends to linger over descriptions of objects. Action (time) does not cease; it is just that it mostly occurs with an emphasized sense of place. And indeed, it is within specific places that time assumes a certain significance for the characters. It is in the space of O'Connel's Pub that events are remembered:

> Samad had suggested Archie's remarriage, 1974. Underneath
> table six in a pool of his own vomit, Archie celebrated the
> birth of Irie, 1975. There is a stain on the corner of the pin-
> ball machine where Samad first spilled civilian blood, with a
> hefty right hook to a racist drunk, 1980. (204)

And it is not just time remembered, or felt time, but time experienced in the actions that happen in different places that is emphasized in the novel. It is during moments when the narrative tends to linger over descriptions of objects. Action (time) does not cease; rather, it mostly occurs with an emphasized sense of place.

This inflects the experience the reader has of the novel: the time it takes to experience the time of the story is governed by the time of the diegesis—those pauses to describe places in the present and in the past, for example. This can stretch out our experience of the character's experience of place as well as the overall sense of time and space of the narrator: "But let's rewind a little" (115), says Smith's narrator, playing with time/space while at the same time guiding us into different times/spaces so as not to leave us too disoriented.

Space is privileged over time in both Kunzru and Smith to intensify the reader's emotional engagement with the characters' relationships to home (family, community, nation). Here, those at the social and racial margins seek some sense of fitting into a place they may call home and work in their different ways to make this place habitable and hospitable. Each path leads to different experiences of characters within places and ultimately to the realizing or not of happiness, hope, home. And it is the realizing or not of these goals by the characters at home, school, or work, in the street, brothel, or mission, and so on that conveys to the reader each novel's powerful critique of social and political forces that disallow their realization of happiness.

Another home also is being shaped in these novels. I mentioned earlier Kunzru's allusions to the canon; he talks about *The Impressionist* as "a book about books." And with Smith, there is strong underlay of Melville's *Moby Dick*. *White Teeth* opens with Archie depressed and about to commit suicide and *Moby Dick* with Ishmael depressed and about to commit suicide.[24] In case the reader fails to make the connection, the narrative supplies us with the necessary signpost: Smith invents a character named Mo Hussein-Ishmael who saves Archie—not out of some sense of benevolence but because, he explains, "We're not licensed for suicides around here" (6). And while one uses the first person and the other the third person, and to varying degrees they both write in playful tone, they also share a propensity for encyclopedic detail and an overall design of social critique. That is, Smith's allusion to and reparticularizing of *Moby Dick* takes some of the schematic features of the precursor work to position her novel within and against a specific narrative system: what we might identify as the "global novel."[25]

Kunzru reparticularizes to the same effect: abstracting the basic blueprints of Conrad, Kipling, Forster to again establish *The Impressionist* within and against a particular tradition. The more the reader can make tangible the abstracted precursor texts, the more puzzle solving is derived. Our memories of Melville's suicidal Ishmael, Forster's caves, Kipling's episodic, adventuring, half-baked Kim allow us to make connections, but connections to novels that collectively make up our social memory of world literature.

But there is more. This reparticularization for Smith and Kunzru carries the added emphasis of raising to the reader's awareness their connections with these precursor world novels. Moreover, there is the strong presence of a will that seeks to direct the reader toward a new evaluative schema of characterization, space, and action and an ethical evaluative framework that allows for a critical awareness of the world as shaped by people living in a divide-and-conquer global capitalist system.

GNASHINGS AND GAPINGS

The narrator's slant, the style of the character's filtering of events, and the way the character speaks all function as markers that

A User's Guide to Postcolonial and Latino Borderland Fiction

allow us to form a better sense of a given character's personality—that is, how and to what extent the funny, serious, disillusioned, passionate, determined, alienated traits manifest in any given character. The particular use of language also allows us to imagine that larger creative entity we tend to call the implied author—that creative force that we imagine is making choices of narrator, plot, character, and so on.

While Smith's and Kunzru's novels solicit a range of emotional responses, at the novels' close the latter is dominated by frustrated jawbone gnashings and the former by wide-gaping laughter. This response reflects more than my own uncontrolled bellyaching laughter when reading Smith's *White Teeth;* it also reflects the response of most of my students. There is a playfulness that intermixes the frustration we feel for Kunzru's Jonathan, but it is not a spontaneous playfulness; its fun lies in its ability to create clever witticisms, smart turns of phrase, grand ironies. Indeed, both authors play with narrative suspense and pause, temporality, and style in ways that turn on and off nonvolitional and volitional forms of laughter. This has several suggestive implications.

First, like other of our evolved capacities (language and theory of mind, for example), our capacity to laugh is necessary for our everyday survival as a species; cross-culturally we all have what has been called a "laughter-coordinating center" that is located in the brain's dorsal upper pons and that is activated by tickling and in response to incongruous or unexpected and recognizably safe stimuli.[26] Laughter works as an everyday destressor. The ritualizing of laughter is a result of a long evolution whereby we—individually and in groups—can take advantage, as neuro- and evolutionary biologists argue, of safe and quiet pauses in our everyday lives; the rituals of laughter offer a type of pause in our work to survive that allows for the development of meaning-making capacities; it can work hand in hand with other active and passive forms of acquiring knowledge of ourselves and the world.

Drawing on research in cognitive, psychobiological, and neurobiological sciences, Matthew Gervais and David Sloan Wilson argue that "incongruity and unexpectedness" cross-culturally undergird all "formal laughter-evoking humor" (398). This "perceived inconsistency between one's current and past experiences" (398) must be formally framed by contexts of safety and play; and rituals of laughter offer an "alternate type of intelligibility, that is, a meaningful interpretation of some stimulus or event that is different from that which was initially assumed" (398).[27] Importantly, Gervais and Wilson distinguish between laughter that is driven more by primitive (prelanguage) stimuli and is more emotionally charged from a self-generated and emotionless (postlanguage) laughter that began to manifest and evolve during the neurocognitive revolution approximately 10,000 years ago. The latter type of laughter is a learned replica of the first type of laughter (mental rehearsal and observation of actions of others), and thus laughter also has necessary implications regarding our capacity to read minds (theory of mind) and empathize.[28]

This empathy and reading of minds comes into play in our ability to tell the differences among types of laughter. A positively valenced laughter acts as a social glue to "synchronize the biological and behavioral state of a group" (406). There is laughter that does the opposite, the "laughing at" that excludes and divides people. Another type of laughter makes people feel safe and inspires confidence, but that type is used to ultimately exploit and take advantage of others (perhaps the way a used car salesman might). Knowing the difference requires sophisticated and continued tuning of our capacity to infer the mental state and intention that elicited the laughter in its context.

What does this have to do with the laughter in *White Teeth* and *The Impressionist*? Kunzru and Smith create situations and contexts and use language (style) differently to elicit a nonvolitional "laughing with" and a more removed "laughing at" (that laughter of wit or cognitive puzzlings). Distinguishing between the two depends on the reader's empathetic and theory-of-mind capacity; each narrative blueprint sets out the terms of its ritualized laughter, and if we fail to read the terms properly, we will miss out on the way each novel's style and mood (tensions, harmonies, and contradictions) aim to elicit laughter.

Distinguishing the type of laughter also requires knowing the difference between the reality of the fictional world and the reality of the world beyond the text. It requires knowing the difference between fictional and nonfictional modes, between the novel and, say, a scientific or historical treatise.[29] It is our evolved capacity to work with time (our capacity to situate ourselves in chronology and to communicate through mime, say) that allows us to connect to the world in chronological terms and with the added advantage of being able to operate in the world (and situate ourselves) in the world either according to a fictional mode (playful mimesis) or a historical or scientific mode (serious mimesis). Our capacity for laughter is a key ingredient in our evolved ability to distinguish between playful mimesis, which pertains to "imaginary" and manipulates relations of cause and effect (causality), and serious mimesis, those actual or truly operating relations of cause and effect (the basis of all science).

Like all novels, those of Smith and Kunzru are de facto safe spaces. As much as the character might be in a socially absurd or ridiculous situation, nothing in the storyworld proper threatens the personality or social esteem of the reader. However, it is the way the authors choose to create situations whereby characters or narrator descriptions deploy a sense of the socially incongruous that will trigger our laughter mechanism. Smith uses a rhythmic style, playful events, and absurdist characterization to trigger spontaneous laughter. Kunzru uses a methodical and cerebral style, incongruous events and characterization (Jonathan's inability to read a situation of "laughing at") to trigger voluntary laughter. Both are constrained by the basic blueprints of our evolved capacity to laugh (from tickle-play with infants to symbolic humor of adults), but ultimately Smith's novel tickles and Kunzru's quips.

Our ability to engage with Smith's and Kunzru's narratives and our ability to discern different types of laughter are all part of our ability to know ourselves and others in the world better. That we laugh, even if in a subdued manner in reading Kunzru, brings us full circle: it is this residual, resonating mood that characterizes the universal playful-mimesis mode of the comic.

WRAP-UP

Perhaps it is in the way this reparticularization constructs evaluative scaffolds and moves readers that makes *White Teeth* and *The Impressionist* engaging novels. Does it make them also postcolonial? Gerald Prince, for example, in his "On a Postcolonial Narratology,"[30] identifies the uniqueness of postcolonial narrative in its expression of experiences of "boundaries, crossings, transfers, dispersions, marginalizations, decks and holds, fields and jungles created by or related to colonialism" (375). A postcolonial narrative would be Smith's or Kunzru's narrative texturing of a "multitopicality—here (and here and here) [as well as] mixtures and inconsistencies, of gaps, breaches, and cracks within spaces or between them" (ibid.). It would be how characters inhabit such cracked or multitopical spaces that inflect their perceptions, utterances, thoughts, "and feelings, their motivations, their interactions" (379) that make their novels postcolonial.

Perhaps *White Teeth* and *The Impressionist* are more than postcolonial. Perhaps they are simply the latest shape of a long tradition of what we might call the global novel, one with a transgeographic reach that offers schema for critically evaluating a world beyond the individual; we see that reach already in the fifteenth and sixteenth centuries with *Don Quixote* and *Gargantua and Pantagruel*. We could also include Voltaire's *Candide*, Smollett's *Roderick Random*, Joyce's *Ulysses*, Woolf's *Orlando*, Nabokov's *Ada*, Fuentes's *Christopher Unborn*, Fernando del Paso's *Palinuro de Mexico*, Timothy Mo's *Renegade or Halo 2*, and Zulfikar Ghose's *Triple-Mirror of the Self*, among many others. While they exist within this continuum of the global novel, the worlds into which each text stretches differ; so too do their characters. The worlds of *White Teeth* and *the Impressionist* are shaped by centuries of colonial violence and exploitation. And Smith and Kunzru write in a historical epoch shaped by global capitalism and its colonial, imperial appendages. As we see in *White Teeth*, global circumnavigations of yesteryear's global novel are no longer necessary; such transgeographic movements can take place within London itself.

The novel has always been worldly, not only in its production and global circulation since the invention of the print culture but because of its plasticity of form. The novel can tell of all things and all experiences and assume nearly any shape. Perhaps this is why the novel today is most recognized as representing the postcolonial condition. It is capacious enough to give texture to particulars of colonial and postcolonial experience and to universals that are the foundations of the human condition. It is perhaps its seemingly limitless capacity that allows the novel to move so readily among places, languages, and cultures and to exist within that "sphere of world literature," as described by David Damrosch in *What Is World Literature?* (6).

Instead of asking what makes the postcolonial novel tick, perhaps I should be asking how certain narratives like *White Teeth* and *The Impressionist* continue to participate in the making of world literature.[31] They add significantly to world literature in the way they use prototypes to reschematize narrative and character scripts and types in their innovative refashioning of imaginary worlds and the way they make fresh the reader's encounter with generic convention, narrative techniques, style, and characterization. They make literature worldly by innovatively combining comic, heroic, and tragic narratives that push us to our emotive and cognitive limits in newly pleasurable and surprising ways.

In recognizing how Zadie Smith and Hari Kunzru variously *make* world literature in sharing with readers worldwide their complex postcolonial imaginings and ultimate affirmation of the human spirit, we ourselves become more worldly as readers and critics.

Five

THIS IS YOUR BRAIN
ON LATINO COMICS

LATINOS IN THE SLIPSTREAM

Historically, few Latino superheroes have appeared in mainstream comic book worlds. The Latino comic book author-artists working today simply enjoy the other worlds the mainstream comics present. Many consider such mainstream characters, settings, and adventures as escapes from their very real and ragged everyday environs. Not surprisingly, such first encounters with a DC or Marvel superhero acted as a formative impulse and initial influence in their work. In the late 1970s, the first Latino TV superhero, El Dorado, was introduced on the television show *Super Friends*. Named after the myth of the city of gold in Peru yet supposedly Mexican, El Dorado sports an Aztec solar calendar on his chest, speaks in a heavily accented Spanglish, and acts as south-of-the-border tour guide for his Anglo team of Super Friends.

In 1976 Marvel already had introduced its first Latino superhero, Hector Ayala, the White Tiger, in a story by Bill Mantlo and George Perez that appeared in *Deadly Hands of Kung-Fu* (issue 19). In 1981 Marvel introduced to *The Incredible Hulk* series (volume 2, issue 265) a north-of-the-border Latina superhero, the devoutly Catholic social worker Bonita Juarez, known as Firebird, in a story by Bill Mantlo and Sal Buscema. The readers learn via an interior monologue that she acquired her superpowers when struck by a fireball that dropped from "the heavens" (6). Catholic through and through, she considers her power as sent from God to be used as a "force for good" (ibid.).

The story unfolds in various parts of the Southwest and follows the rescue of the all-Anglo Teen Brigade that was being held hostage by the Corruptor in a secret lab hidden under an old Spanish mission. Rescuing at-risk youth in her hometown, Buenavista—"an optimistic name for a dirt-poor Mexican American village on the outskirts of Albuquerque, New Mexico" (5)—Firebird transforms into "a great blazing bird-form" (6). Juarez as Firebird and Will Talltrees as Red Wolf (fully tapped into his wolf-spirit power) are outwitted and outperformed when the Anglo superheroes Night Rider, Texas Twister, and Shooting Star arrive on the scene; Firebird and Red Wolf are referred to here as "the Mex-Chick" (16) and "Redskin" (14) and are asked to stand aside while they rescue their Anglo team members. In 1979 Marvel's introduction in *Power Man and Iron Fist* (issue 58) of the urban-crime fighter and *criollo* swashbuckler Alejandro Montoya as El Águila (the eagle) did not much improve the representation of Latinos.

Nor did Latino representations improve with DC comics. After a first appearance in DC's *Justice League of America* in 1984 (annual issue 2) by Gerry Conway and Chuck Patton, Paco Ramone as Vibe—a Puerto Rican gang leader turned break-dancer extraordinaire—appears more regularly in the series. On the cover of the first issue in which he regularly appears (issue 233, 1984), he is dressed in break-dance regalia: baggy yellow pants, vest bearing the letter "V," red bandanna around his neck, green gloves, and yellow wrap-around sunglasses. For that finishing ethnic touch, he sports an under-chin goatee and is colored a slight shade of brown. Splashed across the cover appears: "He's going to *shake things up!*" Set in Detroit, the story begins with Vibe snapping his fingers and moving his feet to a "Do-Da-DA-Do" rhythm. The narrator announces: "They call him Vibe. He's special" (2). After the African American villain Crowbar calls him a "greaseball," Vibe responds: "Whatchu think chu *doin*" (8). Vibe's ability to control a "single vibration wave—a pulse of energy like a one-man earthquake" (11) is no match for Crowbar and other villains he encounters—at least until that day when he is strangled to death by Professor Ivo (issue 258). In 1987 DC buried Vibe.

In 1988 Vibe was reintroduced to readers as one of an immortal team called "The Chosen" in the DC *Millennium* series by Steve Englehart and Joe Staton. Recruited "to advance the human race" (issue 1, 4), the team includes, among others, an Australian aboriginal woman, Betty; a Maoist from mainland China, Xiang Po; an Iranian, Salima Baranizar; an Afro-Caribbean Brit, Carla; and the Peruvian-born and -raised Gregorio de la Vega. The story conveys an explicit critique of U.S. imperialism, and the characters are for the most part interestingly fleshed out. On one occasion, Celia remarks, "What futures *dat, mon?* No future 'roun' *here!* Jus' waitin' for da end oo' da *world*, mon—cmin' any day, day way bloody America carries on!" (issue 1, 16). But Gregorio de la Vega, known as Extraño, leaves much to be desired. He is presented as a limp-wristed Latino who speaks in truncated half-sentences, refers to his team members as "Honey," and is more concerned with color coordination than using his superpower as an illusionist to fight Western imperialism. de la Vega does not last long; he is bitten by the villain Hemo-Goblin, contracts HIV, and soon dies.

In 1989 DC tried the Latino superhero once again with the introduction of Rafael Sandoval as El Diablo in his own self-titled comic. Writer Gerard Jones attempted to root him in the community as a public defender in Dos Rios, Texas (other community-based roles like that of social worker are reserved for Latinas like Bonita Juarez). As public defender elected to office, he moves easily between different social scenes; on the streets he code-switches: *órale, vato,* and *ese* easily fall from his tongue, for example. Like Bonita Juarez, he is connected to the Catholic Church; he is trained by Father Guzman to avenge the poor. In issue 1 Sandoval confronts the big capitalist owner of Muhlback Imports for "lying to the artesanos about the resale of their work" and for "supporting non-union factories in the guise of cottage industries" (17). However, hot temper and lust for the blonde, blue-eyed, and leggy Virginia demonstrate all sorts of clichéd stereotypes. His brown skin color does little, however, to offset his Caucasian superhero chiseled features. And the visuals that describe a Southwestern landscape—cactus, brown dusty roads, and adobe buildings aplenty—fall short when mostly *taquerias,* jails, and check-cashing buildings appear.

It does not help, either, that other Latino characters who appear, like the arch villain El Eskeleto's love interest, Yolanda Ybarra, speak with heavy accents. When she first meets El Diablo she says, "nice to mee-tchoo" (31). Finally, there is a certain conservative element to El Diablo's waxing nostalgic about bygone times when kids could play in parks without being accosted by drug dealers and the homeless. That is, as much as he acts in the present to vanquish crime, there is a certain conservative inflection to his yearning for those bygone days when people knew their place in the socioeconomic hierarchy. Regardless of political sensibility, El Diablo only made it to issue 16 before being canned.

The hot-tempered Latin lover (El Diablo) and the selfless Latina (Firebird) gave way to more of the barrio-born gangbanger type in the 1990s. In the series *West Coast Avengers* by Roy Thomas, Dann Thomas, and Paul Ryan we see the appearance in 1990 of Miguel Santos as Living Lightning (issue 63). He was born and raised in East Los Angeles, comes into his superpower (he wears a containment suit that allows him to control electrical energy and hurl lightning bolts), attempts to avenge his father's death, breaks his bonds of enslavement to Doctor Demonicus, and returns to East L.A. to help his family. His sister is murdered by the Snakes street gang, and his brother, José, has joined another gang, the Jaguars. Living Lightning is later revealed to be gay.

In 1994 Scott Lobdell and Joe Madureira introduced in their *Uncanny X-Men* series (issue 317) the smooth-talking, car-thieving Angelo Espinosa as Skin. Here it is not skin that identifies him as Latino. He remarks, "About a year ago, my skin started turning grey—sagging . . . Growing! For the most part I can control it . . . when I concentrate" (issue 318, 14). He uses his skin to battle foes by suffocation. Marvel let us know that he is Latino in his use of Spanglish (*"muy* educational," "Madre de Dios," *chica, buenos dias*) and his background story: his father was murdered in a drive-by shooting in East L.A.; his girlfriend, Tores, is a chola (Chicana gangbanger); his overprotective mother forced Skin to become a member of Father Miguel's Catholic Youth; and he is continually at the edge of gangbanging. Skin was a major protagonist in *The Uncanny X-Men* series who first appeared in issue 317 (1994) and was later crucified by the Church of Humanity in a mutant hate crime in issue 423 (2003). In *X-Men* (second series, issue 65) Scott Lobdell and Carlos Pacheco introduced a Puerto Rican doctor, Cecilia Reyes, who has mutant energy-field powers. In *X-Factor* (first series, issue 17), Louise Simonson and Walt Simonson give life to Julio Esteban Richter as Rictor, a former mutant who later admits his own bisexuality.

In the new millennium, Marvel began introducing readers to mixed-race Latinos. In 2001 Marvel's series *X-Force* by Peter Milligan and Mike Allred introduced a mixed Irish and Latina superhero, the green-eyed Saint Anna (issue 117). They provide some background to her character: she was conceived when an Argentinean priest crossed the line with an orphaned Irish girl in a mission. Anna's superpower is to heal the "sick and sad" as well as to move objects with her mind. In no time, however, Anna was killed off. She died during an X-Force mission to rescue Paco Perez—a character whose parents were killed by a truck when they tried to cross the U.S.-Mexico border. While *X-Force* killed off Anna pretty swiftly, the comic book is deliberately self-conscious about identity politics and token representations: when a second African American character is introduced, the first starts to fear for his life.

In 2004 Marvel introduced a Latina superhero called Araña (spider) in a new title, *Amazing Fantasy* (second series, issue 1), that recalled the look of the comic book in which Spider-Man debuted. After six issues Araña was given her own self-titled comic book. Written by Fiona Kai Avery and illustrated by Mark Brooks, *Araña* aimed to appeal to a fast-rising middle-class Latino demographic (young and old). Not only is the character more fully fleshed out than her mainstream Latina predecessors—she is connected to her cultural roots via the memory of her Mexican mother, Sofia, and learns much from her smart, sensitive, and strong Puerto Rican father, an investigative reporter for *New York Herald*—but she is the central protagonist of her own generously expansive story. She is smart, strong, culturally aware, determined. In high school by day she crosses all sorts of racial, gender, and faith-based lines in her friendships, including the more heavily charged one of Islam. By night as Araña she sports urban baggy streetwear (and not the usual spandex) and spider-exoskeleton armor, and she wields heavy industrial throw-discs in her battles with the Sisterhood of the WASP. Just as her story brings the worlds of adults and teenagers into contact, so too does it rub her contemporary urban New York up against a mythically dimensioned past: she is recruited by the Spider Society—a nine-hundred-year line of matrilineal fighters of WASP supervillains— to become their hunter to fight to preserve world peace. Her story ended after a twelve-issue run, and Marvel republished the issues of *Araña* in three manga-sized pocketbook volumes, most likely in an attempt to capture a teenage audience that tends to gravitate toward Japanese manga-style comics. Araña continues to guest-star in Spider-Man comics and has a recurring role in *Ms. Marvel*.

In 2005, second-generation Cuban American author-artist (and Marvel editor in chief) Joe Quesada introduced *Daredevil: Father* (issue 2)—and with it the Latino superhero team the Santerians. The team leader, Nestor Rodriguez, or NeRo, is by day a multibillion-dollar entrepreneur with a successful hip-hop label and cologne line for men and by night Eleggua with superpowers like those of his Yoruban deity namesake that include being able to scramble thoughts and communication. Notably, during the day he sports a distinctive goatee, and by night he is smooth-shaven but with a slick of hair over one eye.

NeRo's motivation to set up a vigilante super team spins out of his disillusionment with civil rights activism—his own as a young teen in the shadow of his father before the father was murdered. And the others of his team also derive their powers from the orishas of santeria religious rituals. Quesada provides a glossary of the traits that characterize the deities, or orishas, at the end of the collected issues 1–6 of *Daredevil: Father*. We also learn that Quesada's mother practiced santeria. As this Latino vigilante team fights crime, the superheroes also tangle with Daredevil, code-switching all the while.

On January 1, 2007, Marvel released a newly resuscitated *White Tiger.* Fantasy and young-adult fiction author Tamora Pierce co-authors with Timothy Liebe the story of a street- and book-smart, Bronx-born, gutsy Latina, Ángela Del Toro, as White Tiger. She has a bachelor's degree in political science and a master's in criminology. The niece of the original White Tiger, Del Toro was introduced as an FBI agent tracking the superhero Daredevil (*Daredevil,* volume 2, issue 79, by Brian Bendis and Alex Maleev); after her uncle was killed, she inherited the artifacts that gave him his powers.

Her own adventure begins with bringing down the killer of her uncle Hector, Sano Orll, who works for the transnational mafioso Chaeyi; Chaeyi does not peddle drugs but rather contraband passports and green cards. Del Toro as White Tiger struggles with her own identity issues, both expected and unexpected. For instance, when street thugs dare to call her "Mutie," she reminds them with a drop kick: "Superhuman, estúpido! I'm superhuman!" (issue 1, 31). Pierce and Liebe reflect the contemporary concerns regarding Latinos and immigration in the United States when Ángela passes a newsstand with a newspaper headline "House Debates Registration Act." She reflects, "Great, I was born in the Bronx—but if I put on a costume, I still have to get a green card" (issue 1, 20).

DC also has shown a renewed interest in creating Latino superheroes. DC moved from the backdrop of the 1992 *Batman* (volume 1, issue 475) to the foreground in the 2003 *Gotham Central* (issue 6) Paul Dini's invented Dominican-identified police detective, Renee Montoya. She also appeared that same year in *Batman: The Animated Series.* In addition to being a central protagonist in *Gotham Central* she is one of the protagonists of DC's best-selling comic, *52.*

In DC's major publishing event of 2006, Geoff Johns and Phil Jimenez's *Infinite Crisis* (issue 3) debuted the new Blue Beetle as Tejano teenager Jaime Reyes. In May 2006 *Blue Beetle* appeared; it was created by Keith Giffen, John Rogers, and Cully Hamner. As the issues of this self-titled comic unfold, we discover more and more the complex everyday life of Jaime, his mom (a nurse), father (a mechanic), and sister Milagro, but also the day-to-day existence of those living along the U.S.-Mexico border. In issue 5, Jaime Reyes crosses over to Mexico, where he learns that his nemesis is his Tia Ampero, otherwise known as La Dama; she uses profits generated from high-interest loans borrowed by undocumented people to pay coyotes to get them across the border to build a super army of "Magic-Metas" (issue 6, 28). The series makes several moves to complicate Latino identity and experience. For instance, the writers create a Latina, La Dama, as the big capitalist exploiter of the economic imbalance between Mexico and the United States—her coyote profiteering—and we learn in issue 8 that Jaime's sidekick, Paco, has to make up a class because he flunked Spanish for speaking Spanglish. A stretched panel depicts Jaime and Paco crossing the border from the United States. They walk without much ado in the foreground into Mexico; in the background appears a seemingly immovable cluster of people waiting to enter the United States (issue 5).[1]

Certainly there have been some strides forward into the mainstream world of comic book storytelling. However, most of the Latino characters and stories in circulation remain uninteresting stereotypes. In 2006 Ed Brubaker's and Michael Lark's *Daredevil* (second series, issue 82) visually described a chiseled, clean-cut, and buff Matt Murdock, who encounters in prison an unshaved, slick-haired, and tattooed Latino, Carlos LaMuerto as Black Tarantula. LaMuerto only speaks in laundry lists made up of *ese, vato,* "dawg," "you off the hook," and "knowhut I'm sayin" (18).

Certainly some of the above-mentioned mainstream comic books like *Araña* and *Blue Beetle* offer more engaging depictions and stories about Latinos. This is often the result of these comic books using a greater variety of storytelling devices, more complex characterizations, and a richer array of settings. It is because certain mainstream comic books show a greater sense of commitment to detailing Latino cultural particularities.[2]

LATINOS STRIKE BACK

The first Latino superhero *by* a Latino appeared in 1977 when Tejano Judge Margarito C. Garza produced his comic book, *Relampago.* Garza inked the black-and-white adventures of the morally complex Tejano Marcos Zapata. Raised from the dead and given superpowers by a local *bruja* (witch), he turns his thieving ways around once she is out of the picture and he finds guidance from a local priest. By day Zapata uses law books to defend his community. And by night, with truth, justice, and the Latino way fully embraced and wearing form-fitting spandex from head to toe topped by a cape, he keeps an eye on the community, sweeping in to help the underdog, the stranded child, even endangered birds (issue 3). However, *Relampago* was a proverbial flash in the pan. Not until the 1990s did other Latino caped crusaders begin to appear. One of the main catalysts was Milestone.

The Milestone publishing house produced *Blood Syndicate* and, riding on its coattails, *Kobalt,* a sixteen-issue series introduced in 1993 that ran for two years. Milestone's editor Dwayne McDuffie brought together writer John Rozum and inker Robert Quijano to add to their City of Dakota universe—which includes the African American character Static and the characters of *Hardware* and *Blood Syndicate*—the psychologically compelling beefcake Kobalt, a long-haired, masked vigilante who battles street thugs and corporate multinational evildoers with fists and a steel pole as weapons. In the final panels of the last issue of *Kobalt,* author-artist team Rozum and Quijano reveal his identity. After a near-death battle with a nonmortal villain, he arrives in Mexico City, where for the first time we see him out of mask with his brown skin coloring and identified as Miguel (issue 16, 46). He is home to rest and retrain in order to return to save the City of Dakota. This final striptease enlarges retrospectively the reader's understanding of Kobalt: his unstated but strongly felt sense of alienation, his deep empathy for the racially victimized and down-and-outs, his distaste for those underworld kings like Milton St. Cloud and capitalist ventures like turning a barrio into Utopia Park. Perhaps, too, this Latino identity gives him a sense of right and wrong that is less clear-cut than Superman's. Kobalt often finds himself on the wrong side of the law.

Latino unmaskings happen much more swiftly in Milestone's 1993 publication of *Blood Syndicate,* which ran for three years. Here, Ivan Velez Jr. and artist CrissCross quickly introduced readers to a series of barrio-made, gritty, blaxploitation-styled multiethnic superheroes: "a street gang like no other," one character announces (issue 1, 3), they are bound in their defense of "turf and loyalty" (26). Reflecting on the lack of adequate social representation in comic books, at the end of issue 2 Velez writes that if one can "do anything in a comic book, then why not put a mirror up to American society and show it the way it 'really is?'" (28). The Milestone editors explain:

> We like the world inside our books, and we want everybody
> to know about it. Why? Because we feel that the City of
> Dakota resembles the real world more than other comics do.
> Diversity's our story, and we're sticking with it. The variety
> of cultures and experiences Out There make for better

comics In Here. When people get excited about the diversity In Here, they'll get just as excited about the diversity Out There. (13)

But *Blood Syndicate* is not a mirror held up to the world; it is not exactly social realism. It is still all comic book superhero, epic adventure stuff. The characters variously use their superpowers: supercharged electricity and the ability to turn time backward, among many other powers, are used to battle arch enemies like the hybrid voodoo and digital technologically savvy Soul Breaker, the local mob, and corporate elites who send drugs into the barrio to kill off the poor to buy and develop land.

At the same time that this is superhero adventure, each Milestone superhero comes with a unique set of problems, and enemies materialize also in the form of addiction, greed, religious fundamentalism, sexism, racism, and so on. Each team member struggles with his or her ethnic identity—and some even struggle with sexual desire and orientation. Wise Son must learn to temper his African American Islamic nationalist zeal; Korean American Third Rail becomes more inclusive; the Dominican-identified Afro-Hispanic sister and brother Sara and Carlos Quiñones as Flashback (who steals crack to feed her addiction) and Fade (who struggles with his closeted gay sexuality) "deal with the reality of being black and Latino at the same time" (issue 2, 28). Puerto Rican character Brickhouse struggles to remember her past; and the other Puerto Rican character, Rolando Texador as Tech9, drowns his abusive upbringing in alcohol. There is the Haitian American, Masquerade, and in issue 8 the creators introduce Chinese superhero Nina Lam as Kwai, who struggles with her family's strict cultural values.

Diversity is not just skin deep; it is also how one self-identifies and uses language to announce group affiliation. For example, Boogieman struggles to fit in as an Anglo who identifies with the street and as African American. After an initial upset—the others discover that he is Anglo posing as African American, Boogieman declares: "I am down with all of you. That's the way I talk!" (issue 23, 25). Yet in the end, all his ethnic posturing is forgiven. The characters code-switch with ease between English and Spanish (*que mierda; coño, puñeta,* and *pendejito*); they do not speak in that broken English of DC's Vibe.

In *Blood Syndicate* Velez also revises the reader's expectation of gender as early as issue 1. The story opens with the blonde, purse-toting reporter of the *Dakota Chronicle* identified as Rob Chaplik. While from the clothes and accessories we might infer the character to be a woman, her physique, angular facial features, muscled legs, and name suggest otherwise. The artist CrissCross's visual portrayal and Velez's text work together to bend the reader's gender expectation. Likewise when Velez and CrissCross introduce the character Brickhouse, the visuals and text work together to obscure the reader's identification of gender: Brickhouse is built like the Fantastic Four's character Thing, has corn-row-braided hair, and shows a penchant for romance. Finally, the author and artist interweave into their visual and verbal play with gender (and sexuality and race) complex interior states of mind. Brickhouse struggles to overcome a deep denial over her past as a slave; Fade eventually overcomes his fear of being gay in a straight macho superhero world; Wise Son works through an Islamic nationalist zealotry that becomes a form of bigotry.

Milestone was not the only comics producer in the early 1990s to create complex Latino superheroes and compelling stories. In 1994 Richard Dominguez introduced *El Gato Negro,* published by Azteca Productions. Set in an everyday Edinburg, Texas, the protagonist, Francisco Guerrero, works as a public defender by day and mentors youth of color parolees; by night he busts U.S.-Mexico drug cartels as the masked El Gato Negro. In homage to Judge Garza's Relampago, Dominguez's El Gato Negro has as his consigliere a priest. Guerrero is deeply rooted in his culture and language, speaking to the priest in Spanish. That El Gato Negro is middle-class and Catholic does not mean he is above Chicano slang, often peppering his phrases with *pendejo, ese,* and the like. The bad guys buy rocket launchers over the counter, while El Gato Negro trains in the ways of the ancient warrior's fighting arts, only using in defense of himself and the community the power of his sharply focused mind, kinetic body action, and martial arts weaponry like his flying cat's claws to battle evil. When not fighting the likes of college-educated El Graduado or the capoeira-trained El Observador, El Gato Negro is helping documented and undocumented Latinos in the community. But Dominguez does not make him an undefeated saintly do-gooder. El Gato Negro is often defeated and calls on the power of the Virgin Mary to help him out of a tough situation—and his nice-guy front with the character Narci is merely a means to an end: to woo her to the bedroom.

In a turn from middle-class to blue-collar superhero, in 1996 Fernando B. Rodriguez created *Aztec of the City* at El Salto Comics. Here the reader-viewer meets nineteen-year-old Chicano construction worker Tony Avalos eking out a living in San Jose, California. After a life-threatening accident on the worksite, Avalos wakes from a monthlong sleep in which he journeyed to the Aztec underworld. While he does not recall details of his journey, he does discover from his hospital bed his pre-Columbian-rooted, shape-shifting superpower—Cuauhtémoc reincarnate. Newly self-identified as Aztec of the City, or AOC, he battles various community-threatening enemies—from mobsters to more mythologically dimensioned foes. In issue 2, *Enter La Llorona,* AOC uses his street smarts to sleuth out the villain behind a recent spate of killings of homeless people and the disappearance of orphaned girls. La Llorona is otherwise known as the Cryptic Queen of Creekside Chaos (23).

And there is Laura Molina's *Cihualyaomiquiz, the Jaguar,* originally published in 1996 by Insurgent Comics. Before the story begins, on the inside of the front cover Molina announces:

> ¡Orale! Gente, It takes near super-human strength to get through these oppressive/regressive times. . . . This little book is dedicated to those of you who have experienced and survived racism and discrimination. (No, I'm not talking about White boys whining about women and minorities "taking over.") If you've ever been denied a job, a promotion or a fair trial because of the color of your skin or if you've ever been pissed on because you're poor, you know what I'm talking about.

Indeed, Molina's Chicana protagonist, Linda Rivera, is driven to study law to help defend her community against a militarized police and Immigration and Naturalization Service as well as corporate capitalists. By night as the Jaguar, empowered by her Chicana ancestral roots, she takes down local neo-Nazi villains.

SPANDEX ALTERNATIVES

Superhero-driven comics are one of many routes Latino (and non-Latino) author-artists can choose to follow. Latino author-artists like Wilfred Santiago, Roberta Gregory, and Los Bros Hernandez radically extend what is known as the "alternative" comic book storytelling mode. The alternative (represented by Spiegelman and Eric Droroker) took up where the "underground" (such as Harvey Pekar and R. Crumb) left off, following day-in-the-life stories of characters otherwise invisible to the mainstream. We see this alternative mode weave itself into the work of many Latino comic book author-artists. We see it in Jaime Hernandez's stories that follow decades' worth of the development of a panoply of characters who age, gain and lose pounds, have straight and queer romances, grow apart and together again.

In Jaime Hernandez's *Locas in Love,* issues of race, gender, and sexuality powerfully murmur in the background: we learn of Hopey's frustration at not being able to fit in as a young Latina when we see a flashback of her decapitating a blonde Barbie; we learn of the difference between her carefree approach to her lesbian sexual identity and that of the more uptight Maggie. And we feel an underlying frustration in most of the characters as they grow older and realize they have not fulfilled their dreams. During the twenty-five years that Jaime Hernandez has been creating these characters, they have all been transformed by their many experiences in growing older. In Gilbert Hernandez's *Palomar* and *Luba* storyworlds we follow several generations of Latinos south and north of the U.S.-Mexico border; the reader-viewer is invited into the lives of characters like Luba, Ofelia, Pipo, Fortunato, Tonantzin, and Casmira who also age, struggle with life-changing events, even transform into their total opposites: many react violently to Pipo's coming out of the closet; happy-go-lucky Tonantzin becomes a lost soul who commits suicide by flame; Sergio becomes so enraged that he and his father beat Sergio's childhood friend Fortunato to death.

The "alternative" comic book storytelling mode finds unique expression in Ivan Velez Jr.'s *Tales of the Closet: Volume 1.* Set in Queens in 1987, this story follows the lives of a handful of closeted Latino, Anglo, and Asian teens struggling with either unsympathetic or absent parent figures, school bullies, and hormone-driven desires. Velez's use of a series of narrations filtered through the eyes of Ramona, Kyle, Mary, Jenny Chin, Scotty, and the jock Ben immerse the reader-viewer into the minds of these characters, serving up less a voyeuristic thrill and more a deeply moving portrait. On one occasion we overhear Tony's thoughts: "No college is gonna give a sports scholarship to some fag! God I hate lying! It feels so damn wrong! I got no choice. I either act straight or don't play!" (11). In a postscript Velez tells of struggling against the impulse to write a "pretty or polished" story about the different ways of sexually identifying as a gay or lesbian urban teenager (95).

In Wilfred Santiago's *In My Darkest Hour: A Graphic Novel* the alternative mode takes the shape of a highly self-aware, bitingly paranoid, and often drug-laden first-person account of urban life for the twenty-something Latino character Omar Guerrero. A hopeless Omar reflects:

> Everyone's on their own little orbit within an orbit, round 'n' round, over and over again without losin' a beat, close but distanced from the other, until we go out with a whimper or with a bang . . . we think that beats the hell out of being alone . . . but we all go alone. And that's the end of it. (8)

At the turn of a page, Santiago joltingly breaks up an already psychologically disturbing story with a series of full-page panels that hit hard with allegorical meaning: an amputated, bound, gagged, headless, blubbery body with a Christ figure strapped between its legs; a grotesquely gargantuan, muscled, bald Captain America who does not use his shield to protect but rather to hold bombs that he spills willy-nilly on a diminutive land. The text reads: "Living countdown servants and spectators of the slave drivers' masquerade ball" (109).

Los Bros Hernandez—Gilbert, Jaime, and sometimes Mario—also break up their more straightforward visual and verbal storytelling with other modes. They spice up their more realistic plot rhythms and characterizations by throwing in curve balls such as the fantastic, sci-fi, and a superhero fly-by—but always with a twist. Even in the more character-driven dramatic work of Gilbert and Jaime Hernandez we see them variously break up story sequences with appearances of alien creatures, anthropomorphic monoliths, anxiety-driven women shrinking and growing gigantic (Izzy Ortiz in *Locas*), the appearance of hyperlibidinous little Hinkenfoffers (aliens) and Latina superheroes like Cheetah Torpeda, who tries to relieve her boredom by watching telenovelas and flying around looking for "someone to save, or an enemy to fight" (13).[3] In another issue, *One More Lady's Man,* we even see Cheetah try out a day job as a stripper.

In the first issue of the Los Bros Hernandez series *Love and Rockets* (1982) we see Jaime Hernandez using the epistolary form—"Well, here we are. Sorry I've taken so long to write" (9) to introduce Maggie's obsession with her weight—but also a self-reflexive and playful sci-fi mode. La Maggie is a mechanic hired to travel the world fixing otherworldly machines like the Legendary Saturn Stiletto used during the Zymbodian Revolution to transport the "biggest load of pito in the world out of Zhato" (10).

Alternative Latino comic book possibilities are wide open. We see in Mario Hernandez's work (Jaime and Gilbert's older brother churned out a couple of stories in the early days of *Love and Rockets*) the texturing of more politically charged stories set in tropical-identified countries run by U.S.-funded dictators. One such narrator begins on "the eve of the union elections in Comprachio . . . The first step, many hope toward loosening the heavy grip of neighboring Marzipan, itself dependent on Comprachio for the production of its official state soft drink, Blik!" (volume 15, 20). His visually bold realism and thickly drawn panels along with the crowding of text depict a suffocating and chaotic world where beneficent *gringo* volunteers put a happy face to capitalist exploitation and oppression.

Such alternatives might also weigh more heavily on the story-about-a-story self-reflexive device. We see this in the above-described work of Wilfred Santiago as well as in the Hernandez brothers' *Satyricon* (the *Love and Rockets: Book 15* collection), where any narrative technique goes. Here we see Los Bros Mario, Gilbert, and Jaime play with the verbal and visual comic book storytelling conventions when, for example, in Mario Hernandez's story titled "Life and Rockets . . . When the Muse Is Not Amused," after a first appearance of an in media res–establishing splash page—Mario-as-character falling into the ocean—the visuals depict a bald mermaid who remarks, "Maybe you should try again"; bubbling underwater, the Mario-as-character responds, "Hey, c'mon! This is gonna be good! Gimme a chance!" (*Satyricon,* 49). Later the bald mermaid appears again, berating Mario as author-artist: "You did that same story last time with the same old weird for weirdness sake sequence" (51). Latino author-artists have radically extended this alternative comic book storytelling mode in the various ways that they detail the everyday as firmly located within a larger society and world generally.

COMIC BOOKS AND THE BRAIN

The development of a Latino comic book and comic strip tradition that flows within and against mainstream currents is more than informative. The more we know of its details, the greater pleasure we reap as reader-viewers. When such a genealogy is identified, it becomes more visibly a part of the social memory we categorize as comics: comic books and comic strips. The more conscious we are of its conventions as such, the more readily we can access how its devices make meaning in our brains. As the Latino comic book ingredients become a part of this social memory, the more reader-viewers encode in their neural networks how Latino author-artists creatively reorganize and deploy comic book techniques, props, characters, and prototype narratives. The more we reader-viewers familiarize (schematize) ourselves with the Latino ingredients that make up the whole pie, the greater the cognitive and emotive payoff for us.[4]

To deepen our knowledge of Latino comics, we can study the narrative elements that comprise them: point of view, width of gutter, voice, balloon type, font size and format, and so on. Many have done this well. Will Eisner, for instance, in *Comics and Sequential Art* considers the repetitive use of devices, images, and symbols as forming a grammar of sequential art. Such a focus on narrative elements can help clarify and distinguish between the goings-on within a given story's content (event, characterization, theme) and the activity that takes place at the level of form (play with time, style, point of view, tempo). This is important as it helps direct reader-viewers away from interpretations that reduce the given narrative only to its content or thematic message. The reader-viewer's experience of the narrative is finally one in which form and content are one.

Latino comic book author-artists use a variety of techniques to move their reader-viewers in specific ways. Cognitive science and narrative theory can be useful here to help us account for making and engaging with Latino comic books. For example, author-artists and reader-viewers know intuitively or consciously why a bold-typed word is louder than a nonbold word, why a handwritten typeface effectively conveys feeling, why those comic books lettered in a more uniform typeface feel cold and calculated. The specific shape of a line over a character's head can convey anger or confusion, and big eyes can convey anxiety. Such visual devices work together with textual elements to nudge us to infer one thing and not another. Advances in cognitive science and the tools of narrative theory can help us understand how far an author-artist can go in creating a distance between a series of panels before pushing us over our critical cognitive threshold. Our minds can infer the passage of time by linking characters who appear in one series of panels to be children, then in another series to be adults, as seen often in the work of Los Bros Hernandez. We know that it is the same character in one panel as in another even when the drawing of the shirt or pants length does not exactly match. Reader-viewers can move from one panel to another and connect disparate scenes through inference—hold them in short-term memory—to be able to create coherent wholes. The frequency of gutter placement (more or fewer panels per page) can slow down or speed up the reader-viewer's sense of the story's pacing. The size of the gap between the panels and their distribution might require more or less of our imaginative filling-in to make the story. A series of distant or closeup shots can create specific moods, and the frame's bordered shape (or absence of one) can heighten or diminish our mood. A panel shot from below can trigger a sensation of fear or anxiety, and we can read from the stylization of body gestures the characters' interior states of mind. We can create from two-dimensional visuals and text four-dimensional holographic spaces in our minds. And for that matter, we can create a sense of motion, time, and space from rather simple and static images.

To understand the particulars of each Latino comic book's expression we need to keep in mind the universal quality of how we are moved by storytelling devices. Thus an approach to Latino comic books and comic strips requires an accounting of the genealogy, nuts-and-bolts comic book narrative theory, and insight from the brain sciences. This will help us understand how each Latino comic book works to engage reader-viewers specifically—and universally.

Latino comic book author-artists use certain techniques, narrative devices, styles, and prototypes to reframe in new and interesting ways not just day-in-the-life experiences but a variety of story types such as the autobiographic, superheroic, epic, fantastic, realistic, and metafictional. In choosing to reframe real and fictional worlds, they also ask the reader-viewer to look upon this newly reframed object with a new angle of vision; in so doing, they amplify the reader-viewer's everyday cognitive and emotive activities. Necessarily, then, I will discuss how these author-artists engage our capacity to infer interior states from outward gesture (theory of mind) and our fictional world-making ability.

Let us first look into this idea of reshaping genre. I mentioned this idea of a Latino comic book tradition—a storehouse of sorts filled with passageways lined with rows of shelves packed with types of stories, boxes filled with tools, and folders filled with characters. Indeed, the shelves extend beyond themselves, touching those built in all other storehouses that collectively make up world fiction. When Gilbert Hernandez writes his *Palomar* stories, they elbow their way onto certain shelves within the Latino-identified storehouse and rub up against those that lie adjacent that share, say, storytelling in the romantic tragicomedy mode.

If we take yet another step back, Hernandez's use of the romantic tragicomedy (again, one of three prototypical genres that Hogan identifies in *The Mind and Its Stories*) is an outward manifestation of something going on more deeply within our cognitive and emotive architecture. As a species we strive for fulfillment and have been doing so ever since our forebears first walked upright. Storytelling genres themselves are constrained manifestations of this universal drive. In this circular, loop-back system, a given emotion prototype governs what types of stories are tellable and what is interesting to the reader and author; a prototype works as a guide to what is ultimately, as Hogan states, "effective and engaging" (88). So when Gilbert Hernandez chooses as the umbrella genre for *Palomar* the romantic tragicomedy, he is putting into play a story type that guides our cognitive processes and emotions.

While we all have prototype emotions and a hard-wired cognitive architecture (the brain's thought, language, memory modules), this does not preclude room for creative play. Within such prototypical constraints is a massive (infinite, even) way a given genre can be freshened up to engage us anew. This can be seen when Gilbert Hernandez decides to employ the prototypical narrative of the romantic tragicomedy and yet innovates this genre by altering its conventions; he infuses the story with a good dose of self-reflexivity to reconfigure the conventions of the romantic tragicomedy and thus readjust the reader-viewer's expectation of and emotional engagement with this prototype genre.

Latino comic book innovation spins out of our universal capacity to imagine other worlds. We share the universal capacity to imagine other worlds (to exist temporally in a past and a future as constructed by someone in the present) as well as to propose and share hypothetical situations with others. When we think of Latino comic book author-artist Rhode Montijo taking up the sacrificial story prototype in *Pablo's Inferno*, we see him tweak and amplify this everyday ability to imagine outside ourselves and to exercise our capacity to solve problems. Montijo dedicates a large portion of his day to becoming an expert at plot, dialogue, drawing, panel layout, and so on in ways that those who do not create comic books have not (see my interview with Montijo in *Your Brain on Latino Comics*). He is familiar with enough contents of the themes, forms, traditions, techniques, plots, characters, narrator, and narratee that fill the storehouse to be able to mix and match to create something novel for a readership. And this means that he looks to storehouses outside of the comic book tradition, to those of art, music, history, and many others. He has an aptness that allows him to engage with respective prototype and schema sets to reach beyond his own set of narrative prototypes in crafting *Pablo's Inferno.*

Latino comic book authors often reach beyond the specific domain (say, the techniques and plots that characterize the epic superheroic prototype) and into other domains (the metafictional, for one) to innovate their comic book forms. In *Sonambulo's Strange Tales,* for instance, Rafael Navarro variously reaches outside of his dominant domain—the techniques that characterize noir—into those of fantasy, horror, and even gothic realms to create what we might call a fantastic-noir style. In his *Palomar* stories, Gilbert Hernandez reaches beyond the domain of realism and into that of metafiction to create an invigorating self-reflexive suprarealism.

Innovation is a cognitive process and not the result of divine inspiration. It entails a Latino comic book author-artist knowing well his or her prototype or schema set that allows for an evaluation of what he or she might employ in shaping imagery and point of view; innovation also requires knowing how the work will appear in relation to other forms that constitute the comic book genre. Finally, innovation entails a sense on the part of the Latino author-artist of how the reader-viewer carries certain domain-specific baggage that will need to be reshaped. That is, an author-artist cannot reach too far from the given prototype or schema set in the innovation; in doing so, the author-artist risks losing the audience. And here it is usually the Latino comic book author-artist's built-in sense of what "feels right" that helps govern how far he or she can innovate, how far to push the reader to reform given prototypes and schema.

COMIC, TRAGIC, AND EPIC

Latino comic book author-artists work with a finite range of prototypical narratives derived from a finite number of cross-culturally universal aspirations: happiness and fulfillment. These authors often (and to varying degrees) mix up the prototypical narratives to vary storytelling rhythms and complicate character types and plots. After exhaustive research in oral and written narratives from all over the world, Hogan has identified the three recurring universal tragicomic narrative prototypes discussed earlier that can be combined and individually shaped in an infinite variety of ways: romantic, heroic, and sacrificial.

A Latino comic book author-artist like Gilbert Hernandez can combine different prototype narratives with their affiliative dominant emotion scenarios (of either happiness or sadness) to intensify specific sequences of events in the story of *Palomar*. In his series *Birdland* he can combine the prototype narrative of the heroic epic—a large part of the plot parallels the structure of world epic journeys like those of Ulysses, Gilgamesh, and Daedalus—with that of the romantic (multiple characters falling in love, conflicts, separations, and reunions) to texture this more erotica-driven story. *Birdland* ends in the characters realizing fulfillment and happiness, but in a polymorphous smorgasbord of sexual interpenetrations and biological transformations (female characters with penises and males with vaginas).

Ivan Velez Jr.'s violent, heroic-dimensioned *Blood Syndicate* mixes in the sacrificial prototype but ends on a romantic note. Going against interracial taboos, Korean American superhero Third Rail couples with Afro-Latino Brickhouse to realize goals of fulfillment—powerfully embodied in the birth of their multiracial, electrically charged, and epidermally bricked child. Romance wins the storytelling day in *Blood Syndicate;* the mood is not one of tragedy and sadness that the reader-viewer feels when closing the final page of the final issue but a sense of having encountered something new and vital:

> Milestone got me interested in superhero comics in a way
> no other comics did. Reading of characters who looked like
> me, talked like me, grew up around the sort of people I did
> and felt the need to make a difference was something I very
> much needed and, perhaps, still need. (31)

The coupling convention is not the only road to fulfillment. As we see in Santiago's *In My Darkest Hour,* Omar ends up reuniting with his girlfriend, but tragedy and sadness permeate the air at the comic book's close. He returns to his love interest not as a means to realize the goal of fulfillment but rather as a way to deaden feelings of a deep estrangement from the world, to temporarily sidetrack his thoughts from an acute sense of his life as a "big waiting room; waiting for a sand nigger to blow himself up, waiting for religious prophecies and ancient predictions to not be right, waiting for old age, waiting for the death of the woman I love, waiting for my turn to rot" (112). *In My Darkest Hour* ends with Omar's coupling, but the narrative leaves the reader somewhere different than at the end of Velez's *Blood Syndicate*. The universal prototype narratives are at play but combined in ways that innovate cognitively and emotively. Others might lean more heavily on the sacrificial prototype.

The sacrificial and heroic epic prototype narratives also abound in Latino comics. We see in Rhode Montijo's *Pablo's Inferno* the emphasis on the sacrificial. Pablo becomes a stand-in for a society ignorant of its history; his journey into the underworld is one in which he learns of his ancestral roots and the bloody history of conquest. His final battle leads to a self-knowledge that ultimately restores a barren earth. The final panels describe Pablo planting corn and then rain falling—a sense of balance has been restored. Many other Latino author-artists choose the epic heroic prototype in following the superhero route, subordinating romance to emphasize the heroic tragicomedy in their creation of superhero stories. The Luna Brothers' Pearl, Oropeza's Amigoman, Javier Hernandez's El Muerto, Rodriguez's Aztec of the City, Saldaña's anthropomorphic Burrito, Molina's Jaguar, and many others all are heroes marked off from society as special and who constantly face threats of being usurped by invading villains. The characters prevail, vanquishing villainous invaders and restoring communal social harmony.[5]

Each Latino comic book author-artist combines tragic moments with happy moments; he or she creates the prototype conditions for happiness and those that lead to sorrow. That is, each uses different emotional scenarios to intensify the dominant prototype narrative's goal. Doing otherwise would make for some rather boring comic book reading.

LOGIC AND EMOTIONAL SYSTEMS

We know that visuals like the use of color or black and white, lighting, shading, points of view, and panel size have some emotional effect on the reader-viewer. When Rhode Montijo draws Quetzal's face in a triangular shape and Pablo's as round, he is doing so to arouse certain subcortical emotional responses. And our emotions will vary in degrees of intensity: we can feel annoyed, but this feeling might not overwhelm us and lead to action—it might simply be a mood that whispers in the background; or sometimes we can be overwhelmed to such a degree that our bodies act seemingly of their own accord, regardless of reasoning. Hogan identifies this latter response as "innately sensitized to particular environmental features" (175) that includes automatic limbic system responses to such stimuli as size (large animals), motion type (reptiles), and sounds (growling). The audience of a Latino comic book like *Aztec of the City* knows that the arch villain La Llorona is not "real," but the way Fernando Rodriguez chooses to draw her (oversized and predatory) along with the pacing of the panel layout when describing her visually trigger subcortical responses of fear. Even before she does something nasty and without a narrator telling us explicitly, we know she is to be feared.

A similar subcortical emotional arousal takes place at the level of character action. Here I do not mean the POW-WHAM-BAM action but rather the reader-viewer's following closely the paths taken and choices made by the character that may or may not lead to positive goal outcomes. Avid reader-viewers of Latino comics are in constantly evaluative mode, considering whether a given event, behavior, or action will lead to the character's goals. The degree to which we are invited into the story and character determines the degree of our emotional arousal.

There is another layer of emotive response that is more supracortical than a response to an oversized, animal-like villain (or the closeup of a panicked face or tragic turn of events). It occurs when a Latino comic book author-artist defies certain conventions: sometimes omitting gutters, using an elongated page (as in *Rocketo*), drawing the same character with a different style, and so on. Such play with convention activates (to different degrees depending on the reader and his or her comic book storehouse) our social memory of the rules of the convention and how they work in relation to the author-artist's current modification—all this elicits an emotional response.

While the Latino comic book narratives move us from one cortically or subcortically aroused peak of emotion (short-lived anger, hate, sadness, laughter) to another as the stories unfold, an overall mood persists. The mood is the gel that fills in between peak emotions; the mood can reinforce such emotions (allowing them to persist in attenuated form over long periods) or run counter to them. A comic book's given mood can be established in the actions of the characters, the events portrayed, and the way the artist-author leans more heavily on one type of panel layout (squashed together or spread apart), one type of color wash or schema (black and white or color), more of one type of line drawing (heavy or light). While we move from one peak emotion to the next, depending on the dominant visual and verbal elements used, the author-artist infuses each of his or her stories with an overall mood.

Now without consistent story logic, some internal coherence to the Latino comic book story, there will be little or no emotional response.

We invest emotionally (wittingly or not) in stories that make sense or in stories that can make sense in their carefully orchestrated incoherence, as with some of Los Bros Hernandez's more metafictional work. If there is no logic-governing perspective, color palette, or characterization, then we tend *not* to invest emotionally in the story. When we enter the world of, say, Frank Espinosa's *Rocketo,* we do not suspend disbelief, as some people might imagine; what really happens is that we constantly evaluate the storyworld's logic system, whether it works and is coherent, whether its smoking guns have been fired. If the logic system works, then we will immerse ourselves in (and only ever partially, as our minds are aware always of real time and spacial surroundings) and be moved by the fictional worlds served up.[6]

We might jump at the action, vocalize delight or disgust, sadness, and the like; here the comic book author-artist is using techniques coherently in ways that trigger our automatic reflex (limbic) system. However, no matter how much an author-artist tries to erase our sense of the difference between reality and fiction, if the internal logic of the story does not work, we are not going to invest in it emotionally; we will not cringe or close our eyes, our legs will not jerk, and our eyes will not fill with tears. We will simply turn off our emotions.

READING MINDS, SORT OF

When I was a kid I would dress up as a Mexican *luchador* (wrestler), usually Blue Demon, with a red cap, red shorts, and blue tights. I thought of myself as a hybrid Superman-*luchador.* This phenomenon of identifying with a fictional character has been taking place since time immemorial. I think here of all those young men who dressed up in black after Goethe published *Sorrows of Young Werther* or today's children and teens who dress up as their favorite superheroes every October 31. In these cases as with comic books generally, the reader-viewer actively empathizes with the character. In identifying, we wish to be like the character; we *feel* for the character in ways that we do not feel toward other characters.

This phenomenon of empathy is the same whether reading a novel like *Sorrows of Young Werther* or a Latino comic book. We know that whatever we are, we are not Batman living in Gotham City. We know when reading *Rocketo* that while we may have adopted temporarily the life and goals of the character Rocketo, we are only Rocketo in "an as if way," as Katja Mellman states of this identification process generally. When I "identify" with Blue Demon and Superman, what I am actually talking about is that I *feel* for these characters; the coherence of their actions and goals leads me to invest empathetically in them. This can even lead to a strong sense of *knowing* characters like we might a real friend whose company we enjoy and miss. Certainly Latino comic book author-artists are adept at triggering this feeling for characters in "an as if way." This in turn requires the reader-viewer's capacity to read the interior states of others and the universal capacity to formulate complex hypotheses of the working of another's mind.

When we read and view a Latino comic book story, we are not only putting ourselves in another's shoes; we are able to imagine from the visual and verbal fragments and signposts provided a character *in* a whole world. The same process goes for the author-artists. For example, even though Carlos Trillo and Eduardo Risso do not live in Brooklyn or New York City (both live in Argentina), they can imagine, distill, and distort details in such a way that in their series *Chicanos* a powerful sense of the city can come alive—for themselves and their reader-viewers. The visual cues allow us to feel the protagonist Alejandrina's movement in and through the differently textured and inhabited spaces of the city. The precise visual markings trigger a process whereby specificity of character, time, and place form in the reader-viewer's mind. This imagery also reinforces our emotional investment in Alejandrina. We *feel* for her when romances fail, crushes shatter, sleuthings lead to dead ends; and when she asks the reader directly, "Do you wanna hear how the story ended?" (issue 6, 24), we nod our heads. We are given just enough information to imagine fully these worlds. Now if we lacked the capacity for empathy, we might not be able to read the interior state of the character from exterior gestures and cues—according to the way the author-artist intends for us to do. We might not be able to make the necessary imaginative and *as if* emotional leaps for such comic book worlds to captivate us.

We share the universal faculty for inferring from exterior gesture, behaviors, and attitudes the interior states of mind of other human beings. Without this capacity that governs perception, inference, and action in our everyday activities, we would be psychologically and physically paralyzed. Even if not 100 percent right 100 percent of the time (we all have had experiences of misreading interior states), this capacity, as Lisa Zunshine sums it up, allows us to "construct and navigate our social environment" (6).

Our capacity to read minds, so to speak, plays a role in our ability to empathize with the characters fashioned by Latino comic book author-artists. By reading the author-artist's cues, we can infer causality, identity, perspective, temporal and spatial relations, and character interaction. And Latino author-artists can play with, tease, even push to its limits our mind-reading capacity to intensify our emotional and cognitive response. Often we see the use of visual signposts that cue us to infer a character's frustration, yet the verbal elements suggest contentment and happiness. Maybe character A does not want character B to know that he or she is unhappy. In the case of Trillo and Risso's *Chicanos*, Alejandrina does not want her friend Marita to know that she has a crush on her, so upon hearing of Marita's sexual exploits, she performs emotional nonchalance. The reader-viewer, however, is given enough information to infer a more complex state of mind. And this can become even more complicated when the author-artist supplies yet another level of interpretation, for example, a third-person narrator telling us that Alejandrina is not aware that Marita is aware of her performing emotional indifference.

Latino author-artists can direct this mind-reading faculty of ours in pleasurable and complex ways. Racial scripts can complicate the mind-reading, such as in *Palomar* when Luba ventures into the town San Fideo to have her movie projector fixed and the guys infer from her gestures (and accent) that she is "a dumb Indian" (*Palomar: The Heartbreak Soup Stories*, 95). I think here of Gilbert Hernandez's *Luba: The Book of Ofelia*, which presents a cast of nineteen fully fleshed-out characters. The reader-viewer must keep track of a dumbfounding number of individual interior states of mind, including when a character reads another character's interior state and acts on it; this often leads to the snowballing of misreadings among characters and of consequent chain reactions. Gilbert plays with this confusion by adding multiple dimensions of verbal gestures that conflict with verbal articulations of interior thoughts, leading to both humorous and tragic misreadings. Pipo acts in ways to cover up her romance with her son Sergio's girlfriend, Fritz, but this action leads Sergio and Pipo's ex-husband, Gato, to infer incorrectly that Pipo loves Fortunato; in a rage, they kill the innocent Fortunato.

The more of the character's personality the reader-viewer comes to know, the more the author-artist can complicate our reading of his or her state of mind. If we know Casmira (from the *Palomar* series) to be prudent and rational, yet she acts hysterically in front of one character and not another, we might infer a certain strategic mind-reading manipulation on her part. Gilbert Hernandez knows that the reader-viewer is storing information (episodic memory) about the character's personality, gestures, and context and that he can constantly add to and subtract from this information as well as send the reader on a wild goose chase. He can create scenes in which the visual and verbal narrative elements lead us to misread a character's interior state. In so doing, he constantly tantalizes and titillates us.

To follow a comic book story involves much more than the full functioning of our theory of mind to unthread layers of intentionality. It is a cognitively complex feat that engages visual and verbal senses to stimulate memories, feelings, thoughts, sounds, tastes, smells, sensations of touch. The comic book cues and triggers these memories, feelings, sensations in its unique configuration of verbal and visual elements. The emphasis on one feeling over another, the tension between our reliable or unreliable reading of a character's interior state are all determined—and this uniquely so with comic books—by the way the visual and verbal elements interact as well as which is dominant. Mila Bongco succinctly remarks: "Reading comics involves the pictures and their meanings in relation to the language, and the key to understanding comics does not lie in the words or pictures themselves but in the interaction and relationship between them" (49). Just as there can be a tension between the verbal and visual narrators, so too can there be tensions within the individual visual and verbal elements that make up a panel.

David Carrier contends that without the verbal (the speech and thought balloons) as well as the visual, there is no comic book. The verbal/visual narrator works as a gestalt, even when the reader-viewer sees first the image, then the text. Given that the comic book narrator is both verbal and visual, Latino borderland author-artists can play with various degrees of presence of one or the other to control the rhythm and flow of the story, the pace at which the reader-viewer constructs a narrative gestalt.

Some comic book author-artists choose to tip the balance toward the visual, as Peter Kuper does in *The System* and *Sticks and Stones*. Such stories read more like those Old Testament triptychs of the Middle Ages or pre-Hispanic codex where there is only a visual narrator telling the story. Conversely, there can be a superabundance of a verbal narrator, as with Andrea M. Gaudiano's *Azteca: The Story of a Jaguar Warrior* and Michael Perry and Lee Ballard's *Daniel's Ride*. In both, the visuals act as background filler, giving over the role of storytelling exclusively to the verbal register. In neither do the visuals contribute to telling the story, and in both the visuals only work as distractions. Frank Espinosa's *Rocketo* takes reader-viewers to the limit of the visual/verbal narrator's use of the visual. Here, however, both the verbal and visual in their pendular swings are fundamental in moving the story forward. Given that the visuals are at the edge of the limits of representation—they are very abstract and expressionist—makes it more difficult for the reader-viewer to fuse this with the verbal. While this lends to a viewing/reading of the visuals more as independent units than we would normally do in a mainstream comic book, Espinosa does not push us so far that we no longer move between the verbal and the visual. The verbal/visual narrator is still working to guide and form the reader's gestalt.

How the Latino author-artist chooses to put into motion the verbal and visual elements determines the overall story coherence and mood of the comic. These decisions can thus even direct us in how we might categorize the comic book: more pedagogical than pleasurable or a more balanced combination of both. The way Gaudiano renders the verbal and visual elements in *Azteca: The Story of a Jaguar Warrior* swings more toward the verbal. Its long descriptions of Aztec legend and the history of genocide in the conquest of the Americas lean us toward the serious and pedagogical. While in *Cihualyaomiquiz, the Jaguar* Laura Molina foregrounds Latino resistance within an oppressive and bigoted Anglo-dominated America, its balance between verbal and visual place gives it a less heavily didactic feel.

In Jaime Hernandez's 2006 comic strip "La Maggie La Loca" in *The New York Times Magazine* we see how a Latino author-artist balances more the presence of the visual narrator and verbal narrator: its heavy inked lines, solid yet subdued palette of colors (brown, yellows, blues) share page space with a verbal narrator's presence in the form of an interior monologue in a subpanel caption box; we overhear Maggie's flashes of thought about herself, her friends, and her surroundings.

"La Maggie La Loca" opens, "I woke up in the morning." As the serialized story of La Maggie unfolds, the reader's brain has already cognitively mapped the verbal narrator's past-tense, first-person voice to the visual narrator's focus on the character Maggie. And here things begin to get interesting. The visual narrator can describe Maggie—facial expression, gesture, behavior—in ways that emphasize or conflict with the textual—the narrator's voice. One can depict happiness and the other frustration, one comfort and the other paranoia. In such cases Jaime challenges—and even plays havoc with—the reader's cognitive schemas that work to infer interior state from outward gesture and that allow one to determine from a smile the character's state of pleasure or contentment. So, the force of the double narrator's pendular swings either toward the verbal or the visual affects the feel and the kinetic quality of the story. As each story unfolds, it acquires its own unique pendular rhythm, swinging between the visual narrator and the verbal narrator in ways that lull and surprise; while there is a rhythm, we are constantly registering minute shifts in the verbal and visual narrative configurations.

We can derive a certain pleasure from figuring out how Jaime creates verbal-narrator and visual-narrator tensions; we can begin to read—and even delight in—unreliability in Maggie's voice. In spite of the primacy given to Maggie's thoughts and impressions, such cognitive movement between the verbal and visual narrators that creates certain tensions allows us to step outside of her positionality, to perhaps not use her as the standard of measure for judging a character like Rena—and there is pleasure in this recognition.

Comic book author-artists have the choice of how they want to configure the verbal narrator and the visual narrator. The degree of presence of either one can vary from panel to panel and from an author-artist's comic to comic. The author-artist has artistic control in choosing to vary the pendular swings, though it appears that this artistic control diminishes when he or she begins to work for mainstream comic conglomerates. The narrators can exist in harmony, in tension, or with one much more prominent than the other. Frank Espinosa's extended wordless sequences in *Rocketo* are a case in point. A heavier or lighter presence of either will affect not only the pacing and rhythm of the story but the feeling we have when encountering individual panels: too much of the verbal narrative element within a panel can create a sense of claustrophobia, and little to none a sense of expansiveness, for example.

In Santiago's *In My Darkest Hour* we see how the visual and verbal narrators work to project the story as if it were a lucid dream. The story begins with Omar waking up—does he ever wake up, or is this a dream of him waking up?—but this is emphasized by the light yellow and gray color wash over the panels along with the juxtaposition of disparate images in a rather haphazard montage: a small-panel subjective filter of a street scene, then a jump to a splash page with a stylized Captain America dropping bombs on Iraq, then to a panel with just an eyeball. Movement in this comic book seemingly defies the laws that govern time and space relations in our everyday waking life. The narrative feels as if we are in a lucid dream where one can be flying with a bird's-eye view of a city one instant, then a closeup of someone walking naked in the street the next. To step into the shoes of Santiago's ideal reader we have to apply the logic of dreams to how we read the plot in the visuals and verbal text. If we do not follow the logic of dreams, then this story will not work for us. The verbal and visual narrators in the Latino comic book storyworld determine how we are to cluster traits for scenes, characters, events; this clustering in turn determines the contract we are to sign when entering into the storyworld. With Santiago, we must sign on as reading/viewing a story told in the mode of a dreamlike subjective realism.

WRAP-UP

As this chapter begins to show, nothing is hands off to these Latino borderland author-artists. Both in form and in content, their comic book narrative fiction can be about anything and can materialize or be expressed in the most surprising and unexpected ways. They can playfully riff on and more seriously allude to one another's work, comic books generally, and universal narratives the world over. They can use the techniques and combinations of visual and verbal narrators to convey particular moods and move readers/audiences to imagine holographically other worlds in specific ways. And the cultural particulars of one comic book narrative might trigger a specific response in one reader and not another. And yet, it is possible for the author-artist to transcend the particular and to transport a reader-viewer from Columbus, Ohio, to the streets of East L.A.

In continuing to develop a method and approach to Latino comic book narrative fiction, we need to consider the specific devices available and used in the comic book medium—the verbal/visual double narrator, for instance—as well as how its devices move the reader-viewer. Therefore, we need to consider how an author-artist distills and distorts to engage our many cognitive faculties (language, memory, emotion, and so on). This means not only that we consider how the will to style creates a gestaltic image of an author-artist persona (the ideal author-artist) but also how flesh-and-blood author-artists transform the everyday activities and events in the world we inhabit into objects that engage us in new and interesting ways.

Six

READING THE LATINO BORDERLAND SHORT STORY

THE SHORT AND THE LONG OF IT

There is a tradition of Latino borderland short story writing in the United States—a rather sparse tradition formed not always by the choice of the authors involved. Until the 1980s many Chicano authors were one way or another directed to publish in magazines and journals. Editors considered Chicano authors unskilled in the ways of the more "sophisticated" novel and so encouraged them to write and publish the lesser art of the short story. (See Mary Louise Pratt's "The Short Story: The Long and Short of It.") The net effect was that the few Chicano/Latino authors publishing in the early twentieth century wrote short fiction, and their work appeared mostly in magazines and journals. Some of the better-known authors include María Cristina Mena, who in 1913 and 1914 published her race-focused, sentimental short stories in the magazine *Century,* and Mario Suárez, who published his *barrio* stories after World War II.

In a post–civil rights epoch and with several Chicano-owned and -operated publishing houses (Quinto Sol, Bilingual Review, and Arte Público, for instance) and journals (*El Grito*) established, more short-story writers (and novelists) were appearing on the map, among them Rolando Hinojosa, with his *Estampas del Valle* (1973) and *Generaciones y semblanzas* (1977), and Estella Portillo Trambley, with her *Rain of Scorpions and Other Writings* (1975). By the early to mid-1980s, the mainstream publishers began to take notice of Latino borderland authors generally. Pat Mora, Denise Chávez, Cherríe Moraga, Ana Castillo, Sandra Cisneros, and Helena María Viramontes used the short story to invent unheard-of characters: border crossers, complex and strong women, lesbians. Mora and Moraga used the short fiction form to explore possible alternative roles for Chicanas to those defined by a restrictive Virgin/

Malinche paradigm that permeates Chicano culture. For Latino border-land authors, the short story form has been a main vehicle for authors to draw readers into fictional worlds informed deeply by the Chicano experience and cultural identity. Many used the short story form to tex-ture the lives of figures traditionally swept to the sidelines of literary representation: the old and the very young.

This brief overview illustrates several important issues. Mena, Tram-bley, Cisneros, Mora, and many more were authors of their time. María Cristina Mena, writing in the early twentieth century, was marked by this sociohistorical moment in ways that differ from those of the 1970s that marked Portilla Trambley's work; and Portillo Trambley's 1970s was an epoch very different from the 1980s when Cisneros published *The House on Mango Street*. Living and breathing as a Latina author in each distinctive historical era not only gave rise to an appetite for different imaginative tastes—themes that the author aesthetically shapes, reshapes, and shapes again—but significantly affected those authors as Latinas liv-ing in the United States. When Mena was writing, the strength of the workers' struggle had ensured massive gains in civil rights, but by the 1960s workers were still struggling to grasp those gains.

Latinas and Latinos in the early twentieth century were barely visible as an ethnic group, unlike the Irish and Jewish ethnic groups. While clearly marked off from the "mainstream," the demographics across the country were such that as an "ethnic group," Latinos remained largely invisible. The 1960s changed this, not just with the ongoing civil rights struggles but specifically with the late 1960s Brown Power movement. With a Chicano ethnic group identity forged in the Southwest, a shared cultural heritage (and history of racism) was set into stark opposition to a mainstream United States. By the 1980s Latinos across the board were beginning to become a part of the mainstream. Today, we see many La-tinos and Latinas holding high positions in administrative offices: Linda Chavez (an official in the Reagan administration) and Henry Cisneros (secretary of Housing and Urban Development in the Clinton adminis-tration), among others already mentioned.

The historical circumstances and particularities of Chicanos in the 1910s, the 1960s, the 1980s, and today are very different. We see more Chicanos in upper offices than in the earlier epochs, and along with this integration of Chicanos into the mainstream, we also see Chicano and Latino authors increasingly writing only in English with a few speckles of Spanish. Latino authors are not writing in Spanish as did Rolando Hinojosa. The technological and societal moments influence directly the tools and even worldviews of Latino borderland authors writing today and must be kept centrally in mind. Latino borderland authors today are as likely to write about the experiences of a suburban Latino living in a tract house as they are to write about a construction worker or a gangbanger.

My objective here is not to theorize about the Latino borderland short story by presenting classifications that tie technique, theme, and genre to ethnic identity and experience (for such see Nagel and Pratt). I am not interested in determining how the short story's DNA somehow fits best with the Latino borderland experience. Instead, I propose that we go straight to the authors and their stories to see how they give shape to—and transcend—a contemporary sociohistorical reality. We can see how authors such as Luis Rodriguez and Dagoberto Gilb put into play certain devices available to English-language authors of narrative fiction that engage their readers—their ideal readers. Certain experiences, visions, worldviews, and general knowledge are acquired differently in different sociohistorical epochs, and these specific experiences are conveyed to the reader. Authors like Gilb and Rodriguez use their creative capacity to create distinctive implied authors with distinctively identifiable ideal readers.

To explore the devices used by Dagoberto Gilb and Luis Rodriguez is not to restrict our interpretation to any one formal element (narrator or character filter, for example) or to thematic elements (the particulars of life as a Tejano construction worker in El Paso, for example) but rather to see how each of the ingredients—and there are many—that make up their short stories work to engage their ideal readers in specific ways. A story might use the third person to foreground the sense of alienation felt by a Latino character living in a racist Los Angeles, or this same device could amplify the sense of connection between a father and a son. Each narrative's fictional world can be thematized, as Lubomír Dolezel writes, "in many different ways, depending on the purpose of its representation. . . . Fictional representation generates the richest and most varied set of themes because it strives to perform all possible thematizations on all possible worlds" (38). That is, while the themes are infinite and storytelling devices abundant, often what is most interesting about Rodriguez's and Gilb's short stories is not the themes in and of themselves—many of their readers know well and firsthand the themes explored—but how the writers use techniques to give a particular texture to these themes and to richly texture the particulars of time and place. This approach also keeps us on the straight and narrow path, resisting an evaluation of these Latino borderland authors strictly on the basis of measuring an ethnic quality and type. We might read and analyze the straightforward, realistic stories of Rodriguez alongside those of John Steinbeck, Joyce Carol Oates, or Richard Wright. We might read the minimalist, nearly behavioristic realism of Gilb's stories in concert with those of Ernest Hemingway, John Dos Passos, or Raymond Carver. Why? Because Rodriguez and Gilb choose in many of their stories a third-person narrative voice that refuses to slip into the point of view of the characters and thus refuses the reader a privileged access into the protagonists' states of mind. We see such a voice among writers' preferred techniques to convey a worldview as well as move the reader.

What is interesting about Gilb and Rodriguez is how they choose to distill, stylize, and creatively reorganize certain parts that refer to everyday issues and experiences. Approaching Gilb's and Rodriguez's short stories, then, requires us to think about how the writers use language, genre, and storytelling technique—the building blocks for authors to invent new worlds and for us to imagine and engage with their fictional storyworlds.

WILL TO STYLE

In Dagoberto Gilb's *The Magic of Blood* and *Woodcuts of Women* and Luis Rodriguez's *The Republic of East L.A.* we see that these Latino borderland authors choose primarily to write about issues and experiences of Chicanos in the Southwest, Rodriguez mostly around Los Angeles and Gilb in El Paso. In their fiction making both draw from, distill, and distort the autobiographical—Gilb's working as a journeyman carpenter for sixteen years in El Paso and Rodriguez's running with gangs as a teenager in East L.A.—as well as the indirectly experiential through the stories of others. Rodriguez speaks to how he drew from creatively reimagined as-told-to stories while working with at-risk Chicano youth, for instance:

> The stories are based on real people that I knew or on my own experiences—but they've been all re-imagined. So for some stories, I'd have a general idea of the plot, but would let loose so as to delve deep into the characters and the situations; the characters would then begin to take on a life of their own and take over the story, re-shaping the plot

and ending. This was a good process, finding that balance between controlling the story and letting the characters find their own way and determine their own ending. (In Aldama, *Spilling the Beans in Chicanolandia*, 238)

In this same interview, Rodriguez mentions how the fiction of John Fante, Dagoberto Gilb, and Anton Chekov, among others, helped provide the tools and blueprints that he made his own in crafting his short stories. Moreover, in speaking to his choice of particular devices like first- and third-person narrations, Rodriguez declares, "Ultimately, then, it's how you want to convey the content of the stories that helps direct your decision" (240).

Gilb likewise speaks to reshaping and imagining more fully the men he encountered on construction sites; he made it a habit to take a pad of paper with him to work and rough out stories inspired by fellow workers. He studied carefully the craft of fiction by reading closely and over and over again authors including Fyodor Dostoevsky, André Malreaux, Albert Camus, Thomas Mann, and Günther Grass to be able to identify his own likes and dislikes in terms of technique and style.

The important part of their making fictional the lived (directly or vicariously) experience is the individual and unique way in which each strips down the experience to its bare bones, then reorganizes, amplifies, and stretches it out in ways that move readers. This complete transformation of the nuts and bolts of experience into an aesthetically organized whole is what I refer to as "the will to style" described earlier. Their different uses of narrative techniques transform their knowledge of particular aspects of the world into fictional narrative objects that pull their readers in. It is this will to style that also highlights just how each short story constructs its own implied author—that image formed in our minds of the master of ceremonies of each of the narrative's parts—with a distinctive personality. It is also this will to style that allows us to form an image of the ideal reader who *gets* all the textual cues as well as the beliefs and knowledge conveyed by the implied author.

In each of their stories, Gilb and Rodriguez make certain choices—titles, words, syntax, images, characters, temporal order, and point of view, among others—to control the rhythm and pace that also convey a worldview. And in each story, the authors control how much work the reader does to imagine the storyworld. Rodriguez tends to provide more information about character and setting than Gilb does, requiring the reader to do less work filling the gaps. Gilb's short stories that have minimal detail require much more gap-filling to imagine his worlds. Yet, both give us that "Aha" when their stories come to an end: Rodriguez tends to deliver this in a character's epiphany and Gilb in fitting together details that finally cohere into a whole. These endings are part of their will to style, part of what makes them different from one another even though they often write about urban working-class Latinos struggling to survive.

There are many reasons we might select one collection of short stories to read and not another. We might have read the author before and been drawn to particular phraseology, the play with temporality, or any number of elements—all elements that make up his or her will to style. I have an uncle in Mexico, for example, who is an avid reader of Ian Fleming precisely because he enjoys the kinds of lines James Bond delivers; my sister buys Mary Higgins Clark novels because she is engaged by the way Clark's mysteries unfold. I enjoy Gilb and Rodriguez because of the way they spin phrases, as well as how they use different devices to guide my gap-filling schemas—and sometimes radically redirect this activity—in fitting together the pieces into a whole. We come to expect certain turns of phrase and the use of certain narrative devices and tricks from authors we like. That is, we frame and schematize their work.

FRAMES FOR READERS

The conventionalizing of an author also takes place in the way a publisher markets his or her books. Before even reading the first sentence of the first story in Rodriguez's collection *The Republic of East L.A.* the reader is already prepped and primed by the peritexts: the title and subtitle, the author's name, genre category, jacket-cover blurbs, cover art, author photo, publisher's imprint, and description of the contents. All this and more begins to shape the cognitive schemas— the conventions—by which the reader will engage with its narrative fiction contents.

The Republic of East L.A. as a title resonates less with fiction narrative and more with a document designating a geographically bound space, with its own people and political and judiciary mechanisms to control those people. The *American Heritage Dictionary* confirms this sense, defining "republic" as "an autonomous or partially autonomous political and territorial unit belonging to a sovereign federation." Alongside *The Republic* we read *East L.A.,* getting an even stronger sense of the place and its people (Latinos). Along with the information, there is a certain rhythmic resonance: the abbreviated "L.A." gives the title that ring that "Los Angeles" cannot, and it identifies a certain L.A. insiderness; only outsiders would say "East Los Angeles." As we apprehend the front-page peritexts, we also read the name Luis Rodriguez. The author's name further solidifies this connection between place and people, East L.A. and Latinos, in our minds. On the Rayo first-edition hardback there appears an airbrush painting, styled in a low-rider art manner, of an Impala at a slight angle, with chrome bumper, white-wall tires, and slick blue body paint. In the background we see a breeze-block wall and only a sliver of blue sky. The art pulls the ideal reader even more into a particularized and bounded urban space: the East L.A. Latino low-rider subculture. Thus far, then, the peritext preps and primes the reader for stories that will be situated in a specific place, East L.A. And with it, the title conveys a political worldview: an autonomous, self-ruled territory within a particular geographic space in the United States where the majority is Latino.

Following *The Republic of East L.A.* appears the subtitle, *Stories.* The ideal reader will readjust his or her cognitive frame so as not to expect to read within the book's pages a political document but rather narrative fiction. Expectations of genre are established. The conventions of reading the pages within *as* fiction are set up. If we flesh-and-blood readers step into the ideal reader set up here, we will not burrow into its pages looking for only information that will have some one-to-one correspondence with truth (memoir, autobiography, historical document). This expectation is further solidified when we read on its back cover the category "fiction."

Along with the title, a series of laudatory blurbs appears. On this Rayo first-edition hardback one such blurb reads: "Author of the critically acclaimed bestseller *Always Running: La Vida Loca: Gang Days in L.A.*" Referencing Rodriguez's earlier *Always Running* as a critically acclaimed bestseller provides the seal of quality assurance, in essence saying, "If you buy this book, you won't be disappointed." *Gang Days,* however, focuses even more sharply on an expectation: that this book's stories will gravitate around gang life. A reader who knows anything about the author's life might be less likely to step into the ideal reader spot established by the title; instead this reader might expect an encounter with the autobiographical and factually verifiable. When this nonideal reader opens *The Republic of East L.A.* to a story, he or she might come across a third-person narrative that tells the story of a limo driver or a woman who dances in the street with a watermelon atop her head—and turn off.

There is also a context beyond the peritext at work in marketing and even constructing an ideal reader of Rodriguez's short stories. The hypercontext comes in the form of advertising, book reviews, and, after some time has passed, academic articles. In a review for the *Milwaukee Journal Sentinel,* Daniel Foley identifies the collection's major themes: "the tensions throughout Mexican American society—there are color and class issues, and conflicts between the first- and second-generation Mexican-Americans and the new immigrants." Foley celebrates Rodriguez's "deft" ability to capture the "rhythm of vibrant Mexican-English slang" as well as his "blow[ing] apart the stereotypes of Mexican life in Los Angeles." Foley concludes, "The barrios in his mind pulsate with opportunity, culture and eccentric characters." In the *Los Angeles Times* of May 5, 2002, Jonathan Kirsch writes how the collection "delights in exploring the cross-wired cultures that sizzle and pop on the streets of East Los Angeles." Cecilia Gomez declares in the Riverside, California, *Press-Enterprise* of the same date that the stories resound with "real people, with real strength, in very real predicaments."

The reviews work as publicity, with both good and bad write-ups translating into book sales. They also, however, provide a hypercontext that, much like the peritexts, can establish readerly contracts even before the reader opens to its stories. Kirsch's advertisement that the stories are about "cultures that sizzle and pop" might sell more copies, but it might set up false expectations, both for the reader who expects pepperings of a sizzling exotic and who finds nothing of the sort within the book and for the review reader who decides not to take a chance on the stories for fear of encountering the sentimental and exotic. Notably, the marketing mechanism—the publisher's sending out advance copies to reviewers before the book is bound, printed, and shipped—allows for a type of bridge making between hypercontext and the peritext. Daniel Foley's review, for example, is excerpted and printed within the book's pages just before the copyright information and dedication page.

The peritexts of Dagoberto Gilb's *The Magic of Blood* also set up various readerly expectations. The front cover carries an embossed gold star stamp that assures its quality—"PEN Hemingway Award"—and increased sales. The award situates the collection within a mainstream-recognized convention: Hemingway's fictional minimalism driven by masculine characters. This contract with the reader proves valid once the reader enters Gilb's storyworlds, but with one crucial difference from Hemingway's: Gilb's characters are working-class Chicanos living in the Southwest.

As in the Rodriguez collection, here too we see a nearly immediate formation of a hypercontext that solidifies a masculinist and minimalist contract with the reader. For example, in a book review for the academic journal *MELUS* Barbara J. Sáez identifies as Hemingwayesque Gilb's use of "sparse" and "uncluttered" phrasing that gives shape to an "environment with a language and image all its own and a world where women are only peripheral" (160). In their more extensive and scholarly response, Robert Beuka and Gerald Kennedy find that Gilb's stories make visible and create communities that "challenge even as they supplement the dominant discourse of nationhood" (10). His stories provide, they continue, an "ironic, supplementary relationship to the national master-narrative, which in the United States idealizes New World settlement ordained by God, heroic revolution against colonial oppression, and establishment of a democratic republic ensuring pursuit of the 'American Dream' of prosperity" (11).

Once again, peritext serves a multiple-pronged purpose: to legitimate the text for mainstream readers, to pre-establish the contours of an ideal reader, and to hypostatize (ascribe a material existence to) themes of exclusion and resistance. This third purpose functions as a prescriptive guide to reading—but one that is sorely misguided. Not only is there very little, if any, irony in Gilb's stories, but they have nothing to do with resistance and everything to do with the down-and-out, exploited, and oppressed.

The peritext's creation of an implied reader happens, but the actual reader does not have to accept the role. Indeed, the more the reader reads (and accumulates knowledge more generally of how the world works) and is attuned to how these peritexts work, the less likely it is that he or she will follow the peritexts' prescripts. Once we enter Gilb's fictional worlds we see absolutely no irony and no textual cues that might trigger an allegorical reading—of nation or whatever. As Sáez writes, Gilb carves out of reality and the virtual reality created by writers like Hemingway to create storyworlds filled with "rough-hewn characters" and to invent "piece by piece, what it feels like to live in the margins" (162).

POINT OF VIEW

Luis Rodriguez and Dagoberto Gilb both refrain from using point-of-view pyrotechnics such as narrated monologue and psychonarration. Neither uses that third-person narrator with the felt presence of a character's voice embedded seamlessly within. Rather, they tend to swing between using an objective third-person narrator and a first-person narrator, often a narrator-as-character who makes extended use of interior monologue.

Rodriguez uses the character-as-narrator along with extended monologue in several of his stories, including "My Ride, My Revolution," which seemingly begins in the third person: "The long sleek limousine lays into the curved street as kids of all sizes, of many coughs and giggles, skirmish around it, climb its blinding chrome and white armor, smearing dirt and fingerprints on its tinted windows" (1). The description is rhythmic and figurative of a "long sleek" limousine built of "blinding chrome and white armor" that "lays into the curved street." Here the reader "hears" the voice of the narrator, but because the narrative has yet to identify a first-person narrator position, it conveys a sense of being part of the community—a collective narrative voice. Then Rodriguez identifies the "I" of the narrator, Cruz Blancarte—an East L.A. Chicano working temp jobs and with the dream of making it big as a musician. The second paragraph begins,

> I'm awake, sitting at the edge of my bed with my hands on
> my head, startled by the wedges of daylight through torn
> curtains, by the voices and inflections, their wild abandon,
> and by the men's search for living poignancy from the
> polished enormity in their midst. (1)

Delaying identification of this "I" perspective and voice in the seemingly third-person, objective opening solidifies Cruz's position as a ventriloquist, a "we" narrative of sorts of the community. The narrator also waxes philosophical: "men's search for living poignancy from the polished enormity." As a bridge narrative voice, Blancarte is at once inside and outside the community. And Rodriguez makes sure there is a logic within the story that allows us to see why this is. We learn that the twenty-nine-year-old Blancarte is a musician, self-taught philosopher, and politically aware Chicano (raised by a Chicana activist) who lives in the *barrio* and works part-time jobs including as a limo driver—hence the "ride." With the "we" point of view established, the logic system of the story—the background—has to hold up. The reader understands where the curious mixture of philosophical musing, colloquial expression, and "we" omniscience comes from. And from this unique perspective, the reader gets to go on a ride, seeing L.A. from this "I/we" East

L.A. Chicano perspective. He gives a ride to a prostitute and rather than judge sees instead a "sad lonely person" who "made some wrong turns, met some wrong people, and now she can't see her way out of this except in a dream of money—what everybody tends to do" (14).

Rodriguez uses the third-person-narrator device in many of his stories. This allows him to create certain tensions and even frustrations between how we as readers (in the role of the ideal reader) interpret and judge a character and the way the implied author of the story does. In the story "Las Chicas Chuecas" Rodriguez uses the third-person point of view (largely filtered through an as-told-to perspective) to tell the story of sixteen-year-old Noemi and her older sister, Liver—a member of Las Chicas Chuecas gang. As the story unfolds we learn of Noemi's uncaring and abusive mother, her run-in with drugs as well as her rape, pregnancy, and miscarriage. Within this violent and destructive setting where there is seemingly no room for the imagination—in fact, all those around Noemi lack completely this faculty—Noemi has imagination in spades. In the first paragraph of the story the narrator tells us one of her fantasies: "like the many she's always had, where she fought off armies of skeletons and goblins with swift thrusts of sword and powerful kicks" (45). The story establishes Noemi's escape mechanism early on and reminds us of this at several moments in the narrative.

This, however, is rather odd. That the implied author would invest Noemi with such daydreams—fairy-tale fantasies filled with knights slaying monsters and goblins and her imagining herself to be an Aztec princess—conflicts with Noemi's everyday reality. The ideal reader of the story is supposed to feel and understand that she lives in a world filled to the brim with violence, exploitation, oppression—a decrepit society in which people have had their emotion and empathy sucked out of them. Within this world, one individual still has the capacity to feel, imagine, and create. And we see this well when Noemi writes a poem for Ms. Matsuda:

> There are girls that are poems
> Like a smile is a poem
> Girls who laugh their song
> Thru their eyes
> There are girls who see a world
> But touch beneath it
> And there are girls who are too much hurt
> Too much reality for dreams (58)

This imagery fits with Noemi's personality and environment. We believe in the creativity and imagination of the character. So when the implied author leans us more toward a Noemi who imagines in rather prosaic, never-never-land ways, we are frustrated, even angry. The short story ends with just such a fairy-tale resolution. With Noemi lying in a hospital bed after her miscarriage, the narrator tells us, "As Noemi's mind drifted into sleep, she saw herself dueling against giant mutant knights, cutting their bodies in half or handing them back their arms. She was a striking and valiant figure" (71). This last paragraph of the story follows right on the coattails of her decision to turn her life around, go back to school, and eventually become a high school counselor. The implied author wants us to understand that it is from this never-never-land place with duels against giant mutant knights that Noemi finds refuge and empowerment. Given Noemi's life context, this does not work.

A flesh-and-blood reader like me will not put himself in the place of the narrative's ideal reader: one who would believe this to be the character's source of strength. Instead, the actual reader will fit together all the pieces of Noemi's life—a sixteen-year-old girl struggling to survive in a modern-day East L.A.—and look for a young girl who turns to writing poetry as a way to "touch beneath" the violence of her world. When the narrative details Noemi and her life and the implied author's worldview of fairy tale as an escape and a source of strength do not match up, an actual reader might not step into the shoes of the ideal reader and instead could back off frustrated and angry.

GAP FILLING

This gap-filling process occurs also when we encounter a fictional character. Indeed, authors like Rodriguez and Gilb (and their narrators and characters) and their readers are always filling in gaps and therefore always reading the individual's gestures, attitudes, and behaviors against a larger set of conventions established at the social level. Dagoberto Gilb's story "Maria de Covina" unfolds as follows: "I've got two sports coats, about six ties, three dressy pants, Florsheims I polish *a la madre,* and three weeks ago I bought a suit, with silk lining, at Lemonade for Men" (3). There is enough narrative detail—first-person narrative with a syntax that pushes the rhythm of the words forward confidently, seamless code switching, and content—for a reader to infer a psychological type. As I mentioned, this is a self-assured fellow who likes to look good. However, Gilb plays with this automatic script and framing of the reader, soon turning this image of the narrator upside down and inside out. While this is a first-person narrator as protagonist who talks much of his mind, the reader would not be able to infer psychological nuance if not for a systematic overlap and intersection of the individual (internal) and the social (external) perspectives. This also demonstrates not only how thought (internal) and action (external) are linked in borderland narrative fiction but that they exist along a continuum: they can be very close together or very far apart, but always linked by a thread. Indeed, Gilb's stories are mostly thought-driven.

There is very little actual action in the stories, and when there is action, it is not action for action's sake; the action is the seed for some kind of turn in thought and even a paralysis of action in a protagonist's obsessive thinking. The protagonist of Gilb's story "Nancy Flores" cannot get over his failure to get the girl, the title character. His remembrance of things past—actions never taken—lead to a psychological paralysis and his eventual complete isolation and undoing.

Social (external) thought is also at play when the implied author presents an implied moral norm or worldview (and this can shift throughout any given story), with its attendant ideal reader, that ultimately does not match a real reader's response. In Rodriguez's "Las Chicas Chuecas" the implied author's fairy-tale worldview appears systematically so as to shape an ideal reader who will not be surprised at the never-never-land ending, and this leads to frustration and rejection on the part of a real reader like myself. This acceptance or rejection of an implied author's worldview results from our ability to constantly measure the implied author's worldview against or within norms of behavior and common knowledge. We can accept the invitation to take the role of the ideal reader or not if we judge the worldview of the implied author to be wrong or misguided. The individual reader, like the individual author, is constantly configuring the narrator and characters within a larger context of social memory—norms of behavior and knowledge about how our world actually works.

TEMPORAL ORDER

While both use the device of slowing down and speeding up the pace of the narrative in their various reorderings of the way events unfold in the storyworld, Rodriguez tends to use the device of the flashback (and flashforward within a flashback) more than Gilb. Rodriguez's story "Shadows" opens with the third-person narrator describing a homeless character asleep in a cemetery after a bad night of drinking. Swiftly the temporal order shifts, detailing the young life of the character, Rudy. The close juxtaposition of disparate entities—the older drunkard and his younger self, described as "a decent student" who was "fluid and graceful with a strong athletic build and sharp facial features" (29).

As more of the story unfolds, we take the role of the ideal reader and ask how this athletic and graceful young man ended up a drunkard sleeping in a cemetery. However, the narrator provides little in the way of events that may have led to this turn. What the narrator does provide is a sentence or two describing the odd contradiction between the image of Rudy as reflected by a social mirror (family, school, friends) and his own self-image: "he lacked poise and confidence" (29). Later his mother would read Rudy's low self-esteem as a despondent mood inherited from his grandfather who "never seemed to respond to anything around him" (30–31), but the ideal reader knows the picture is at once more complicated, and simpler. Despite a series of flashforwards within the flashback—we learn of Rudy's move into his first apartment, his turn to alcohol to inundate himself in a sense of "emptiness, the shame" (36), and how his love interest, Fabiola, pulls him temporarily out of an alcoholic haze—the narrator never describes an event or events that might have led to his demise and does not deliver any psychological detail.

The flashback provides a back story but no tangible cause. That soap-operaesque psychopathological script is never delivered. And in its absence, the narrative opens for another kind of reading—an allegorical one, if you will. This is a story about society today and how it is making individuals, family, communities more estranged from one another, how it is creating emotionally and empathetically dead people. In our contemporary world we cannot point a finger at a physical or psychological event as the cause of Rudy's demise; the deadening of our emotional and empathetic capacities grows from the social fabric itself—a social fabric stitched together by a fragile and decrepit capitalism. The narrator reflects on just such a fracturing of family and community as they sacrifice all "to find 'the good life' in America" (27). In the flashback where we expect back-story details, Rodriguez's narrator holds back. As such the narrator guides its ideal reader to consider Rudy's condition not as isolated and atomized but rather as deeply woven into the collective experience of our reified reality today.

SENSE OF PLACE

The characters we meet in Gilb's and Rodriguez's short stories are strongly rooted in very specific places that are very much shaped by time. The characters' thoughts, actions, dilemmas directly grow out of and respond to their living in these specific locales (in time). The readers of their short stories feel this distinctiveness of a character's existence in a place (in time) through various descriptive means: in the topographic long shot and pan and through a more narrowly focused, subjective and localized, street-level view, to borrow some film terminology.

Dagoberto Gilb's story "Mayela One Day in 1989" in *Woodcuts of Women* literalizes the technique of the topographic with the localized presentation of place. The story begins:

> I'm in a city called El Paso. I could point it out on a map.
> Right here, here it is. There is longitude, latitude. For most
> this is enough, a satisfactory explanation. But say we don't
> use all these imaginary concepts. Say there is no west of or
> east of or north of or south of. Forget all that. Forget these
> legalistic boundaries. No Texas here, no Mexico there, no
> New Mexico. Forget all that. (19)

Here the narrator wants the reader to forget about all those artificially imposed markers that create un*natural* divisions. In this first instance, the narrator asks that we pull away and abstract those details that give a contour to different landscape spaces. But this only takes the reader even more forcefully into a lived place that has nothing to do with drawing-room pens. With an even stronger sense of the presence of a narrator located in this space at the ground level, the description continues:

> Here's a river. Here are mountains. A sky above. Night, day.
> Sun and moon. Where there are people, there are build-
> ings, and streets, and walkways. There are colorful and not
> so signs with messages that can be reduced to words. Eat.
> Sleep. Money. Work. Play. (Ibid.)

As place becomes more and more concrete as a lived-in space, the ideal reader can imagine more tangibly the figure of the narrator in this place, gesturing to the left, to the right, telling us all about what makes a place: its mountains and its people eating, sleeping, working, playing. And by the end of the paragraph when the narrator announces, "I walk on the streets" (ibid.), the narrative point of view and the reader along with it are firmly grounded in this place. It is the narrator's walking or driving within this space that sparks a memory of a woman from his past, Mayela. Without shifting into past tense, as we might expect, the narrator stays in present tense:

> We drive past the lights and the well-known streets. Past the old courthouse and the new jail into the dark, oldest part of town, where frail tenements are without plumbing or electricity, where the Spanish language is spoken and in its most idiomatic form, so close to roots of meaning and sound that words breed like simple cells. (22)

The narrator's present-tense description of movement in this place in the past fuses in the reader's mind past and present and how lived experiences past and present within this place fuse in the mind of the narrator. Place is at least as much a shaper of the narrator's consciousness as his memory of one day with Mayela in 1989.

In Rodriguez's stories we encounter third-person narrators that describe localized places *as if* from within; and the title of the collection *Republic of East L.A.,* already does some of the work in identifying these places. In "Las Chicas Chuecas" the sense of place moves from outside— the mention of Pomona Freeway (45)—to the inside, those spaces in East L.A. inhabited by the sixteen-year-old protagonist, Noemi. And by using the as-told-to narrative form—Noemi tells her story to her high school counselor, Ms. Matsuda, "hired to help at Garfield High School" (ibid.)—the narrative conveys how different places (Garfield High, home, and the streets, shops, and markets in between) within an East L.A. space shape Noemi's thoughts and actions and her identity.

The narrator describes Garfield High as inanimate: "a beige three story building pushed back from the street by a swath of grass" and surrounded by a "high chain-link fence . . . like a prison" (55). It is also a lived space: "a crowded interchange at rush hour. Inside the school, teachers, parents, and administrators admonished students who lingered in the hallways to get to their classrooms" (57). Claustrophobia, suffocation, and restriction characterize this space. Conversely, when Noemi walks home, the narrator gives the sense of freedom and play:

She particularly liked to visit El Mercado on First and
Lorena to hear mariachis, eat tacos, and locate some hard-
to-find Mexican music and clothing. Other times she'd
stop at La Curandera Doña María's Botánica ("daily *limpias*
and spiritual readings guaranteed!") on Chavez Avenue
near Eastern to eye the elaborate and colorful *velas,* herbs,
and spiritual items. Noemi also liked to observe the street
peddlers as they sold mangoes on a stick, elotes con chile,
churros, and raspadas on street corners, in parking lots, and
parks. (60)

Along with contrasting the way Noemi experiences different places,
the narrator infuses a certain geographical, architectural, and historical specificity. For instance, Noemi's house is given a specific location:
"Dittmann Avenue, a few houses from Hubbard Street" (59). The narrator tells us that it is in a neighborhood filled with "older stock wood-
frame houses and duplexes, some with pots of flowers on windowsills
and scattered gardens in backyards" (59). Finally, the reader learns that
Noemi's neighborhood was at the

epicenter of the 1970 East L.A. riot [that] began when armed
sheriff's deputies attacked a crowd of around thirty thousand
protesting the Vietnam War at Salazar Park (when it was
called Laguna Park)—ending in the deaths of several people,
including Chicano journalist Ruben Salazar. (60)

The narrator as outsider (third person) and at the same time insider
(knowing that where Chavez intersects Eastern Noemi can look at colorful *velas,* or candles) is further solidified in the reader's mind by the
language and phrases used, not just the sprinkles of Spanish but also
in qualifying the chain-link fence "like a prison" and using the phrase
"administrators admonished students." This is a narrator very close to
Noemi's perspective of the world.

Knowledge of place, language, and perspective gives texture to the
narrator's outsider/insider sense of place in time—a time when all that is
left of the civil rights and antiwar movements is the name of a park after
a fallen journalist; a time of chain-link fences around centers of education; a time when a generation of Chicanas like Noemi has fewer and
fewer choices in the world.

Rodriguez's and Gilb's stories deal with family: family ripped apart, family about to rip apart, family destroyed, family physically together but emotionally removed. Even the most isolated and atomized characters are somehow still tied to a world beyond themselves (society), and this usually takes the form of family. In Gilb's "Mayela One Day in 1989" we learn from the character-as-narrator that the seemingly free-floating and independent Mayela married at sixteen and has two children. Moreover, the narrator informs us that Mayela has told him "stories of men: fathers, brothers, cousins, lovers" (20). Even in this story that does not gravitate around a family per se, family is present.

Another of Gilb's stories, "Shout," in *Woodcuts of Women,* focuses more directly on family as social nexus. The story unfolds one hot, humid evening when the construction-worker protagonist returns home to his wife and three boys. They live in an apartment building surrounded by all sorts of people and their noise; and this apartment building, as the narrator describes, exists within a "huge city out there groaning its sound" (50). The unnamed protagonist arrives angry and shouting at a wife who is also angry and shouting. With economic pressures, children, the heat, and a looming sense that the unnamed protagonist is about to be fired—"It was a job neither of them wanted to end too soon" (51)—the wife announces that she is pregnant. As this story foregrounds the impact the economic (job uncertainties) and social (family members and the people in the apartment building within a huge city) setting has on the behavior between husband and wife, parents and children, family is intimately woven into the tissue that wraps around the world.

As I mentioned earlier, morals are those internalized rules concerning the relationships between individuals that first take shape in the family. Not surprisingly, it is within this nucleus of the family as social nexus that we see Gilb's and Rodriguez's characters internalize or reject a series of rules about how to interact with others. The first-person narrator and protagonist of "Mayela One Day in 1989" knows that she is married but does not care. The narrator-character, Cruz Blancarte, of Rodriguez's story "My Ride, My Revolution" knows that the woman he is driving somewhere is a prostitute, but he does not care. In Gilb's "Shout" the couple shouting at one another know that living in an apartment building means that they are disturbing others, but they do not care. Noemi's mother shoots heroine, but she does not care. In all cases, we have behavior that goes with or against a set of norms, and we have emotion.

Noemi is upset when she discovers her mother high, for instance. She knows this is wrong and that it will destroy her mother. Without emotions, we would not need rules of behavior toward others that we internalize to a greater or lesser degree of consciousness. The social situations (with their attendant moral dilemmas) that these stories texture also differ depending on the place *in* time (sociopolitical and historical).

WRAP-UP

What makes the study (and teaching) of Latino borderland short stories such as those of Gilb and Rodriguez interesting is not to focus exclusively on the thematic elements and issues nor to focus only on the devices used to organize and convey this information. While it is important for us to pay attention to style, point of view, temporal order, peritexts, and hypercontexts, it is just as important to keep the themes in mind all along as well. After all, when we read a story by Gilb or Rodriguez, theme and technique fuse into a gestalt in our mind.

This is also why it is important to keep in mind the main objective: to understand better how borderland narratives tick—through the authors and their choices—and how they in turn move the reader. It is crucial to think of Latino borderland authors as participating actively in shaping world literature—and being shaped by world literature. Gilb and Rodriguez, like some other Latino borderland writers, touch on subjects and issues in ways that we do not see in María Cristina Mena, Mario Suárez, or Sandra Cisneros. Gilb and Rodriguez are of their time and therefore touched by very different social and political historical climates. So Rodriguez uses certain narrative techniques to texture the story of a young Chicana barely surviving in a decrepit East L.A., while Suárez uses the barbershop as a conceit to tell multiple stories of a handful of relatively fulfilled characters with very different economic and social concerns. Rodriguez writes in another time, in which the disease of capitalism has infected and rotted to the core today's social tissue.

While Rodriguez and Gilb are of their time, their deft use of storytelling techniques they use to convey themes and issues—place in time—throws down the gauntlet to other authors, now and tomorrow. It is the unique imprint—their will to style—they give to their fiction that transcends the particulars of their flesh-and-blood existence in time and place. This is what makes the difference between Latino borderland authors who particularize character experience in places *in* time with a clear will to style and those who abstract character experience in places *out of* time. So, in reading Gilb and Rodriguez we would do well to attend to the formal features involved in the writing of the story (its the universal infrastructure) and how they work to particularize features contained in the subject matter (themes, places, and time). Finally, we would do well to keep in mind how their stories are felt (the making of the implied author and ideal reader) and how this springs from our capacity for emotion, empathy, and behavior as flesh-and-blood readers situated in a place *in* time.

NOTES

1. In *Fictions of India: Narrative and Power* Peter Morey critiques Jameson for collapsing different Indias into one Third World imaginary space. "If we consider the 'Indian national allegory' less as the *story* of the nation in a finite, self-contained textual space than as the proliferation of *stories* that go to make up India, we enrich our understanding of cultural diversity beyond the bounds of that often negative social unit privileged above all others in the rise of capitalism" (185). However, Morey falls into the trap of reading postcolonial novels as allegories of what he identifies as an "ongoing narrative of India" as played out "on the bodies of their central characters in a landscape ribbed by a railway which conveys those bound for their own undiscovered countries" (ibid.).

2. Though Bhabha's formulation lacks even a modicum of common sense, he has been followed by many. R. Radhakrishnan theorizes the nation as narration to theorize a "radical postponement of *identity*" in the celebration of "displaced hybridities" (54). And R. Radhakrishnan's Bhabha-like move to identify all colonial power structures as discursively constructed leads him to posit a textual resistance and destabilizing of "the sovereignty of nationalism" (54). On one occasion, he confuses narrative fiction with historical and ontological fact to conclude of one of Amitav Ghosh's earlier novels, *Shadow Lines*, that it is "real precisely because [it is] imagined" (62). And although Meenakshi Mukherjee does not participate in this conflation of the imaginary with the real and the real with the imaginary, Mukherjee nonetheless reads the novel in reductive terms. In *The Perishable Empire: Essays on Indian Writing in English,* Mukherjee writes, for example, that "the reality represented in the novel is not an unmediated reflection of what actually existed, but an ideological reconstruction moulded by an implicit political agenda in which language has . . . a determining role" (9).

3. In *White Mythologies* Robert Young begins to level a similar critique against Bhabha's formulation of a subaltern *inter dicta* textual resistance to colonialism as erasing real political agency in the world (149–152). It is also note-

worthy that almost all poststructuralist postcolonial critics and cultural studies practitioners refer only to de Saussure (whose *Course in General Linguistics* is based on notes taken by several of his students who had attended the various series of lectures he gave on the subject between 1907 and 1911), as if linguistic studies had made no significant progress since the beginning of the twentieth century. It is very doubtful that the great majority of "theories" developed by poststructuralist postcolonial critics and cultural studies practitioners could have even been formulated if they had resorted to contemporary linguistic science as represented, for instance, by Noam Chomsky.

4. In a short, erudite, and witty essay titled "Pascal's Sphere," Jorge Luis Borges traces the history of godlike metaphors, from Xenophanes of Colophon (sixth century BCE) to Blaise Pascal (1623–1662). In the last chapter of the last book of Rabelais's *Gargantua and Pantagruel* this metaphor is expressed as follows: "That intellectual sphere, whose center is everywhere and whose circumference nowhere, which we call God" (cited in Borges, 7). Borges identifies just such a period when Rabelais wrote this—that of the late Renaissance—as the moment when such a metaphor was applied to the universe as a whole and when "men felt lost in time and space" (8). He elaborates: "In time, because if the future and the past are infinite, there cannot really be a when; in space, because if every being is equidistant from the infinite and the infinitesimal, there will not be a where" (ibid.). Borges concludes his essay writing, "Perhaps universal history is the history of the diverse intonations of a few metaphors." (9). Interestingly, Michel Foucault's conception of power is identical to this metaphor: "Power is everywhere; not because it embraces everything but because it comes from everywhere" (93–94). Now, if power "comes from everywhere," it cannot have a "where." Power thus becomes a mystical entity and a mystical concept.

5. The home in postcolonial novels is for Rosemary Marangoly George a site that expresses "the ideological struggles that are every day in the construction of the subjects and their understanding of home-countries" (3). Home functions as another localized epistemological space whereby the reader can decode identity formation based on gendered and racialized inclusion and exclusion discursivities and where the postcolonial family (characterized by "hyphenation" and "wandering") can resist "dominant ideologies like nationalism" (5).

6. Another example of this type of textualist idealism runs through the work of R. Radhakrishnan. In his essay "Postmodernism and the Rest of the World," for instance, he celebrates the "embattled rhetoric of home" (39) as just such a resistant site to a homogenizing global capitalist nation-state. The rhetoric of home opens up the possibility and identification of a localized subjectivity and epistemology that can be "deployed strategically to resist the economic impulse toward sameness" (ibid.). Again, however, for R. Radhakrishnan to posit a postcolonial rhetoric of home as "radical epistemology" (48) that resists such oppressive paradigms as the Western postmodern disdain for "the category

home" (ibid.), he must confuse language for cultural phenomena; he must repeat the poststructuralist systematic muddling of signifier with sign, the home of postcolonial fiction with the homes made and inhabited by real subaltern peoples.

7. Aijaz Ahmad, in *In Theory,* proposes a historical critique of postmodern postcolonial theory that stems from a repressive and bourgeois metropolitan literary analytic and that fills the gap left from a cultural imperialism in a post-capitalist age. Neil Larsen is critical of poststructuralist postcolonial theory that proposes a "false or inverted consciousness of the historical reality, that on another, more subjective plane, it desires simply to evade" ("DetermiNation," 143).

8. *The Glass Palace* is a novel and therefore participates in the conventions of this genre that have been traced back to its birth: the moment of sixteenth-century global expansion and the building of the modern form of nation-state—both impulses originating in Europe. However, the novel is not simply a response to nation-building processes. While the spread of the capitalist mode of production led to a massive conceptual, scientific, and cultural revolution in European countries first—and this certainly informed the novel's shape and content—narrative fiction in general and the novel in particular have always projected the imagination beyond the immediate present and sought to represent the human aspiration to a freedom that transcends the shackles of exploitation and oppression as well as the limitations of nation-states.

9. In *Metahistory,* Hayden White blurs the boundary between narrative fiction and historical document to demonstrate how one can decode history as one interprets a literary text; such decodings then reveal history to be a signifying system constructed to naturalize hierarchies of difference. However, to do so White must reductively read narrative fiction as only made up of plot and not a complexly organized interaction of mode, tempo, diegetic point of view, theme, and characterization, and so on. It is this complex organization, among other features, that distinguishes historical document from narrative fiction.

10. In case the reader fails to pick up on the contract that asks him or her to read *The Glass Palace* as primarily a fictional construct and not a historically verifiable document, Ghosh includes "Author's Notes" at the novel's end: "In attempting to write about places and times that I knew only at second- and third-hand, I found myself forced to create a parallel, wholly fictional world. *The Glass Palace* is thus unqualifiedly a novel and I can state without reservation that except for King Thebaw, Queen Supayalat and their daughter, none of its principal characters bear any resemblance to real people, living or deceased" (549).

11. In *The Glass Palace,* the history migrates into fiction to add emotional depth, create dramatic effect, and enliven the reader's imagination. This is not to say that the novel pretends that the historical record is always an unbiased telling of events or that fiction does not migrate into fact for propagandistic ends. The sepoy Indian revolt against the British in 1857 is mentioned several times throughout the course of the novel (on pages 26, 29, 44, 49, 222, and

417, for example). On one occasion, a fictionalized British major relates the event, referring to it not as a "mutiny," which would connote organization and resistance, but as an uprising formed by an "unruly" mob of Indians (44). Conversely, when Indian characters recall the event, it is referred to as "the Mutiny of 1857" and embraced as the expression of Indian dignity and will to survive within violent colonial oppressive conditions. As remembered by Anglo and Indian characters, the event is given a different ideological tinge. This difference does not alter the facts of the event of 1847; it simply sheds light on how the relating of a historical event can be given a bias based on ideological interest.

12. Ghosh's narrative presents us with the flip side to biological or cultural remaking of family. At one point, it is revealed that Rajkumar uses the concept of family to justify the exploitation of others. And for the fallen Queen Supayalat, her sense of obligation to family is so entrenched in old racist social orders—she remarks with disgust at the "smell of miscegenation" that is in the air and cannot stand the idea of her lineage leading to her daughter's birth of a "half-caste bastard" (173)—that she ultimately destroys her family.

13. Some postcolonial theorists might be critical of Ghosh's choice of the romance as his vehicle to tell his story. Likened to that of myth or escapist fantasy, the romance genre is often set up in contradistinction to facing reality directly in a mode like realism. In *Cultural Imperialism and the Indo-English Novel,* Fawzia Afzal-Khan identifies realism as "a generic strategy of hope, for it allows the writer to construct a world that can be made whole, a world where people can achieve a harmonious balance between self and society and thus give some meaning to their existence and their culture. Realism is thus, ultimately, a 'healing' fictive strategy for Third World writers, though certainly a more 'progressive,' less petrified one than that of myth" (178). As Ghosh proves with *The Glass Palace*—and his many other novels that employ a variety of storytelling modes and genres—postcolonial writers can use any number of conventions and techniques to texture how their characters can gain a sense of meaning and belonging in the world.

14. Narrative fiction and ontological fact are similarly confused by Doris Sommer. In her essay "Irresistible Romance" (and later her book, *Foundational Fictions*), Sommer reads a number of nineteenth-century historical novels written by Latin American politician-authors as romances that unfold as love stories but whose "star crossed lovers [actually] represent particular regions, races, parties, or economic interests which should naturally come together" (75). The novel of romance in Latin America, then, is a genre that Sommer identifies as yoking together the "historical allegory" (84) with the sentimental. That these novels appeared at the moment of postcolonial nation formation in Latin America leads Sommer to decode their subtextual, political agenda: "Their passion for conjugal and sexual union spills over to a sentimental readership in a move that apparently hopes to win partisan minds along with hearts. The

undeniable burden for new novelists, then, was formal, sentimental, and politi-cal at the same time" (75). Finally, then, Sommer's "foundational fictions" used the romance genre—courting, love, and family—to cover over repressive "leg-islative or military campaigns" (73) and to naturalize a "rhetoric of productive sexuality" (73) in the formation of nation.

It is true that many politicians in nineteenth-century Latin America were also writers; this is explained at least in part by the fact that at that time only a very small minority of people knew how to read and write, so for an intel-lectual or a writer to become a politician was commonplace. In countries like Argentina or Mexico with between 20 million and 40 million people, only around 200,000 and 400,000 people were literate at any given time, and only about 20,000 to 40,000 actually read. Moreover, up until the twentieth century, written matter generally was very scarce, and novels even scarcer. So we have to question Sommer's assertion that those "foundational fictions" actually had the power to cover over ideologies of nation formation—as "part of a general bourgeois project to hegemonize a culture in formation" (92), as she states—and we have to ask how many copies of these novels were sold and how many were actually read and by what kind of readers in order to have had such ef-fect. Even today in Mexico—with its more than 100 million inhabitants—it is exceptional for a novel to have a print run of more than 2,000 copies. One can imagine what it would have been like in Sommer's nineteenth century, when many Mexican authors had their books printed in, well, Paris!

CHAPTER FOUR

1. While they are very different in approach, aim, and goal, the reader might wish to consider the arguments put forth regarding genre and ethnic or postcolonial identity in my *Postethnic Narrative Criticism* as well as *Brown on Brown*, M. R. Axelrod's *The Politics of Style in the Fiction of Balzac, Beckett, and Cortázar*, and Monika Fludernik's essay "Imagined Communities as Imaginary Homelands." Axelrod discusses the Latin American Boom authors and their shared "spirit of alienation" that is "vital to the evolution of the novel as a way of undermining the hegemony of the European Realistic novel in general, the English Realistic novel in particular and their canonical ossification" (89). Again, I disagree with Peter Hitchcock's hypostatizing of the theme of disloca-tion that gives the postcolonial novel an existence above and beyond history—and magically outside of literature itself.

2. The narrative takes us back to the mid- to late 1980s as well. At one point the narrator describes this era as a time when "all the shit of the eighties—Irish bombs, English riots, transatlantic stalemates . . . spewed out [on televi-sion and] everyone was weeping for themselves and their children, for what the terrible eighties was doing to them" (114). The general mood the novel

conveys is shaped by walls falling, borders opening, and political correctness ablaze alongside Thatcher's increased attacks against trade unions and the welfare state, censorship (burning of *Satanic Verses*), racism, and class oppression and exploitation.

3. On another occasion, the narrator describes Clara's first love interest, Ryan, as having freckles that "were a join-the-dots enthusiast's wet dream" (25).

4. Irie ventures into the white-owned PK's with her "half-caste hair" to realize "the impossible desire for straightness" (231). Here, "ammonia, hot combs, clips, pins, and simple fire had all been enlisted in the war and were doing their damnedest to beat each curly hair into submission" (229). With her hair burnt off, she is given a voucher to buy "eight packets of number-five-type black hair" (231) from an Indian woman who peddles in a global trade of selling hair weaves—real and artificial.

5. Smith's narrator recounts:

> This has been the century of strangers, brown, yellow, and white.
> This has been the century of the great immigrant experiment. It
> is only this late in the day that you can walk into a playground
> and find Isaac Leung by the fish pond, Danny Rahman in the
> football cage, Quang O'Rourke bouncing a basketball, and Irie
> Jones humming a tune. Children with first and last names on
> a direct collision course. Names that secrete within them mass
> exodus, cramped boats and planes, cold arrivals, medical checkups.
> It is only this late in the day, and possibly only in Willesden, that
> you can find best friends Sita and Sharon, constantly mistaken
> for each other because Sita is white (her mother liked the name)
> and Sharon is Pakistani (her mother thought it best—less trouble).
> (271–272)

6. The narrator describes Magid's malaise as symptomatic of his desire to be middle-class English:

> He wanted to own cats and not cockroaches, he wanted his mother
> to make the music of the cello, not the sound of the sewing ma-
> chine; he wanted to have a trellis of flowers growing up one side
> of the house instead of the ever-growing pile of other people's
> rubbish; . . . he wanted his father to be a doctor, not a one-handed
> waiter. (126)

7. In "New Ethnicities, the Novel, and the Burdens of Representation" James Proctor reads *White Teeth* as indifferent to difference and thus in "the refusal to worry about 'race' . . . or to invest in insurrectional forms of violence as

progressive alternatives [as] not necessarily a retreat from politics [as much as it is a] sign of the margins' incorporation into a commodified mainstream" (119).

8. While several critics like Clare Squires have expressed dismay at Smith's lack of development of the young feminist lesbian character Neena (a.k.a. Niece-of-Shame), I argue that this would have given the novel a too-clear-cut and dogmatic worldview. The novel does better when filtered through the perspective of a deeply conflicted and complexly contradictory character like Irie. The different worldviews and sensibilities are foregrounded readily in the post–hair-straightening scene when Neena tells Irie: "you've been taught all kinds of shit. You've got to reeducate yourself. Realize your value, stop the slavish devotion, and get a life, Irie . . . The truth is the Barbara Streisand cut you've got there ain't doing shit for you. The Afro was cool, man. It was wicked. It was *yours*" (237).

9. More exactly, composing a literary work involves a number of stages, with complex procedural schemas operating at each stage. Different procedural schemas may have different levels of activation at different stages. For example, there is usually a period of preparation for a work. In this period, the author does his or her normal activities with an especially attuned awareness to them as well as to other cultural phenomena (novels, art, music, and the like) that might also be used as scripts and scaffoldings in the making of the new work. Thus an author at this stage may find his or her attention focused on particular scenes, faces, bits of overheard (or read) dialogue, and so on. Whether reading a novel or listening to a conversation on the train to work, the author's focus on the world around him or her to mine for schemas (themes, scenes, characterization) might be at work simultaneously. For more on how authors work with different real and fictional ingredients as well as how certain event schemas attract certain scene-construction schemas see Hogan's *The Mind and Its Stories* and *Cognitive Science, Literature, and the Arts*.

10. In *Why We Read Fiction*, Lisa Zunshine uncovers the layers of mind-reading activity that a given number of cultural representations elicit, from television sitcom to *New Yorker* cartoon. She proposes that certain complex layerings of emotions in any given representational sequence "push our mind-reading adaptations to what feels like their limits (within particular historical milieus, that is)" with the consequence of leaving us "in rather emotionally suggestive moods" (31).

11. Memory is both an individual neurobiological and a social phenomenological reality. Discussing how Smith's and Kunzru's novels admix dominant elements of the picaresque or the Rabelaisian requires the use of language— a social memory of symbolic registers with agreed-upon meanings that communicate ideas and emotions. Memory also requires a certain degree of disciplinary knowledge whereby "picaresque" and "Rabelaisian" define specific narrative traits of particular storytelling modes. This is to say, the reading experience

is at once personal (activation of individual memory) and social (activation of larger memories of language and literature). This personal and social memory provides the key by which we can feel at liberty to relish in the experience of the narrative world as fictional; contractually, the social memory in this case is telling us that we do not need to verify events, actions, existence of characters, and so on, as real.

12. Playful mimesis is exemplified in Miguel de Cervantes, the anonymous author of *Lazarillo de Tormes,* François Rabelais, Joseph Fielding, William Thackeray, Joaquim Maria Machado de Assis, James Joyce, Henry Miller, Djuna Barnes, Jorge Luis Borges, Juan Rulfo, William Burroughs, William Gass, Ishmael Reed, and many others.

13. The picaresque schema exhibits a sense of fatedness and affirms the corporeal; it typically focuses on a protagonist who hails from unknown origins and survives on cunning and a chameleonlike ability to blend into alien cultures and who usually is restless but does not experience grand epiphanies—this is often why many critics consider such characters flat. The picaresque is typically a narrative that sympathizes with a worldview at odds with society (racially, socially, sexually, gendered, and so on) that thus offers the reader a new perspective on that society and its many social hierarchies and types. Here, too, because the character typically does not experience grand moments of consciousness change, the reader remains more focused on objects and people outside of the protagonist's interiority. Otherwise stepped over and ignored underworlds are revealed, and in the revelation the ideological veneers that cover exploitation and oppression in a global capitalist system become apparent. See Christopher Ehland's *Picaresque Perspectives—Exiled Identities* and Timothy G. Compton's *Mexican Picaresque Narratives.*

14. See Howard Mancing's "Prototypes of Genre," in which he discusses continuums that tend more toward prototypical categories than oppositions between categorical/generic groups.

15. Not all readers will be *ideal* readers. Bruce King concludes a review of *White Teeth:* "It is too long for the characters to be merely amusing, and I found myself reacting against many of their stupidities. I am also uncomfortable when minorities are portrayed as nonstop foolish" (118). Likewise, Askhari Hodari writes, "More than 400 pages in length, the book is large, but the concepts explored are larger still. Smith's writing style multiplies the plot with each word. In the hands of a less generous editor, the novel might have had more focus" (27). Anita Mathias writes of how Smith's "relentless sly wit . . . can be wearing" (28) and how the inner lives of her characters are "reduced to blurbs" (ibid.). Unlike the "iridescent prose and inventive, anguished meditations on history, love, evil, and God" (ibid.) seen in the likes of Rushdie and Toni Morrison, Mathias concludes, "*White Teeth* is slight" (ibid.). While the novel "can hurt your sides from laughing," Greg Tate considers *White Teeth* lacking in emotional resonance; "it doesn't haunt you" (75). Finally, Zenga Longmore

writes in her piece "Fairy-Sweary-Land" that while it is "refreshing to read descriptions of Harlesden with no mention of crack cocaine or gunfights, the heavy, jargonised style dulls the bite of *White Teeth*" (47). Bryan Walsh considers Kunzru's *The Impressionist* the work of a "brilliant literary impressionist who hits every symbol, fulfills every gesture, while missing something essential beneath the shining surface." A reviewer for *The Economist* considers *White Teeth* "a little derivative" and even "Rushdie-ite." It is "soulless," according to Shailaja Neelakantan of the *Far Eastern Economic Review.* She concludes:

> Even when he travels to the "heart of darkness" in Fotseland, Africa, to study his "whiteness," the darker inside we discover is hardly worth the journey. Most of the attendant characters are not fully drawn, given—like Privett-Clampe—to shouting "Tally Ho," "On! On! On!" and "View Halloo" in the throes of sexual passion. A more experienced novelist would have lent muscle to these sly takes on colonialism and colour, which appear only in glimpses in the novel. *The Impressionist,* which lacks a coherent theme or a character of compelling humanity, is entertaining but strangely empty.

16. Oddly, Squires is critical of Smith's lack of development of certain characters, including Clara, whose introduction to the secret fruits of feminist books by Neena is not taken up:

> It is ironic that Smith, as a young female writer, makes a brief nod to feminism and then leaves Clara without a voice. While this could be seen as typical of the novel's rejection of politically correct representations (Samad's tribulations with his faith being another), it is not sufficiently explored for it to be anything other than a throwaway piece of characterization, an example of the subjugation of character to plot. (59–60)

Clara's interest in Archie is unbelievable, though.

> The "believability" of Clara's motivation hinges, then, on the impact of comic representation. Whether the characters are locked into stereotypes, and the extent to which their actions are reliant on the demands of the plot, is regulated by the novel's genre definition. (60)

Also oddly, Squires talks of the narrative negotiating "between the modes of realism and magic realism" that "lends the narrative its generous, inclusive tone" (66).

17. The reparticularizing of Conrad's *Heart of Darkness* arrives at the novel's

end. All Pran/Jonathan's preparations for Africa, from his studies in the university library to his mentorship with ethnographer Professor Chapel fixed in his mind the image of the "lone adventurer, heroically, inscribing the English character on a blank land" (*The Impressionist* 345). Upon his approach, the narrator describes his "waiting to be swallowed by towering forest trees, to feel he is approaching the primeval heart of a little-known continent: this is what happens when you go up an African river" (348). However, the narrator does not leave us with a *Heart of Darkness* schema unaltered. The narrator further describes how "instead of closing in, the country opens up, the skies widening and the foliage on the banks thinning to tracts of low acacia scrub" (348). Moreover, his experience in Africa leads neither to a Kurtz-styled narcissistic collapse nor to a Marlowe-like self-righteousness but a vision-quest–induced transformation of self.

18. The examples of Smith's use of this talk style abound. On one occasion, the narrator describes Samad on his way to see his mistress, Poppy, about to cross paths with his son:

> Unbeknownst to all involved, ancient ley-lines run underneath these two journeys—or, to put it in a modern parlance, this is a rerun. We have been here before. This is like watching television in Bombay or Kingston or Dhaka, watching the same old British sitcoms spewed out to the old colonies in one tedious, eternal loop. Because immigrants have always been particularly prone to repetition—it's something to do with that experience of moving from West to East or East to West or from island to island. Even when you arrive, you're still going back and forth; your children are going round and round. There's no proper term for it—*original sin* seems too harsh; maybe *original trauma*. (136–137)

19. In *Talk Fiction* Irene Kacandes discusses an "interactional" model to understand better how certain authors create a "participant-narrator through the text-as-statement, not as reading in the subjective will of an individual reader" (29). These fictions engage readers in the way they ask us to respond to their talking; that is, they expect the reader to be affected. They seek to absorb the reader and, according to Kacandes, to act in the "wor(l)d" (217).

20. Given that the dominant universal narratives are generated from the prototypical structures of our emotional concepts, we see how these genres are ultimately based on prototypical emotional scenarios. For example, falling in love and reuniting with a lover lead to our happiness. Indeed, as Hogan's research suggests, this romance prototype triggers the strongest, most salient memory because of how it parallels our own personal experiences of realizing goals of happiness.

21. If the plot contained only events that realized happiness constantly—or

characters who were perennially euphoric—the narrative would be indistinguishable and boring. Any narrative that has anything interesting cannot simply be a series of events more or less causally related and tending toward an aim or goal.

22. In *The Mind and Its Stories* Patrick Hogan clarifies: "The prototypical narratives have a telic structure including an agent, a goal and a causal sequence connecting the agent's various actions with the achievement or non achievement of the goals" (205). He continues,

> The goal is anything an agent might strive to achieve. As we have already discussed, what an agent strives to achieve is happiness. This is trivially true. It is part of what we mean by "happiness." Even when a masochist strives for the experience of pain, he/she is striving for happiness. Thus, technically, an agent's goals are always imagined to be eliciting conditions for happiness, or means to the eliciting conditions for happiness (221).

23. Wesley Kort argues of space-dominant narratives generally: "Actions and events are more causally related to the conditions than to one another. Rather than having a significance of its own, the time of the narrative can easily become the time it takes for the conditions to expose themselves and to exert their effects or the time it takes for the characters and narrator to explore the environment" (17).

24. *Moby Dick* begins:

> Call me Ishmael. Some years ago—never mind how long precisely—having little or no money in my purse, and nothing particular to interest me on shore, I thought I would sail about a little and see the watery part of the world. It is a way I have of driving off the spleen, and regulating the circulation. Whenever I find myself growing grim about the mouth; whenever it is a damp, drizzly November in my soul; whenever I find myself involuntarily pausing before coffin warehouses, and bringing up the rear of every funeral I meet; and especially whenever my hypos get such an upper hand of me, that it requires a strong moral principle to prevent me from deliberately stepping into the street, and methodically knocking people's hats off—then, I account it high time to get to sea as soon as I can. This is my substitute for pistol and ball. With a philosophical flourish Cato throws himself upon his sword; I quietly take to the ship. (1)

25. In 1987 Maxine Hong Kingston declared in an article for *Mother Jones* magazine that the "next step" should not be to write the great American novel

but rather to write the global novel (Seshachari, n.p.). The novel has always been global; authors read authors from around the world. However, authors can choose to have a greater degree of globalness present in their novels. Namely, the global novel is not born with Kingston's declaration nor with Smith's or Kunzru's novels. The authors simply choose to participate, extend, and complicate a tradition of novel writing that circumnavigates global narrative aesthetics.

26. While there are culturally learned specific dimensions to humor (a joke in Mexico might not get the same laughs as in the United States) as stimuli of laughter, laughter itself is a universal human behavior found in all cultures the world over.

27. Gervais and Wilson cite the example of infants at prelanguage ages of two to six months who spontaneously laugh when they perceive unexpected stimuli in nonserious contexts (398). They argue that the first type of laughter and "its associated positive effect also enable infants to maintain interactions with novel, mildly stressful stimulation so that they can cultivate world knowledge and develop social competence" (403).

28. Gervais and Wilson discuss lab experiments on laughter that reveal how the supplementary motor area (SMA, Brodmann's Area 6 of the brain) has been implicated in all the "requisite aspects of laughter phenomena" (405) and result from activation of our mirror neuron system. The SMA is active during: "(i) laughter production; (ii) imagined or internal laughter; (iii) laughter perception, although to varying degrees; and (iv) humor appreciation" (ibid.).

29. We might speculate further here. With the shift to a more sophisticated hunter-gatherer society and then to one that practiced forms of crop cultivation, figures who were gifted at storytelling (shamanlike figures) were supported with food, shelter, and so on by the labor of the group. Indeed, as adaptationists argue, if selection favors those who experience positive emotions and play, then such nonlaboring figures would most likely be individuals who could tell a good story (manipulate time and space for audiences) and solicit emotions that would glue the group together. Arguably, they were the figures who were most skilled at ritualizing laughter in ways that abstracted and decontextualized the stimuli of social play (physical and/or emotional response to perceived incongruity). Adept at manipulating time (past, present, and future), they must have been skilled at triggering laughter, as Gervais and Wilson argue, "by a more generalized type of nonserious social incongruity" (414). They must have been more adept at abstracting aspects of everyday activities and potential sources of stress (accidents and bodily expulsions, for example) to make them seem funny. They were adept at transforming such potential daily stressors, stated in more technical terms, "to elicitors of social play and positive emotion" (414). Thus narrative and laughter go hand in hand.

30. Prince concludes the following in "On a Postcolonial Narratology":

As a theory (or science, or poetics) of narrative, (postcolonial) narratology differs from postcolonial narratological criticism. The first characterizes and articulates narratively pertinent categories and features in order to account for the ways in which narratives are configured and make sense; the second uses these categories and features in order to specify the configuration and sense of particular narratives. Of course, apart from constituting a tool kit for criticism and because it explores potentialities of narrative (post-colonial) narratology can not only permit the (re)assessment of indefinitely many texts; it can also, perhaps, function as a rhetoric and indicate hitherto unexploited narrative forms. (379)

31. While Djelal Kadir focuses her analysis on a series of other narratives, her identification of "narratives of worlding" (3) nicely describes Smith's and Kunzru's novels. In contrast to these two, the novels she describes participate in a "beneficent world literature (the cosmopolitan) [that] simply covers over and sanitizes a militarized violence and fragmentation of peoples that occurs every day" (5), such worldly narratives as *White Teeth* and *The Impressionist* reach out into and complicate understandings of the world.

CHAPTER FIVE

1. There have been other DC and Marvel Latino characters, including Marvel's Brazilian identified Roberto da Costa, the son of a CEO who was introduced as Sunspot in the *New Mutants Graphic Novel* (1982) by Chris Claremont and Bob McLeod. And Judd Winick reveals the father of the Green Lantern figure Kyle Rayner to be a Latino.

2. The creator of *El Diablo*, Gerard Jones, takes the opportunity to inform his readers that he grew up Anglo but was fascinated by Chicanos and Chicano culture; this allowed him, he argues, to bring a greater realism to his work. Ultimately, however, he states, "none of that matters [because] the whole Latino thing, is just background. We're all just doing *people* stories here, human dramas and comedies that are only incidentally about place and race" (issue 1, 40).

3. Jaime Hernandez's character Maggie is into superhero comics. In the first issue of *Locas in Love* she mentions how in pulling out a "Doomsday depression emergency kit (six pack) and my favorite stack of super hero comics, I came across an old Ultimax comic I really never looked at in detail (the art wasn't very good)" (51). In interviews Jaime and Gilbert Hernandez have said they often gorged themselves on the massive piles of comics passed down by their mother and older brother, Mario (Aldama, *Your Brain on Latino Comics*).

4. We know from everyday experiences that our individual and social

memories are tied intimately to our emotional systems. The emotion center (the amygdala) and the memory center (the hippocampus) sit adjacent to one another, and neuroscientific research has determined that the firing in the memory neural network occurs most dramatically when attached to a strong trace emotion. Indeed, we cannot talk about comic book genres—rules and form—without talking of memory and therefore also emotion.

5. The superhero can be stripped down to the following bare bones: an outsider to society, he uses his powers to ingratiate himself within society by defeating villainous interlopers. See also Richard Reynolds's *Super Heroes: A Modern Mythology*.

6. When we turn a comic book page—or any page of narrative fiction or any sequence from a movie for that matter—our brains are constantly telling us that this is not the real world. This must be a powerful product of our evolution. Already at a young age we know how to distinguish fiction from reality; it is because we know the difference that as children we can enjoy so much the make-believe worlds of narrative fiction.

WORKS CITED

Abbott, Porter H. "The Evolutionary Origins of the Storied Mind: Modeling the Prehistory of Narrative Consciousness and its Discontents." *Narrative* 8, no. 3 (October 2000): 247–256.

Abraham, Taisha. "An Interview with Arundhati Roy." *Ariel* 29, no. 1 (1998): 89–92.

Acosta, Oscar "Zeta." *The Autobiography of the Brown Buffalo.* New York: Vintage, 1989.

Afzal-Khan, Fawzia. *Cultural Imperialism and the Indo-English Novel.* University Park: Pennsylvania State University Press, 1993.

Agarwal, Ramlal. Review of *The God of Small Things. World Literature Today* 72, no. 1 (Winter 1998): 208–209.

Aguirre Beltrán, Gonzalo. *Regiones de refugio: El desarrollo de la comunidad y proceso dominical en mestizo América.* Mexico City: Instituto Indigenista Interamericano, 1967.

Ahmad, Aijaz. *In Theory: Literatures, Classes, Nations.* London: Verso, 1992.

———. "Reading Arundhati Roy Politically." *Frontline* 14, no. 15 (July 26–August 8, 1997): 103–108.

Aldama, Frederick Luis. *Brown on Brown: Chicana/o Representations of Gender, Sexuality, and Ethnicity.* Austin: University of Texas Press, 2005.

———. "Hari Kunzru in Conversation." *Wasafiri: The Transnational Journal of International Writing* 45 (July 2005): 11–14.

———. "An Interview with Amitav Ghosh." *World Literature Today* 76, no. 2 (Spring 2002): 84–90.

———. *Postethnic Narrative Criticism.* Austin: University of Texas Press, 2003.

———. "The Pound and the Fury." *Poets and Writers Magazine* 29, no. 5 (September–October 2001): 34–36.

———. *Spilling the Beans in Chicanolandia: Conversations with Writers and Artists.* Austin: University of Texas Press, 2006.

———. *Why the Humanities Matter: A Common Sense Approach.* Austin: University of Texas Press, 2008.

————. *Your Brain on Latino Comics: From Gus Arriola to Los Bros Hernandez.* Austin: University of Texas Press, 2009.

Alter, Robert. *Imagined Cities: Urban Experience and the Language of the Novel.* New Haven, CT: Yale University Press, 2005.

————. "Reading and Style in Dickens." *Philosophy and Literature* 20, no. 1 (1996): 130–137.

————. Review of Zadie Smith's *On Beauty. New Republic,* October 3, 2005, 29–32.

Alter, Stephen. "A Few Thoughts on Indian Fiction, 1947–1997." *Alif: Journal of Comparative Poetics* 18, no. 1 (1998): 14–28.

Anzaldúa, Gloria. *Borderlands/La Frontera: The New Mestiza.* San Francisco: Aunt Lute, 1987.

Appadurai, Arjun. *Modernity at Large: Cultural Dimensions of Globalization.* Minneapolis: University of Minnesota Press, 1996.

Apter, Emily. "Comparative Exile: Competing Margins in the History of Comparative Literature." In *Comparative Literature in the Age of Multiculturalism,* ed. Charles Bernheimer, 86–96. Baltimore: Johns Hopkins University Press, 1995.

Armstrong, Nancy. *Desire and Domestic Fiction.* New York: Oxford University Press, 1987.

Arteaga, Alfred. "Gun." In *House with the Blue Bed,* 57–58. San Jose, CA: Mercury House, 1997.

Ashcroft, Bill. *On Post-Colonial Futures: Writing Past Colonialism.* London: Continuum, 2001.

Austen, Chuck, Ron Garney, and Mark Morales. *The Uncanny X-Men: Holy War,* issue 423. New York: Marvel Comics, 2003.

Avery, Fiona Kai, and Mark Brooks. *Amazing Fantasy,* 2d series, issue 1. New York: Marvel Comics, 2004.

————. *Araña,* vol. 1: *The Heart of the Spider.* New York: Marvel Comics, 2005.

Axelrod, M. R. *The Politics of Style in the Fiction of Balzac, Beckett, and Cortázar.* New York: St. Martins Press, 1992.

Bal, Mieke. *Narratology: Introduction to the Theory of Narrative.* Trans. C. van Boheemen. London: University of Toronto Press, 1985.

Bartolovich, Crystal, and Neil Lazarus, eds. *Marxism, Modernity and Postcolonial Studies.* Cambridge, England: Cambridge University Press, 2002.

Bedford, James Gavin, director. *Street King.* Mistral Pictures, USA Home Entertainment, 2002.

Bendis, Brian, and Alex Maleev. *Daredevil: The Murdock Papers, Part 4,* vol. 2, issue 79. New York: Marvel Comics, 2005.

Beuka, Robert, and Gerald Kennedy. "Imperiled Communities in Edward P. Jones's *Lost in the City* and Dagoberto Gilb's *The Magic of Blood.*" *Yearbook of English Studies* (2001): 10–23.

Bhabha, Homi. "DissemiNation: Time, Narrative, and the Margins of the Modern State." In *Nation and Narration,* ed. Homi Bhabha, 291–322. New York: Routledge, 1990.

———. Introduction to *Nation and Narration,* ed. Bhabha.

———. *The Location of Culture.* New York: Routledge, 1994.

Bhatt, Indira, and Indira Nityanandam, eds. *Explorations: Arundhati Roy's* The God of Small Things. New Delhi: Creative Books, 1999.

Boehmer, Elleke. "East Is East and South Is South: The Cases of Sarojini Naidu and Arundhati Roy." *Women: A Cultural Review* 11, nos. 1–2, 2000: 61–70.

———. *Stories of Women: Gender and Narrative in the Postcolonial Nation.* Manchester, England: University of Manchester Press, 2005.

Bongco, Mila. *Reading Comics: Language, Culture, and the Concept of the Superhero in Comic Books.* New York: Garland Press, 2000.

Booth, Wayne. "Why Ethical Criticism Can Never Be Simple." In *Mapping the Ethical Turn: A Reader in Ethics, Culture, and Literary Theory,* ed. Todd F. Davis and Kenneth Womack, 16–28. Charlottesville: University Press of Virginia, 2001.

Borges, Jorge Luis. "Pascal's Sphere." In *Other Inquisitions: 1937–1952,* 6–9. Austin: University of Texas Press.

Brubaker, Ed, and Michael Lark. *Daredevil: A New Beginning,* 2d series, issue 82. New York: Marvel Comics, 2005.

Campos, Mark. *Moxie, My Sweet.* Seattle: FineComix, 2005.

Camus, Albert. *The Stranger.* New York: Knopf, 1988.

Cantú, Hector, and Carlos Castellanos. *The Lower You Ride, the Cooler You Are: A Baldo Collection.* Kansas City: Andrews McMeel, 2001.

———. *Night of the Bilingual Telemarketers.* Kansas City: Andrews McMeel, 2002.

Carrier, David. *The Aesthetics of Comics.* University Park: Pennsylvania State University Press, 2000.

Castillo, Ana. *Loverboys. Stories.* New York: Plume, 1997.

Chatman, Seymour. *Coming to Terms: The Rhetoric of Narrative in Fiction and Film.* Ithaca, NY: Cornell University Press, 1990.

———. *Story and Discourse: Narrative Structure in Fiction and Film.* Ithaca, NY: Cornell University Press, 1978.

Chatman, Seymour, and Willie van Peer. *New Perspectives on Narrative Perspective.* Albany: SUNY Press, 2001.

Chomsky, Noam. *Current Issues in Linguistic Theory.* The Hague: Mouton, 1964.

Cockrum, Dave, and Mary-Jo Duffy. *Power Man and Iron Fist,* issue 58. New York: Marvel Comics, 1979.

Coetzee, J. M. *Boyhood: Scenes from Provincial Life.* New York: Viking, 1997.

———. *Disgrace.* New York: Viking, 1999.

Cohn, Dorrit. *The Distinction of Fiction.* Baltimore: Johns Hopkins University Press, 1999.

————. "Narrated Monologue." Excerpted from *Transparent Minds: Narrative Modes for Presenting Consciousness in Fiction* (1978) in *Theory of the Novel: A Historical Approach*, ed. Michael McKeon, 493–514. Baltimore: Johns Hopkins University Press, 2000.

Compton, Timothy G. *Mexican Picaresque Narratives*. Lewisburg: Bucknell University Press, 1997.

Conway, Gerry, and Chuck Patton. *Justice League of America*, series 1, annual issue 2 (October) and issue 233 (December). New York: DC Comics, 1984.

Cortázar, Julio. *Blow-Up and Other Stories*. New York: Pantheon, 1985.

Craig, Amanda. "But What About This Year's Barbados Novel?" *New Statesman*, June 27, 1997, 49.

Damasio, Antonio. *Looking for Spinoza: Joy, Sorrow, and the Feeling Brain*. Orlando, FL: Harcourt, 2003.

Damasio, Antonio, and Hanna Damasio. "Minding the Body." *Daedalus*, Summer 2006, 14–22.

Damrosch, David. *What Is World Literature?*. Princeton, NJ: Princeton University Press, 2003.

Danielewski, Mark Z. *Mark Z. Danielewski's House of Leaves*. New York: Parthenon, 2000.

Derrida, Jacques. *Grammatology*. Baltimore: Johns Hopkins University Press, 1997.

Desai, Anita. *Baumgartner's Garden*. New York: Knopf, 1989.

————. *Fasting, Feasting*. London: Chato and Windus, 1999.

de Saussure, Ferdinand. *Course in General Linguistics*. New York: McGraw Hill, 1966.

Dharwadker, Vinay. "The Internationalization of Literatures." In *New National and Post-Colonial Literatures*, ed. Bruce King, 59–77. Oxford: Clarendon, 1996.

Dhawan, R. K., ed. *Arundhati Roy: The Novelist Extraordinary*. London: Sangram, 1998.

Díaz, Roberto Ignacio. *Unhomely Rooms: Foreign Tongues and Spanish American Literature*. London: Associated University Presses, 2002.

Dodiya, Jaydipsinh and Joya Chakravarty, eds. *The Critical Studies of Arundhati Roy's* The God of Small Things. New Delhi: Atlantic, 1999.

Dolezel, Lubomír. "Fictional and Historical Narrative: Meeting the Postmodernist Challenge." In *Narratologies: New Perspectives on Narrative Analysis*, ed. David Herman, 247–273. Columbus: Ohio State University Press, 1999.

Dominguez, Richard. *El Gato Negro*. Comic book series. Dallas: Azteca Productions, 1994.

————. *Team Tejas*. Comic book series. Dallas: Azteca Productions, 1997.

Durant, Sam. *Postcolonial Narrative and the Work of Mourning: J. M. Coetzee, Wilson Harris, and Toni Morrison*. Albany: SUNY Press, 2004.

Eakin, Emily. "What Is The Next Big Idea? The Buzz Is Growing" *New York Times*, July 7, 2001.

Easthope, Antony. *Privileging Difference*. New York: Palgrave, 2002.

Economist. "Rainbaby; New British fiction." April 6, 2002, 363.

Edel, Uli, director. *King of Texas*. Burbank: Warner Home Video, 2002.

Eggers, Dave. *Dave Eggers's A Heartbreaking Work of Staggering Genius*. New York: Simon and Schuster, 2000.

Ehland, Christopher. *Picaresque Perspectives—Exiled Identities*. Heidelberg: Winter, 2003.

Eisner, Will. *Comics and Sequential Art*. Tamarac, FL: Poorhouse Press, 1985.

Englehart, Steve, Joe Staton, and Ian Gibson. *Millennium: The Summoning,* issue 1. New York: DC Comics, 1988.

Espinosa, Frank. *Rocketo*, vol. 1: *The Journey to the Hidden Sea*. Berkeley, CA: Image Comics, 2006.

Fludernik, Monika. "Identity/Alterity." In *The Cambridge Companion to Narrative Theory,* ed. David Herman, 260–273. Cambridge, England: Cambridge University Press, 2007.

———. "Imagined Communities as Imaginary Homelands." In *Diaspora and Multiculturalism: Common Traditions and New Developments,* ed. Fludernik, 261–285. Amsterdam: Rodopi, 2003.

———. *Towards a 'Natural' Narratology*. New York: Routledge, 1996.

Foley, Daniel. Review of *The Republic of East L.A.* by Luis Rodriguez Jr. *Milwaukee Journal Sentinel,* April 7, 2002.

Foucault, Michel. *History of Sexuality,* vol. 1. Trans. Robert Hurley. New York: Random House, 1980.

Fraser, Robert. *Lifting the Sentence: A Poetics of Postcolonial Fiction*. Manchester: Manchester University Press, 2000.

Friedman, Susan Stanford. "Spatial Poetics and Arundhati Roy's *The God of Small Things.*" In *A Companion to Narrative Theory,* eds. James Phelan and Peter J. Rabinowitz, 192–205. Oxford, England: Blackwell, 2005.

Gallese, Vittorio, Christian Keysers, and Giacomo Rizzolatti. "A Unifying View of the Basis of Social Cognition." *Trends in Cognitive Science* 8, no. 9 (September 2004): 396–403.

Garcia, Cristina. "Inés in the Kitchen." In *Little Havana Blues: A Cuban-American Literature Anthology,* ed. Virgil Suarez, 152–157. Houston: Arte Público Press, 1996.

Garro, Elena. *Recollections of Things to Come*. Trans. Ruth L. C. Simms. Austin: University of Texas Press, 1969. Originally published in 1963 as *Los recuerdos del porvenir.* Mexico City: Joaquin Moritz.

Garza, Judge Margarito C. *Relampago,* issue 3: *America's First Mexican-American Super-Hero Battle "El Pájaro Grande."* Corpus Christi, TX: Mesloh, 1977.

Gates, Henry Louis Jr. *"Race," Writing, and Difference*. Chicago: University of Chicago Press, 1992.

Gaudiano, Andrea M. *Azteca: The Story of a Jaguar Warrior*. Denver: Denver Museum of Natural History, 1992.

Genette, Gérard. *Narrative Discourse. An Essay in Method.* Trans. Jane E. Lewin, foreword by Jonathan Culler. Ithaca, NY: Cornell University Press, 1980. Originally published in French in 1972.

———. "Order in Narrative." In *The Narrative Reader,* ed. Martin McQuillan, 91–95. London: Routledge, 2000.

———. *Palimpsests: Literature in the Second Degree.* Lincoln: University of Nebraska Press, 1997.

———. *Paratexts: Thresholds and Interpretation.* Cambridge, England: Cambridge University Press, 1997.

George, Rosemary Marangoly. *The Politics of Home: Postcolonial Relocations and Twentieth-Century Fiction.* Cambridge, England: Cambridge University Press, 1996.

Gerlach, John. *Toward the End: Closure and Structure in the American Short Story.* Tuscaloosa: University of Alabama Press, 1985.

Gervais, Matthew, and David Sloan Wilson. "The Evolution and Functions of Laughter and Humor: A Synthetic Approach." *Quarterly Review of Biology* 80, no. 4 (2005): 395–430.

Ghosh, Amitav. *The Calcutta Chromosome.* New York: Harper Perennial, 2001.

———. *The Glass Palace.* London: HarperCollins, 2000.

Ghosh, Bishnupriya. *When Borne Across: Literary Cosmopolitics in the Contemporary Indian Novel.* New Brunswick, NJ: Rutgers University Press, 2004.

Giffen, Keith, and John Rogers. *Blue Beetle,* issues 1, 5–6. New York: DC Comics, 2006.

Gilb, Dagoberto. *Gritos: Essays.* New York: Grove Press, 2003.

———. *The Magic of Blood.* New York: Grove Press, 1993.

———. *Woodcuts of Women.* New York: Grove Press, 2001.

Gomez, Cecilia M. "Overcoming the Past." Riverside, CA: *Press-Enterprise,* May 5, 2002, F10.

Grant, Alan, and Norm Breyfogle. *Batman,* vol. 1, issue 475. New York: DC Comics, 1992.

Gregory, Roberta. "California Girl." In *Road Trips: A Graphic Journey Across America,* ed. Pete Friedrich, 71–76. San Francisco: Chronicle Books, 2005.

———. *Life's a Bitch: The Complete Bitchy Bitch Stories,* vol. 1. Seattle: Fantagraphics Books, 2005.

Grzegorczyk, Marzena. *Private Topographies: Space, Subjectivity, and Political Change in Modern Latin America.* New York: Palgrave Macmillan, 2005.

Hallet, Cynthia Whitney. *Minimalism and the Short Story—Raymond Carver, Amy Hempel, and Mary Robison. Studies in Comparative Literature,* vol. 28. Lewiston, NY: Edwin Mellen Press, 1999.

Heath, Stephen. "The Politics of Genre." In *Debating World Literature,* ed. Christopher Pendergast, 163–174. New York: Verso, 2004.

Hernandez, Gilbert. *Birdland.* Seattle: Fantagraphics Books, 1992.

———. *Love and Rockets X,* vol. 10. Seattle: Fantagraphics Books, 1993.

———. *Luba: The Book of Ofelia*. Seattle: Fantagraphics Books, 2005.

———. *Palomar: The Heartbreak Soup Stories*. Seattle: Fantagraphics Books, 2003.

———. *Sloth*. New York: DC Vertigo Comics, 2006.

Hernandez, Gilbert, and Jaime Hernandez. *Love and Rockets,* 1st series, issue 1. Seattle: Fantagraphics, 1982.

Hernandez, Gilbert, Jaime Hernandez, and Mario Hernandez. *Love and Rockets, Book 15: Satyricon*. Seattle: Fantagraphics, 1997.

Hernandez, Jaime. *Locas in Love*. Fantagraphics Books, 2000.

———. *Locas: The Maggie and Hopey Stories*. Seattle: Fantagraphics Books, 2004.

———. "La Maggie La Loca." *New York Times Magazine,* April 23, 2006, 35.

Hernandez, Javier. *El Muerto: The Aztec Zombie,* issue 1. Whittier, CA: Los Comex, 2002.

Higashi, Chris. Review of *The Glass Palace*. *Library Journal* 126, no. 11 (June 15, 2001): 132.

Hitchcock, Peter. "The Genre of Postcoloniality." *New Literary History* 34, no. 2 (Spring 2003): 299–330.

Hodari, Askhari. "The Mystique of Zadie Smith." *Black Issues Book Review* 2, no. 5 (September–October 2000): 27.

Hogan, Patrick Colm. *Cognitive Science, Literature, and the Arts: A Guide for Humanities*. New York. Routledge, 2003.

———. *Empire and Poetic Voice: Cognitive and Cultural Studies of Literary Tradition and Colonialism*. Albany: SUNY Press, 2004.

———. *The Mind and Its Stories: Narrative Universals and Human Emotion*. New York: Cambridge University Press, 2003.

Huggan, Graham. *The Post-Colonial Exotic: Marketing the Margins*. London: Routledge, 2001.

Hulme, Keri. *The Bone People: A Novel*. New York: Penguin, 1986.

Jameson, Frederic. "Third-World Literature in the Era of Multinational Capitalism." *Social Text* 15 (Autumn 1986): 65–88.

Johns, Geoff, and Phil Jimenez. *Infinite Crisis,* issue 3. New York: DC Comics, 2006.

Johns, Geoff, Grant Morrison, Mark Waid, and Greg Rucka. *52.* New York: DC Comics, 2006–2007.

Jones, Gerard. *El Diablo,* issue 1. New York: DC Comics. 1989.

Kacandes, Irene. *Talk Fiction: Literature and the Talk Explosion*. Lincoln: University of Nebraska Press, 2001.

Kadir, Djelal. "To World, to Globalize—Comparative Literature's Crossroads." *Comparative Literature Studies* 41, no. 1 (2004): 1–9.

Kafalenos, Emma. *Narrative Causalities*. Columbus: Ohio State University Press, 2006.

Kakutani, Michiko. "Melodrama as Structure for Subtlety." *New York Times,* June 3, 1997.

Keen, Suzanne. *Empathy and the Novel*. New York: Oxford University Press, 2007.

———. *Narrative Form*. New York: Palgrave, 2003.

King, Bruce. "New Centers of Consciousness." In *New National and Post-colonial Literatures,* ed. Bruce King, 3–26. Oxford, England: Clarendon, 1996.

———. Review of *White Teeth*. *World Literature Today* 75, no. 1 (2001): 116–118.

Kirsch, Jonathan. "Westwords." *Los Angeles Times,* May 5, 2002.

Knight, Charles A. *The Literature of Satire*. Cambridge, England: Cambridge University Press, 2004.

Kort, Wesley A. *Place and Space in Modern Fiction*. Gainesville: University Press of Florida, 2004.

Krupat, Arnold. *The Voice in the Margin: Native American Literature and the Canon*. Berkeley: University of California Press, 1989.

Kumar, Akshaya. "Creative Dynamics: Prettifying the Small." In *The Fictional World of Arundhati Roy,* ed. R. S. Pathak, 60–69. New Delhi: Creative Books, 2001.

Kuper, Peter. *Sticks and Stones*. New York: Three Rivers Press, 2004.

———. *The System*. New York: Vertigo, 1997.

Kureishi, Hanif. *The Buddha of Suburbia*. New York: Viking, 1990.

———. *Intimacy*. London: Faber, 1998.

Kunzru, Hari. *The Impressionist*. New York: Dutton, 2002.

———. *Transmission*. New York: Dutton, 2004.

Larsen, Neil. "DetermiNation: Postcolonialism, Poststructuralism, and the Problem of Ideology." In *The Pre-Occupation of Postcolonial Studies,* ed. Fawzia Afzal-Khan and Kalpana Seshardi-Crooks, 140–156. Durham: Duke University Press, 2000.

———. *Nationalism and Cultural Practice in the Postcolonial World*. Cambridge, England: Cambridge University Press, 1999.

Leal, Luis. *A Luis Leal Reader*. Ed. Ilan Stavans. Evanston, IN: Northwestern University Press, 2007.

LeDoux, Joseph. *The Self: From Soul to Brain*. New York: New York Academy of Sciences, 2003.

Lindenberger, Herbert, Alban K. Forcione, and Madeline Sutherland, eds. *Leo Spitzer: Representative Essays*. Stanford: Stanford University Press, 1988.

Lobdell, Scott, and Joe Madureira. *The Uncanny X-Men: Phalanx Covenant,* issue 317. New York: Marvel Comics. 1994.

Lobdell, Scott, and Carlos Pacheco. *X-Men,* 2d series, issue 65. New York: Marvel Comics, 1997.

Lodge, David. *Consciousness and the Novel: Connected Essays*. Cambridge: Harvard University Press, 2002.

Longmore, Zenga. "Fairy-Sweary-Land." *Spectator,* January 29, 2000, 47.

Lunsford, Andrea A., and Lahoucine Ouzgane, eds. *Crossing Borderlands: Composition and Postcolonial Studies*. Pittsburgh, PA: University of Pittsburgh Press, 2004.

Mancing, Howard. "Prototypes of Genre in Cervantes's *Novelas ejemplares*." http://www.cognitivecircle.org/ct&lit/CogCircleResearch/CogCircle _research.html.

Mantlo, Bill, and Sal Buscema. *The Incredible Hulk*, vol. 2, issue 265. New York: Marvel Comics, 1981.

Mantlo, Bill, and George Perez. *The Deadly Hands of Kung-Fu*, issue 19. New York: Marvel Comics, 1975.

Manzanas, Ana María, and Jesús Benito. "Introduction: Trickster Mediations." In *Intercultural Mediations: Hybridity and Mimesis in American Literatures*, ed. Ana María Manzanas and Jesús Benito, 1–9. Munich: Lit Verlag, 2003.

Margolin, Uri. "Cognitive Science, the Thinking Mind, and Literary Narrative." In *Narrative Theory and the Cognitive Sciences*, ed. David Herman, 271–294. Stanford, CA: Center for the Study of Language Information (CSLI), 2003.

Mathias, Anita. "View from the Margins." *Commonweal* 127, no. 14 (August 11, 2000): 27–29.

McDuffy, Dwayne, and Denys Cowan. *Hardware*. New York: DC/Milestone, 1993–1997.

McGinn, Colin. *The Power of Movies: How Screen and Mind Interact*. New York: Pantheon, 2005.

McHale, Brian. *Postmodernist Fiction*. New York: Metheun, 1987.

McPherson, James Alan. *Elbow Room*. New York: Fawcet, 1986.

Mellmann, Katja. "E-Motion: Being Moved by Fiction and Media? Notes on Fictional Worlds, Virtual Contacts, and the Reality of Emotions." *Psyart: An Online Journal for the Psychological Study of the Arts* (2002), Article 020604. http://www.clas.ufl.edu/ipsa/journal/2002_mellmann01.shtml.

Melville, Herman. *Bartleby, the Scrivener: A Story of Wall-Street*. New York: Simon and Schuster, 1997.

———. *Moby Dick, or, The Whale*. New York: Modern Library, 2000.

Mignolo, Walter D. *Local Histories/Global Designs: Coloniality, Subaltern Knowledges, and Border Thinking*. Princeton, NJ: Princeton University Press, 2000.

Miles, Robert. "What is a Romantic Novel?" In *Novel: A Forum on Fiction* 34, no. 2 (Spring 2001): 180–201.

Miller, David. *On Nationality*. New York: Clarendon Press, 1995.

Milligan, Peter, and Mike Allred. *X-Force*, issue 117. New York: Marvel Comics, 2007.

Minhas, Nisha. *Sari and Sins*. London: Pocket Books, 2003.

Mishra, Pankaj. "There'll Always Be an England in India." *New York Times Book Review*, February 11, 2001, 7.

Molina, Laura. *Cihualyaomiquiz, the Jaguar.* Arcadia, CA: Insurgent Comics, 1996.

Montijo, Rhode. *Pablo's Inferno.* Oakland, CA: Abismo, 2004.

Moretti, Franco. *Atlas of the European Novel 1800–1900.* London: Verso, 1998.

Morey, Peter. *Fictions of India: Narrative and Power.* Edinburgh, Scotland: Edinburgh University Press, 2000.

Moss, Laura. "'The Plague of Normality': Reconfiguring Realism in Postcolonial Theory." *Jouvert: A Journal of Postcolonial Studies* 5, no. 1 (Autumn 2000): N.p. http://social.chass.ncsu.edu/Jouvert/v5i1/con51.htm.

Mukherjee, Meenakshi. *The Perishable Empire: Essays on Indian Writing in English.* New Delhi: Oxford University Press, 2000.

Mullaney, Julie. *The God of Small Things: A Reader's Guide.* New York: Continuum International, 2002.

Nagel, James. *The Contemporary American Short-Story Cycle: The Ethnic Resonance of Genre.* Baton Rouge: Louisiana State University Press, 2001.

Naipaul, V. S. *A House for Mr. Biswas.* New York: McGraw Hill, 1961.

Nasta, Susheila. *Home Truths: Fictions of the South Asian Diaspora in Britain.* New York: Palgrave, 2002.

Navarro, Rafael. *Sonambulo's Strange Tales.* La Habra, CA: Ninth Circle Studios, 1999.

Needham, Anuradha Dinwaney. *Using the Master's Tools: Resistance and the Literature of the African and South-Asian Diasporas.* New York: St. Martin's Press, 2000.

Neelakantan, Shailaja. Review of *The Impressionist. Far Eastern Economic Review* (Hong Kong), July 25, 2002, 52.

Nelson, Tim Blake, director. *O.* Trimark Home Video, Lions Gate Entertainment, 2001.

Okri, Ben. *Songs of Enchantment.* London: Jonathan Cape, 1993.

Palmer, Alan. *Fictional Minds.* Lincoln: University of Nebraska Press, 2004.

———. "Mind Beyond the Skin." In *Narrative Theory and the Cognitive Sciences,* ed. David Herman, 322–348. Stanford, CA: CSLI Publications, 2003.

Pathak, R. S., ed. *The Fictional World of Arundhati Roy.* New Delhi: Creative Books, 2001.

Pavel, Thomas. *Fictional Worlds.* Cambridge: Harvard University Press, 1986.

Pérez-Torres, Rafael. *Mestizaje: Critical Uses of Race in Chicano Culture.* Minneapolis: University of Minnesota Press, 2006.

Perry, Michael, and Lee Ballard. *Daniel's Ride.* San Francisco: Free Will Press, 2001.

Phelan, James. *Experiencing Fiction: Judgments, Progressions, and the Rhetorical Theory of Narrative.* Columbus: Ohio State University, 2007.

Pierce, Tamora, and Timothy Liebe. *White Tiger,* issue 1. New York: Marvel Comics, 2007.

Pihlainen, Kale. "The Moral of the Historical Story: Textual Differences in Fact and Fiction." *New Literary History* 33 (Winter 2002): 39–60.

Pratt, Mary Louise. "The Short Story: The Long and Short of It." *Poetics* 10, nos. 2–3 (1981): 175–195.

Prince, Gerald. "Introduction to the Study of the Narratee." In *From Modernism to Postmodernism: An Anthology,* ed. Lawrence Cahoone, 99–103. Oxford, England: Blackwell, 2003.

———. "On a Postcolonial Narratology." In *A Companion to Narrative Theory,* ed. James Phelan and Peter J. Rabinowitz, 372–381. Oxford, England: Blackwell, 2005.

Proctor, James. "New Ethnicities, the Novel, and the Burdens of Representation." In *A Concise Companion to Contemporary British Fiction,* ed. James F. English, 101–120. Oxford, England: Blackwell, 2006.

Quesada, Joe, Danny Miki, and Richard Isanove. *Daredevil: Father.* Collection of issues 1–16. New York: Marvel Comics, 2007.

Radhakrishnan, R. "Postmodernism and the Rest of the World." In *The Pre-Occupation of Postcolonial Studies,* ed. Fawzia Afzal-Khan and Kalpann Seshadri-Crooks, 37–70. Durham, NC: Duke University Press, 2000.

Ramachandran, Vilayanur S. "The Artful Brain." BBC Reith Lecture Series, 2003: *The Emerging Mind.* At http://www.bbc.co.uk/print/radio4/reith2003/lecture3.shtml?print.

Ray, M. K. "*The God of Small Things:* A Feminist Study." In *The Fictional World of Arundhati Roy,* ed. Pathak, 95–107.

Rechy, John. *The Miraculous Day of Amalia Gómez.* New York: Arcade, 1991.

Reynolds, Richard. *Super Heroes: A Modern Mythology.* Jackson: University Press of Mississippi, 1994.

Richardson, Brian. "Singular Text, Multiple Implied Readers." *Style* 41, no. 3 (Fall 2007): 259–274.

———. *Unnatural Voices: Extreme Narration in Modern and Contemporary Fiction.* Columbus: Ohio State University Press, 2006.

Rios, Isabella. *Victuum,* Ventura, CA: Diana-Etna, 1976.

Robbins, Trina. *From Girls to Grrlz: A History of Women's Comics from Teens to Zines.* San Francisco: Chronicle Books, 1999.

———. *The Great Women Super Heroes.* Northampton, MA: Kitchen Sink, 1996.

Rodriguez, Abraham Jr. *The Boy Without a Flag: Tales of the South Bronx.* Minneapolis: Milkweed Editions, 1992.

Rodriguez, Fernando B. *Aztec of the City: Enter La Llorona,* issue 2. San Jose, CA: El Salto Comics, 1996.

Rodriguez, Luis. *The Republic of East L.A.: Stories.* New York: Rayo/Harper Perennial, 2003.

Romanow, Rebecca Fine. *The Postcolonial Body in Queer Space and Time.* Newcastle-Upon-Tyne, England: Cambridge Scholars, 2006.

Roy, Arundhati. *The End of Imagination.* Kottayam, India: D. C. Books, 1998.

———. *The God of Small Things.* New York: Random House, 1997.

————. *An Ordinary Person's Guide to Empire*. Cambridge: South End Press, 2004.

————. *Power Politics*. Cambridge: South End Press, 2001.

————. *War Talk*. Cambridge: South End Press, 2003.

Rozum, John, and Robert Quijano. *Kobalt,* issues 1–16. New York: DC/Milestone, 1993–1995.

Rucka, Greg, and Michael Lark. *Gotham Central,* issue 6. New York: DC Comics, 2003.

Rushdie, Salman. *Imaginary Homelands: Essays and Criticism 1981–1991*. London: Granta, 1991.

————. *Midnight's Children*. London: Jonathan Cape, 1981.

————. *The Satanic Verses*. New York: Vintage, 1989.

————. *Step Across This Line: Collected Nonfiction 1992–2002*. New York: Random House, 2002.

Rutman, Paul. "The Indians Are Coming." (London) *Electronic Telegraph,* January 4, 1997, 585.

Sáez, Barbara J. Review of *The Magic of Blood* by Dagoberto Gilb. MELUS 22, no. 1 (1997): 159–163.

Said, Edward. *Orientalism*. New York: Vintage, 1979.

Saldaña, Carlos. *Burrito: Jack-of-All-Trades,* issue 1. Glendale, CA: Accent! Comics, 1995.

Santiago, Wilfred. *In My Darkest Hour: A Graphic Novel*. Seattle: Fantagraphics, 2004.

Seshachari, Neila C. "Reinventing Peace: Conversations with Tripmaster Maxine Hong Kingston." *Weber Studies* 12, no. 1 (Winter 1995): N.p. http:// weberstudies.weber.edu/archive/archive%20B%20Vol.%2011-16.1/Vol.% 2012.1/12.1KingstonInterview.htm.

Seyhan, Azade. *Writing Outside the Nation*. Princeton, NJ: Princeton University Press, 2001.

Shamsie, Kamila. *salt and saffron*. New York: Bloomsbury, 2000.

Shklovsky, Victor. *Theory of Prose*. Elmwood Park, IL: Dalkey Archive Press, 1990.

Simonson, Louise, and Walt Simonson. *X-Factor: Die, Mutant, Die,* 1st series, issue 17. New York: Marvel Comics, 1987.

Singh, Anita. "Margin at the Center: Reading of *The God of Small Things*." In *The Fictional World of Arundhati Roy,* ed. Pathak, 132–136.

Sinha, Yogesh, and Sandhya Tripathi. "A Postmodernist Reading." In *The Fictional World of Arundhati Roy,* ed. Pathak, 151–157.

Smith, Zadie. *White Teeth*. London: Hamish Hamilton, 2000; London: Penguin, 2001; New York: Vintage, 2001.

Sodhi, Meena. "*The God of Small Things:* Memory and Art." In *The Fictional World of Arundhati Roy,* ed. Pathak, 39–50.

Sommer, Doris. *Foundational Fictions: The National Romances of Latin America*. Berkeley: University of California Press, 1991.

———. "Irresistible Romance: The Foundational Fictions of Latin America." *Nation and Narration,* ed. Homi Bhabha, 71–98. New York: Routledge, 1990.

Spivak, Gayatri. "Can the Subaltern Speak?" In *Marxism and the Interpretation of Culture,* ed. Cary Nelson and Lawrence Grossberg, 271–313. Champaign: University of Illinois Press, 1988.

Spolsky, Ellen. "Narrative as Nourishment." In *Toward a Cognitive Theory of Narrative Acts,* ed. Frederick Luis Aldama. Austin: University of Texas Press, forthcoming.

Squires, Claire. *Zadie Smith's White Teeth: A Reader's Guide.* New York: Continuum International, 2002.

Stein, Mark. *Black British Literature: Novels of Transformation.* Columbus: Ohio State University Press, 2004.

Swami, Praveen. "'A Tiger Woodsian Debut': Arundhati Roy's Novel Goes International." *Frontline* 14, no. 15 (July 26–August 8, 1997): 100–102.

Syal, Meera. *Anita and Me.* New Delhi: Indus, 1996.

Tate, Greg. "Fear of a Mongrel Planet." *Village Voice,* May 16, 2000, 75.

Thomas, Dann, Roy Thomas, and Paul Ryan. *West Coast Avengers: The Original Human Torch vs. the Living Lightning,* issue 63. New York: Marvel Comics, 1990.

Timm, Bruce, and Eric Radomsk. *Batman: The Animated Series.* Los Angeles: Warner Brothers, 1992.

Todorov, Tzvetan. "Reading as Construction." In *Essentials of the Theory of Fiction,* ed. Michael J. Hoffman and Patrick D. Murphy, 258–272. 2d edition. London: Leicester University Press, 1996.

Treuer, David. *Native American Fiction: A User's Manual.* St. Paul, MN: Graywolf Press, 2006.

Trillo, Carlos, and Eduardo Risso. *Chicanos,* issue 6. San Diego: IDW Publishing, 2006.

———. *Chicanos,* vol. 1. San Diego: IDW Publishing, 2007.

Truax, Alice. "A Silver Thimble in Her Fist." *New York Times Book Review,* May 25, 1997, 5.

Updike, John. "Mother Tongues: Subduing the Language of the Colonizer." *New Yorker,* June 23–30, 1997, 156–159.

Velez, Ivan Jr. *Tales of the Closet: Volume 1,* New York: Planet Bronx Productions, 2005.

Velez, Ivan Jr., and CrissCross. *Blood Syndicate.* New York: DC/Milestone, 1993–1996.

Walsh, Bryan. "The Smooth Surface." *Time International,* June 24, 2002, 72.

Walsh, Richard. "Dreaming and Narrative Theory." In *Toward a Cognitive Theory of Narrative Acts,* ed. Frederick Luis Aldama. Austin: University of Texas Press, forthcoming.

———. "Fictionality and Mimesis: Between Narrativity and Fictional Worlds." *Narrative* 11, no. 1 (2003): 110–121.

————. "The Narrative Imagination Across Media." *Modern Fiction Studies* 52, no. 4 (2006): 855–868.

White, Hayden. *Metahistory: The Historical Imagination in Nineteenth-Century Europe.* Baltimore: Johns Hopkins University Press, 1974.

Williams, Patrick. "Post-Colonialism and Narrative." In *Routledge Encyclopedia of Narratology,* ed. David Herman, Manfred Jahn, and Marie Laure-Ryan, 451–456. New York: Routledge, 2007.

Winterson, Jeanette. *Written on the Body.* London: Jonathan Cape, 1992.

Wood, James. *The Irresponsible Self: On Laughter and the Novel.* New York: Picador, 2004.

Wortham, Frederic. *Seduction of the Innocent.* New York: Rinehart, 1953.

Wright, Bradford W. *Comic Book Nation: The Transformation of Youth Culture in America.* Baltimore: Johns Hopkins University Press, 2001.

Young, Robert. *White Mythologies: Writing History and the West.* London: Routledge, 1990.

Zunshine, Lisa. *Why We Read Fiction.* Columbus: Ohio State University Press, 2006.

INDEX

Eisner, Will, 121
"Elbow Room" (McPherson), 37
El Dorado (TV superhero), 107
Electric Moon, 53
Electronic Telegraph, 54
Eliot, George, 12, 35
Eliot, T. S., 10
El Salto Comics, 116–117
emotions: and emotive and narrative
    prototypes, 44–45, 97–98, 164n20;
    and empathy, 11, 17, 42–43, 47, 95,
    104, 128–130; intensity of, 126–127;
    and Kunzru's *Impressionist*, 96–98,
    103–105; and Latino comic books,
    126–128; and memory, 167–168n4;
    and mind-reading faculty, 161n10;
    and mirror neuron system, 17; and
    narrative techniques, 10–11, 17;
    neuroscience on, 16–17, 126–127;
    and postcolonial and Latino border-
    land fiction generally, 10–11, 40–42;
    as second-order narrative tool,
    40–42; and sentimentality, 43; and
    Smith's *White Teeth*, 96–98, 103–105,
    162n15. *See also* laughter
emotive and narrative prototypes,
    44–45, 97–98, 123–124, 164n20
empathy, 11, 17, 42–43, 47, 95, 104,
    128–130. *See also* emotions
Empathy and the Novel (Keen), 42–43
Empire and Poetic Voice (Hogan), 51
End of Imagination, The (Roy), 52
Englehart, Steve, 108–109
English language. *See* language
enstrangement, 35–38
Enter La Llorona, 117
Erdrich, Louise, 39
Espinosa, Frank, 14, 128, 132, 133
Estampas del Valle (Hinojosa), 135
ethics and morals, 45–47, 152–153
Experiencing Fiction (Phelan), 45–46
Explorations: Arundhati Roy's The

God of Small Things (Bhatt and
    Nityanandam), 55
exposing the device, 37

fabulism, 86
family: in Ghosh's fiction, 66, 67,
    81–82, 84, 158n12; in Latino border-
    land short stories, 152–153; postcolo-
    nial rhetoric of home, 156–157nn5–6
fantastical storytelling mode, 34
fantastic-noir style, 124
Fante, John, 139
Fasting, Feasting (Desai), 28
Faulkner, William, 12, 51, 54, 59
feminist criticism, 56–58
fiction: conventions of the novel, 157n8;
    global novels, 105–106, 165–166n25;
    history versus, 2, 13, 67–68, 76–81,
    157–158nn9–11; and human aspira-
    tion for freedom, 157n8; Latino
    borderland short story writing
    generally, 135–137; limitless capacity
    of novels, 106; social or political
    impact of, 46–47, 65, 68–76, 84–85;
    stages in composition of, 161n9. *See
    also* postcolonial and Latino border-
    land fiction; world literature; *and
    specific authors and titles of their works*
fictional poiesis, 78
Fictional World of Arundhati Roy, The
    (Pathak), 55
Fictions of India (Morey), 155n1
Fielding, Joseph, 94, 162n12
films, 24, 53
filter and slant, 34
Finnegan's Wake (Joyce), 44, 92
first-order narrative tools. *See* narrative
    tools
Fitzgerald, F. Scott, 59
flashback and flashforward, 25–26, 148
Flaubert, Gustave, 39
Fleming, Ian, 140

preface material in, 79; peritext of, 79; realist storytelling mode of, 82; romance plot of, 80–85. *See also* Ghosh, Amitav

Glissant, Edouard, 30

godlike metaphors, 156n4

God of Small Things, The (Roy): academic scholarship on, 55–57; autobiographical elements in, 59; Boehmer on, 50, 55, 56; Booker Prize for, 52, 54; characters in, 63; commercial success of, 13, 54–55; feminist and postcolonial readings of, 56–58; focus of study of, 2, 13; Friedman on spatial poetics of, 50; hypercontext of, 52–57; literary influences on, 59; mainstream media critics on, 54–55; multiperson character slant in, 60–64; mystery/suspense plot of, 60, 64; narrative techniques of, 57–65; postmodern approach of, 57; publishing advances for, 52; realism of, 58–59, 65; romance plot of, 59–60, 64; sales of, 54; significance of, as catalyst for other writers, 64–65; temporal planes of, 60; and theory of the mind, 43–44; translations of, 52; "we narrator" versus third-person narrator in, 13, 60–64; writing of, 53–54. *See also* Roy, Arundhati

Goethe, Johann Wolfgang von, 128

Gomez, Cecilia, 142

Gonzalez, Alberto, 9

Gotham Central, 112

Goytisolo, Juan, 1

Grass, Günther, 139

Green Lantern character, 167n1

Gregory, Roberta, 117

Grito, El, 135

"Gun" (Arteaga), 40

Hamilton, Hamish, 22

Hamner, Cully, 112

Hardware, 114

Hardy, Thomas, 59

HarperCollins India, 54

Heartbreaking Work of Staggering Genius, A (Eggers), 22

Heart of Darkness (Conrad), 35, 51, 94, 163–164n17

Hemingway, Ernest, 138, 142–143

Herbert, Patricia, 79

Hernandez, Gilbert, 117–120, 122–125, 130–131, 167n3

Hernandez, Jaime, 117–120, 132–133, 167n3

Hernandez, Javier, 126

Hernandez, Mario, 119, 120, 167n3

heroic tragicomedy, 97, 124–126

Higashi, Chris, 76

Hinojosa, Rolando, 135, 136

historical noeisis, 78

History of Sexuality (Foucault), 71

history versus fiction, 2, 13, 67–68, 76–81, 157–158nn9–11

Hitchcock, Peter, 49, 159n1

Hodari, Askhari, 162n15

Hogan, Patrick Colm, 11, 44–45, 51, 97–98, 123, 124, 126–127, 161n9, 164n20, 165n22

Homer, 18

House for Mr. Biswas, The (Naipaul), 69

House of Leaves (Danielewski), 22

House on Mango Street (Cisneros), 136

Hulme, Keri, 42–43

humor, 87, 103–105, 162n15, 166nn26–29

hypercontext: of Gilb's *Magic of Blood*, 143; of Rodriguez's *Republic of East L.A.*, 142; of Roy's *God of Small Things*, 52–57

idealism, 72–73

ideal readers: definition of, 27–28; of Kunzru's *Impressionist*, 92, 93–96; of Latino borderland short stories,

Joyce, James, 32, 35, 44, 54, 92, 106, 162n12

Justice League of America, 108

Kacandes, Irene, 164n19
Kadir, Djelal, 167n31
Kapur, Manju, 64
Kapur, Sekar, 53
kathakali (Kerala storytelling tradition), 51, 59
Keen, Suzanne, 42–43
Kennedy, Gerald, 143
Keysers, Christian, 17
Kiely, Robert, 83
Kim (Kipling), 95, 102
Kincaid, Jamaica, 59
King, Bruce, 162n15
King Lear (Shakespeare), 97
King of Texas, 24
Kingston, Maxine Hong, 165–166n25
Kipling, Rudyard, 95, 102
Kirsch, Jonathan, 142
Knight, Charles, 90
Kobalt, 114
Kort, Wesley, 165n23
Krishen, Pradeep, 24, 53
Krupat, Arnold, 20
Kumar, Akshaya, 57
Kunzru, Hari: narrative approaches and techniques of generally, 14; and theory of the mind, 44; *Transmission* by, 46; and will to style, 96, 102. *See also Impressionist, The* (Kunzru)
Kuper, Peter, 131
Kureishi, Hanif, 1, 4, 5, 10, 43

language: bilingual word play, 38; Dolezel on, 77; English language used by authors of postcolonial and Latino borderland fiction, 10, 13, 86, 136; identity politics of, 86; in Latino comic books, 115, 116; Spanglish in mainstream comic books,
110, 113; Spanish language and Latino authors, 136. *See also* code switching
Lark, Michael, 113
Larsen, Neil, 6, 157n7
Latin America, 158–159n14
Latin American Boom authors, 159n1
Latino borderland fiction. *See* postcolonial and Latino borderland fiction; *and specific authors and titles of their works*
Latino comic books: "alternative" comic book storytelling mode in, 117–120; by Azteca Productions, 116; cognitive science on, 121–122; diversity among, 134; by El Salto Comics, 116–117; emotional responses to, 126–128; gay and lesbian characters in, 115, 116, 118; ideal readers of, 134; innovation in, 124; by Insurgent Comics, 117; language in, 115, 116; by Milestone publishing house, 114–116; and mind-reading faculty, 128–134; mood of, 127; narrative elements of, 120–124, 134; and narrative prototypes, 123–124; racial scripts in, 130; superheroes in, 113–117, 126; and theory of mind, 122, 131; and universals, 122–124, 129, 134; visual elements of, 121–122, 126–127, 131–133; visual/verbal double narrators of, 13, 34, 131–134. *See also* comic books; *and specific author-artists and titles of their comic books*
Latinos, mainstreaming of, 9–10, 136
laughter, 87, 103–105, 166nn26–29
Lazarillo de Tormes, 162n12
Leal, Luis, 20
LeDoux, Joseph, 17
Lindenberger, Herbert, 31–32
literacy, 159n14
Llorona, La, 117, 127

Mora, Pat, 135–136
Moraga, Cherríe, 135–136
morals. *See* ethics and morals
Moretti, Franco, 83–84
Morey, Peter, 155n1
Morrison, Toni, 162n15
Moss, Laura, 49–50
Mother Jones, 165–166n25
movies. *See* films
Ms. Marvel, 111
Mukherjee, Meenakshi, 155n2
Mullaney, Julie, 59
multiple implied or ideal readers, 28–29
music, 16
"My Ride, My Revolution" (L. Rodriguez), 144–145, 152

Nabokov, Vladimir, 94, 106
Nagel, James, 137
Naidu, Sarojini, 56
Naipaul, V. S., 69
"Nancy Flores" (Gilb), 147
narrated monologue, 31–32, 60–64
narratee, 27–28, 34–35
narration as nation, 68–76, 84–85, 155n2
"Narrative Imagination Across Media, The" (Walsh), 23
narrative prototypes. *See* prototype narratives
narrative tools: cognition and emotion, 40–42; duration, 24; and emotions, 10–11, 17, 40–42; emotive and narrative prototypes, 44–45, 97–98, 164n20; empathy, 42–43, 47, 95, 104, 128–130; enstrangement, 35–37; ethics and morals, 45–47, 152–153; exposing the device, 37; filter and slant, 34; first-order narrative tools, 21–40; flashback and flashforward, 25–26; genre, 39–40, 49;

ideal reader, 27–28; implied author, 26–27; intermental minds, 32–33; of Latino comic books, 120–124, 134; mode, 25; multiple implied or ideal readers, 28–29; narrated monologue, 31–32, 60–64; narratee, 34–35; palimpsest, 35; partial suspension of disbelief, 40; peritext, 21–23; plural narrator, 30–31; puzzle solving, 36–38; second-order narrative tools, 47; story and discourse, 23–24; style, 38–39; theory of mind, 43–44, 104, 122, 131. *See also* narrators; prototype narratives; *and specific authors and titles of their works*
narratology, 14, 16, 20–21. *See also* narrative tools
narrators: character-as-narrator, 29–30, 144, 152; of Ghosh's *Glass Palace*, 77–80; of Gilb's short stories, 143–144, 146–147, 149–150, 152; of historical narrative, 77–78; of Kunzru's *Impressionist*, 87, 89, 90, 94; of Latino comic books, 13, 34, 131–134; narrated monologue, 31–32, 60–64; participant-narrator, 164n19; plural narrator ("we narrator"), 13, 30–31, 60–64, 144–145; of Rodriguez's short stories, 143–146, 148, 150–152; of Smith's *White Teeth*, 88, 89, 90, 95–96, 99; types of, 29–30
Nash, Thomas, 94
nation: Bhabha on, 71–72, 74–76; definition of, 73–74; and democracy, 53, 74–75; narration as, 68–76, 84–85, 155n2; power structure of nation-state, 67; and romance genre, 83–84; and working class, 74–76. *See also* capitalism; *and specific countries*
Nation and Narration (Bhabha), 72
Native American Fiction (Treuer), 7, 39
Native American literature, 7, 20

naturalism, 86
Navarro, Rafael, 124
Neelakantan, Shailaja, 163n15
Nelson, Tim Blake, 24
neurobiology, 16–17, 37, 47, 103–104,
    166nn27–29, 167–168n4. *See also*
    cognitive science
"New Ethnicities, the Novel, and the
    Burden of Representation" (Proc-
    tor), 160–161n7
New Mutants Graphic Novel, 167n1
New Statesman, 54
New Yorker, The, 54
New York Times Book Review, 54
New York Times Magazine, 132–133
Nikaya, Amyutta, 79
Nikaya, Majjhima, 79
Nityanandam, Indira, 55
noir, 124
"Notes on Writing and the Nation"
    (Rushdie), 84
novels. *See* fiction; postcolonial and
    Latino borderland fiction; world
    literature; *and specific authors and titles
    of their works*

"O", 24
Oates, Joyce Carol, 138
Okri, Ben, 30–31
Olivas, Daniel, 10
"On a Postcolonial Narratology"
    (Prince), 11, 105, 166–167n30
On Beauty (Smith), 93
Ondaatje, Michael, 38
One More Lady's Man, 119
On Nationality (Miller), 74
Ordinary Person's Guide to Empire, An
    (Roy), 52
Orientalism (Said), 72
orientalism and neo-Orientalism,
    55–57, 72
Orlando (Woolf), 106

Oropeza, Anthony, 126
Othello (film), 24
Otherness, 5, 6, 8
outsiderness, 89–91, 96, 160–161nn5–8
Ouzgane, Lahoucine, 5

Pablo's Inferno, 123–124, 126
Palestinians, 75
palimpsest, 35
Palinuro de Mexico (del Paso), 106
Palmer, Alan, 32, 33
Palomar, 118, 122–125, 130–131
Parker, Oliver, 24
partial suspension of disbelief, 40
particulars of postcolonial and Latino
    borderland fiction, 2–3, 10–13,
    19–20, 91–93
Pascal, Blaise, 156n4
"Pascal's Sphere" (Borges), 156n4
Passage to India, A (Forster), 35, 95
Pathak, R. S., 55
Patton, Chuck, 108
Pekar, Harvey, 117
Perez, George, 107
Pérez-Torres, Rafael, 5, 20
Perishable Empire, The (Mukherjee),
    155n2
peritext: definition of, 21; examples of,
    21–23; of Ghosh's *Glass Palace*, 79; of
    Gilb's *Magic of Blood*, 142–143; and
    ideal readers, 143; purposes of, 143;
    of Rodriguez's *Republic of East L.A.*,
    140–142
Perry, Michael, 131
Phelan, James, 45–46
phonetics, 16, 17, 21. *See also* narrative
    tools
picaresque, 92–95, 161n11, 162n13
Picaresque Perspectives—Exiled Identities
    (Ehland), 162n13
Pierce, Tamora, 112
Pihlainen, Kale, 78

racism, 10–11, 26, 136
Radhakrishnan, R., 155n2, 156–157n6
radical hybridity, 69, 70, 71, 74–76
Rain of Scorpions and Other Writings
(Trambley), 135
Ramachandran, Vilanayur S., 37
Ramayana, 59, 60
Rao, Raja, 5, 30
Ray, M. K., 56
readers *See* ideal readers
Reagan, Ronald, 136
realism: European/English Realistic novel, 159n1; of Ghosh's *Glass Palace*, 82; of Kunzru's *Impressionist*, 87; postcolonial theories of literature on, 49–50, 86, 158n13; of Roy's *God of Small Things*, 58–59, 65
Rechy, John, 4, 34, 35
Recollections of Things to Come (Garro), 31, 38, 43
Reed, Ishmael, 162n12
Regiones de refugio (Aguirre Beltrán), 18
Relampago, 113–114
Renegade or Halo 2 (Mo), 106
Republic of East L.A., The (L. Rodriguez), 20, 138–142, 150–151
Reynolds, Richard, 168n5
Richardson, Brian, 28, 30, 31, 60–61
Rios, Isabella, 38, 44
Risso, Eduardo, 129, 130
Riverside, Calif., *Press-Enterprise*, 142
Rizzolatti, Giacomo, 17
Robinson Crusoe (Defoe), 49
Rocketo, 127, 128–129, 132, 133
Roderick Random (Smollett), 106
Rodriguez, Abraham, Jr., 38–39
Rodriguez, Fernando B., 116–117, 126, 127
Rodriguez, Jose, 9
Rodriguez, Luis: allegorical reading of "Shadows" by, 148; biographical information on, 138–139; and code switching, 15; English language

used by, 10, 13; ethics and morals in short stories by, 152–153; family in short stories by, 152–153; flashback and flashforward used by, 148; and frames for readers, 140–142; and gap-filling process, 139, 146, 147; ideal readers of, 137, 141–142, 145–148; implied authors of, 137, 145, 147; literary influences on, 139; narrative approaches and techniques of generally, 14, 137–138, 153–154; narrative voice and point of view used by, 138, 143–146, 148, 150–152; and peritexts of *The Republic of East L.A.*, 140–141; readers' reactions to narrative techniques of, 12; reviews of short stories by, 142; and sense of place, 140–141, 149, 150–151; short fiction of, 3, 13, 20, 45, 137–154; and temporal order, 147–148; themes of, 137, 142, 153–154; and will to style, 138–140
Rogers, John, 112
romance genre: and Austen, 83–84; and Ghosh's *Glass Palace*, 80–85; in Latin America, 158–159n14; postcolonial theorists on, 158n13; and Roy's *God of Small Things*, 59–60, 64; Sommer on, 158–159n14
Romanow, Rebecca Fine, 5
romantic tragicomedy, 97, 122–125
Roy, Arundhati: academics and mainstream critics on, 5–9; acting and screenplay writing by, 53; biographical information on, 53, 59; English language used by, 10; narrative approaches and techniques of, 12, 14, 15, 57–65; political essays by, 52–53, 58, 65; readers' reactions to, 12; and will to style, 65. *See also God of Small Things, The*
Rozum, John, 114
Rulfo, Juan, 162n12

Rushdie, Salman: academics and mainstream critics on, 5, 55; Aldama's reading of, 1; compared with Smith's *White Teeth*, 94, 162–163n15; English language used by, 10; on imaginary homelands, 66; *Midnight's Children* by, 28–29, 54; *The Satanic Verses* by, 69; on Smith's *White Teeth*, 22; on social or political impact of fiction, 65, 84; *Step Across This Line* by, 65, 84

Russian Formalists, 36

Rutman, Paul, 54

Ryan, Paul, 109–110

sacrificial tragicomedy, 97, 124, 126

Sáez, Barbara J., 143

Said, Edward, 55, 72

Saldaña, Carlos, 126

salt and saffron (Shamsie), 25, 45

Santiago, Wilfred, 25–26, 117–120, 125–126, 133–134

Sari and Sins (Minhas), 28

Satanic Verses, The (Rushdie), 69

satire, 90–92

Satyricon, 120

second-order narrative tools. *See* narrative tools

self-fiction, 20

self-reflexive device, 120

semantics, 16, 17, 20–21. *See also* narrative tools

sentimentality, 43

Seyhan, Azade, 5, 68, 69, 77

Shadow Lines (Ghosh), 155

"Shadows" (Rodriguez), 148

Shakespeare, William, 23–24, 97

Shamsie, Kamila, 25, 45

Shklovsky, Victor, 36, 42

short stories. *See* fiction; postcolonial and Latino borderland fiction; *and specific authors and titles of their works*

"Shout" (Gilb), 152

sign (signifier and signified), 69–70, 72

Silver Cloud Café (Véa), 37–38

Singh, Anita, 56–57

"Singular Text, Multiple Implied Readers" (Richardson), 28

Sinha, Yogesh, 57

slant and filter, 34

Smith, Zadie: narrative approaches and techniques of generally, 14; *On Beauty* by, 93; photographs of, on book jackets, 22–23, 26; and will to style, 96, 102. *See also White Teeth*

Smollett, Tobias, 106

Sodhi, Meena, 59

Somalia, 74

Sommer, Doris, 83, 158–159n14

Sonambulo's Strange Tales, 124

Songs of Enchantment (Okri), 30–31

Sorrows of Young Werther (Goethe), 128

Spider-Man, 110, 111

Spiegelman, Art, 117

Spilling the Beans in Chicanolandia (Aldama), 138–139

Spitzer, Leo, 31–32

Spivak, Gayatri, 20

Spolsky, Ellen, 43

Squires, Clare, 94, 161n8, 163n16

Staton, Joe, 108–109

Stein, Mark, 22, 90–91

Steinbeck, John, 37, 138

Stendhal, 12

Step Across This Line (Rushdie), 65, 84

Sterne, Laurence, 36, 94

Sticks and Stones, 131

Stories of Women (Boehmer), 5, 50, 55, 56

story, 23–24

Stranger, The (Camus), 33

Street King, 24

style: bilingual word play, 38; and code switching, 10, 13, 15, 38–39, 109, 115, 146; description and examples of, 38–39. *See also* narrative tools

Suárez, Mario, 135, 153
subalterns, 20, 68–70, 74–75, 155n3, 157n6
Super Friends, 107
superheroes: blue-collar superhero, 116–117; female superheroes, 107–108, 110–112, 115, 117; identification with, 128–129; in Latino comic books, 113–117, 126; Latino superheroes in mainstream comic books, 107–113, 168n5
suspension of disbelief. *See* partial suspension of disbelief
Swami, Praveen, 54, 55
Switzerland, 73
Syal, Meera, 8
syntax, 16, 17, 20–21. *See also* narrative tools
System, The, 131

Tales of the Closet, 118
Talk Fiction (Kacandes), 164n19
Tate, Greg, 162n15
television, 107
temporal dimension. *See* time
Thackeray, William, 162n12
theory of mind, 43–44, 104, 122, 131
Theory of Prose (Shklovsky), 36
Thomas, Dann, 109–110
Thomas, Roy, 109–110
time: double temporal sequence, 25–26; flashback and flashforward, 25–26, 148; in Kunzru's *Impressionist*, 100–102; in Rodriguez's short stories, 147–148; in Roy's *God of Small Things*, 60; in Smith's *White Teeth*, 100–102
Todorov, Tzvetan, 25, 47
Tom Jones (Fielding), 94
tragicomic narrative prototypes, 97, 122–126
Transmission (Kunzru), 46
Transparent Minds (Cohn), 31–32

Treuer, David, 7, 10, 39
Trillo, Carlos, 129, 130
Tripathi, Sandhya, 57
Triple-Mirror of the Self (Ghose), 106
Tristram Shandy (Sterne), 36
Trotsky, Leon, 48
Truax, Alice, 54

Ulysses (Joyce), 32, 35, 106
Uncanny X-Men, 110
Unfortunate Traveler, The (Nashe), 94
Unhomely Rooms (Díaz), 5
United States, 73, 74, 75, 136–137. *See also* capitalism; democracy
universals: and Latino comic books, 122–124, 129, 134; and postcolonial and Latino borderland fiction, 11–12, 15–18, 47, 91–93, 103–105
University of California Berkeley, 1–2
Unnatural Voices (Richardson), 30, 60–61
Updike, John, 54

Véa, Alfredo, 37–38
Velez, Ivan, Jr., 114, 116, 118, 125, 126
Victuum (Rios), 38, 44
Viramontes, Helena María, 135
Voltaire, 94, 106

Walsh, Bryan, 163n15
Walsh, Richard, 23
War Talk (Roy), 52, 53, 65
"we narrator," 13, 30–31, 60–64, 144–145
West Coast Avengers, 109–110
Westmoreland, William, 17
What Is World Literature? (Damrosch), 106
When Borne Across (Ghosh), 5
White, Hayden, 157n9
White Mythologies (Young), 155–156n3
White Teeth (Smith): author photographs on jacket of, 22–23; begin-

Index   197

ning of, 14, 87–88, 100–102; body in, 88, 160n4; carnivalesque style in, 87, 92; characters of, 87–88, 90, 94, 98–100, 102, 160n5, 161n8, 163n16; colloquialisms in, 96, 164n18; critics on, 90–91, 93–94, 160–161nn7–8, 162–163n15; emotional responses to, 96–98, 103–105, 162n15; film adaptation of, 24; flashback in, 25–26; as global novel, 105–106; humor in, 103–105, 162n15; ideal reader of, 92, 93–96; implied author of, 22–23, 26; length of, 162n15; literary allusions in, 94, 102; mood of, 159–160n2; narrative styles of, 87–88, 92, 95–96; narrator of, 88, 89, 90, 95–96, 99, 160n3; outsiderness of, 90–91, 96, 160–161nn5–8; palimpsest in, 35; particular/universal dimension of, 2–3, 13, 91–93; peritext of, 22–23; place, time, and social order in, 100–102; plot and agents of, 98–100; prototype narratives of, 91–92, 97–98; sections of, 92, 99; and theory of the mind, 43–44